W9-DCL-809

Sources Of American Spirituality

Rose Hawthorne Lathrop

SELECTED WRITINGS

Edited by Diana Culbertson, O.P.

PAULIST PRESS
New York ♦ Mahwah, N.J.

Book design by Theresa M. Sparacio.

Library of Congress Cataloging-in-Publication Data

Lathrop, Rose Hawthorne, 1851–1926.
   [Selections.　1993]
   Selected writings/Rose Hawthorne Lathrop; [edited by] Diana
Culbertson.
      p.　cm.—(Sources of American spirituality)
   Includes bibliographical references and index.
   ISBN 0-8091-0463-6
   1. Lathrop. Rose Hawthorne, 1851–1926.　2. Servants of Relief for
Incurable Cancer—Biography.　3. Dominican sisters—United States—
Biography.　4. Dominicans—Spiritual life.　I. Culbertson, Diana.
II. Title.　III. Series.
BX4446.8.Z8L3725　1993
271′.97202—dc20
[B]　　　　　　　　　　　　　　　　　　　　　　　　　　93-14622
　　　　　　　　　　　　　　　　　　　　　　　　　　　　CIP

Published by Paulist Press
997 Macarthur Boulevard
Mahwah, N.J. 07430

Printed and bound in the United States of America

CONTENTS

PREFACE

To include Rose Hawthorne Lathrop in an examination of the sources of American spirituality is to recognize her importance not only in the history of spirituality but to contemporary efforts to make social justice a more visible dimension of Christian proclamation and praxis. Much of her story has been told before, but her writings have not been generally available, although her published articles are as compelling now as they were to many of her contemporaries. Her letters and personal papers, moreover, can now be cited freely as we achieve historical distance from the events and people of her cultural and religious milieu. The dynamics of grace, in fact, become visible as we view a personal struggle as part of a tradition longer than a lifetime. Rose Hawthorne Lathrop lived at an extraordinary intersection of American culture when Puritan theology had yielded (among New England intellectuals) to Unitarian optimism, and the impulse to social change was a conspicuous dimension of American civil religion.

The conversion of Mr. and Mrs. George Lathrop to Catholicism in 1891 was not unusual, but it was not typical either, and the realization that so immediate an inheritor of the Hawthorne name should ally herself with a church perceived as non-American came as a *frisson* if not a shock to many of her contemporaries. Once begun, the impulse to conversion in Rose Hawthorne Lathrop was not to stop. In her life, conversion was always process and movement, an energy she never resisted. That she was able to draw so profoundly from her own culture, and immerse herself in a Catholicism then struggling to define itself as American as well as Roman, gives us reason to examine more closely the motions of grace in her particular history. Further, her story, as it is now emerging, helps us to examine the ongoing efforts (and achievements) of women in American church history, offering us an unusual view of two women whose love for each other confirmed them in their love for God and the poor.

All letters indicated as "[Berg]" are from the Henry W. and Albert

1

A. Berg Collection, The New York Public Library, Astor, Lenox and Tilden Foundations. Three letters, Rose [Hawthorne Lathrop] to Lily, Aug 27th [1876], Rose [Hawthorne Lathrop] to George Lathrop [1880] and Sophia [Hawthorne] to Elizabeth [May 20th, 1868] are from the Nathaniel Hawthorne Papers, Essex Institute, Salem, Mass. All other letters designated "[Essex]" are from the Hawthorne-Manning Collection of the Essex Institute. The letter from Rose Hawthorne to Mrs. Fields [1861] is included by courtesy of the trustees of the Boston Public Library, Boston, Mass. Letters designated "[Houghton]" are included by permission of the Houghton Library, Harvard University, Cambridge, Mass. The letter from Sophia Hawthorne to Rose [May 20, 1868] and the September 5, 1852 entry from the *Nathaniel and Sophia Hawthorne Journal 1842–1854,* vol. 2 (accession numbers MA 3400 and MA 580), both cited in the Introduction, are included with the permission of the Pierpont Morgan Library, New York. Letters designated "[RHH]" are in the archives of the Rosary Hill Home, Hawthorne, NY.

My gratitude must be extended to Mother M. Bernadette, O.P., and the Hawthorne Dominicans whose generosity and encouragement have made this book possible. I should like to acknowledge also the support of my friends in the Dominican Order, my family, and my colleagues at Kent State University who have shown so much interest in this project.

INTRODUCTION

When Maurice Francis Egan in a 1922 article in the *New York Times* Book Review considered the spiritual turning points in Rose Hawthorne Lathrop's life, he wanted to cite the death by cancer of Emma Lazarus, the poet whose lyric "Give me your tired, your poor . . ." was eventually inscribed at the base of the Statue of Liberty. Emma Lazarus had been a friend of Rose Hawthorne, and the connection would have been dramatically effective. But Mother Alphonsa, as Rose Hawthorne was known after 1900, less romantic than Egan and more rooted in the reality of events, pointed out that her compassion for the cancer-afflicted poor had been aroused, rather, by the story of a painful and lonely death of a poor seamstress condemned by her cancerous affliction to Blackwell's Island (now Roosevelt Island). Father Alfred Young, C.S.P., who had instructed Rose and her husband George before their entry into the church, had given her an account of the young woman's circumstances. As Mother Alphonsa later wrote, "A fire was then lighted in my heart, where it still burns. . . . I set my whole being to endeavor to bring consolation to the cancerous poor."

But prior to hearing that account, Rose Hawthorne's heart had already been prepared.

THE CHILD AND THE BRIDE: 1851–1871

Rose Hawthorne was born in Lenox, Massachusetts, May 20, 1851, the third and youngest child and the second daughter of Nathaniel Hawthorne and Sophia Peabody. Her mother, herself the daughter of a schoolteacher, the intelligent and socially conscious Elizabeth Palmer Peabody, was extraordinarily well-read, not only in the classics of literature known in English nineteenth century culture, but in the emerging new American literature. The Peabody sisters—Mary, Elizabeth, and Sophia—were very much a part of Boston and Salem literary

3

and artistic society; Sophia, in particular, was deeply influenced by Ralph Waldo Emerson, whom she admired and whose ideas about the divinity in human nature touched her profoundly.[1] Rose's Aunt Elizabeth, by all accounts the most aggressive of the three sisters (and Hawthorne's least favorite), had first noticed the young Hawthorne and lured him to literary gatherings, especially gatherings at the Peabody home. It was she who became famous as an educator and a specialist in children's literature and kindergarten schooling. It was she also who cultivated the friendship of the widower Horace Mann, urged him to run for the Massachusetts State legislature, where he became interested in educational reform, and finally yielded him in marriage to her sister Mary. The famous Aunt Lizzie, moreover, also served for nine years as a secretary to Dr. William Ellery Channing, that great Unitarian challenger of Calvinist pessimism, whose influence on New England intellectuals—and certainly on the Peabody sisters—was immeasurable.

Sophia Peabody owed much of her own early education to her older sister Elizabeth, as well as to her mother, but she was not physically strong and was more socially obscure than her tempestuous and reforming sister. When Nathaniel Hawthorne, the young author of *Twice Told Tales,* arrived at the Peabody home, it was Sophia he noticed and Sophia with whom he fell in love. They were married on July 9, 1842, after Nathaniel returned, disillusioned, from the Brook Farm community. George Ripley's great experiment with communal living and hard labor was no environment for a writer. But Concord was, the young couple decided, and to Concord they moved, living in what subsequently became known as the Old Manse.[2] Hawthorne continued to write, but money enough to support a wife and family did not follow his efforts. When Hawthorne finally secured an appointment in Salem as surveyor, or chief administrative officer of the Salem Custom House, Nathaniel and Sophia returned to what then seemed a dismal city.

When Rose was born the Hawthornes, with seven-year-old Una and five-year-old Julian, had just moved to Lenox from Salem. Hawthorne had lost his position because of political conflict, but he had just completed *The Scarlet Letter,* and found himself suddenly famous. In the late summer of 1852 during one of Nathaniel's absences, Sophia commented with extraordinary prophetic insight on her newest child: "She has scolded a great deal lately—I do not know what I shall do about it. She has an idea of woman's rights, I believe, and means to stand up for them in her own person. She has been very sweet too, going to kiss Julian when he cried and trying to comfort him and displaying a thousand charming little ways."[3]

It was in Lenox that Hawthorne began *The House of the Seven Gables,* and where he formed his long-lasting friendship with Herman Melville, whose home was nearby. Then, dissatisfied with the climate in the Berkshires, Hawthorne soon moved his family to West Newton, a suburb of Boston, and finally back to Concord, where they purchased Bronson Alcott's home, known as the Hillside, and renamed it Wayside. Rose could not have had many memories of that period in the now famous house, for the Hawthornes moved to Liverpool, England, in 1853, Nathaniel having been appointed American consul by his old friend Franklin Pierce. Rose writes of those years in her life with more than a little trace of grief:

> In England he mingled more than ever before with the members of literary and fashionable society. I, who in 1853 was but two years old, had to be satisfied with a glance and a smile, which were so much less than he had been able to give to my brother and sister in their happier days, for they had enjoyed hours of his companionship as a constant pastime. I was, moreover, younger than the others, and was never allowed to grow, as I wished, out of the appellations of Rosebud, Baby, and Bab (as my father always called me), and all the infantine thought which those pet names imply. I longed myself to hear the splendidly grotesque fairy tales, sprung from his delicious jollity of imagination, which Una and Julian had reveled in when our father had been at leisure in Lenox and Concord; and the various frolics about which I received appetizing hints as I grew into girlhood made me seem to myself a stranger who had come too late.

Then, as if to check an unwanted expression of regret in this 1897 text, the mature woman adds: "But a stranger at Hawthorne's side could be very happy, and, whatever my losses, I knew myself to be rich."[4]

The most important part of the riches of Rose Hawthorne was the extraordinary love she witnessed between her parents. Sophia and Nathaniel Hawthorne loved each other with passion and with what can only be called exaltation. Their love was mutual worship, not what we might consider nineteenth century verbal flourishes resembling worship. Every biographer of Hawthorne testifies to the intensity of their relationship, and the letters of this extraordinary couple bear out the testimony. Wagenknecht cites the following passages from early Concord days:

(In the first Hawthorne is responding negatively to his wife's request to burn a portion of one of her letters to him.)

> ... never was a wife's deep, warm, chaste love so well expressed, and it is as holy to me as the Bible. Oh, I cannot begin to tell thee how I love thee.

> If you fail me (but there is no such if) I might toil onward through this life without much outward change, but I should sink down and die utterly upon the threshold of the dreary Future. Were *you* to find yourself deceived, you would betake yourself at once to God and Heaven, in the certainty of there finding a thousand-fold recompense for all earthly disappointment; but with me, it seems as if hope and happiness would be torn up by the roots, and could never bloom again, neither in this soil nor in the soil of Paradise.[5]

After Hawthorne's death, Sophia wrote:

> His own soul was behind the wings of the cherubim,—sacred, like all souls which have not been desecrated by the world. I never dared to gaze at him, even I, unless his lids were down. It seemed an invasion into a holy place. To the last, he was in a measure to me a divine mystery; for he was so to himself. I have an eternity, thank God, in which to know him more and more, or I should die in despair. Even now I progress in knowledge of him, for he informs me constantly.[6]

However much a contemporary reader might flinch at this quasi-divinization of a spouse, Sophia's admiration and love for her husband can scarcely be in question.

The love and care these two extended toward their children is further evidence of the riches Rose described herself as experiencing. What child has ever received a more loving corrective note than the four-year-old Rose from her father when the family was briefly separated:

> DEAR LITTLE PESSIMA,—I am very glad that Mamma is going to take you to see "Tom Thump;" and I think it is much better to call him Thump than Thumb, and I always

mean to call him so from this time forward. It is a very nice name, is Tom Thump. I hope you will call him Tom Thump to his face when you see him, and thump him well if he finds fault with it. Do you still thump dear Mamma, and Fanny, and Una, and Julian, as you did when I saw you last? If you do, I shall call you little Rose Thump and then people will think that you are Tom Thump's wife. And now I shall stop thumping on this subject.

Your friend little Frank Hallet is at Mrs. Blodget's. Do you remember how you used to play with him at Southport, and how he sometimes beat you? He seems to be a better little boy than he was then, but still he is not so good as he might be. This morning he had some very nice breakfast in his plate, but he would not eat it because his mamma refused to give him something that was not good for him; and so, all breakfast-time, this foolish little boy refused to eat a mouthful, though I could see that he was very hungry, and would have eaten it all up if he could have got it into his mouth without anybody seeing. Was not he a silly child? Little Pessima never behaved so,—oh no!

There are two or three very nice little girls at Mrs. Blodget's, and also a nice large dog, who is very kind and gentle, and never bites anybody; and also a tabby cat, who very often comes to me and mews for something to eat. So you see we have a very pleasant family; but, for all that, I would rather be at home.

And now I have written you such a long letter that my head is quite tired out; and so I shall leave off, and amuse myself with looking at some pages of figures.

Be a good little girl, and do not tease Mamma, nor trouble Fanny, nor quarrel with Una and Julian; and when I come home I shall call you little Pessima (because I am very sure you will deserve that name), and shall kiss you more than once.

N.H.

(*Memories of Hawthorne*, 296–97)

To Julian, Sophia, especially, was protective. Writing to him from Lisbon during a visit there in 1855, she urges him to confide to his father in her absence "all your heart and life, so as not to be shut up and alone." And her postscript admonishes, "When you see any spots on your clothes, be sure and ask some one to wash them off for you."[7]

Una was the treasured one, perhaps because of her physical and emotional fragility. She was, judging from her photograph, an extremely beautiful, if sorrowful looking young woman, whose almost fatal illness as a young girl in Rome overwhelmed Hawthorne with sorrow and, by Julian's admission, almost put his mother into head-on conflict with the Providence in which she had always trusted.

The education of the children during the Hawthorne years in England and later on the Continent was supplied by tutors and governesses, as well as by Sophia and Nathaniel themselves. We read in Julian's biography of his parents that he was instructed in both Latin and Greek by his father (although there is little indication that he learned very much, since he was always less than industrious as a student), that he was required to memorize Macauley's Lays of Ancient Rome before leaving for that city, and that for the sake of the children the family was accompanied by the Antioch college graduate, Miss Ada Shepard, both governess and interpreter.[8]

The Hawthornes left England for Europe in 1858. Rose was by then seven years old and her childhood was thus marked by an extraordinary (at least by nineteenth century New England standards) cascade of Italian, thoroughly Catholic religious images. It is difficult to judge what the subsequent impact of such images was but, in retrospect, it is curious to read in Nathaniel Hawthorne's notes of his youngest daughter sketching the designs on the floor of the Siena Cathedral, of scampering around the awesome Santa Maria Novella (Dominican) church in Florence—chasing Julian, it seems, and of having a statue of St. Rose of Lima being called to her attention. Much has been written of the impact of the Italian sojourn on Hawthorne himself, not all of it substantiated, but it seems clear that the siege of Renaissance art and Italian religion he experienced, especially in Florence, did not leave him untouched. Describing the chapter-house of the Church of Santa Maria Novella in Florence where Mass is offered and confessions heard, Hawthorne writes:

The cool dusky refreshment of these holy places, affording such a refuge from the hot noon of the streets and piazzas, probably suggests devotional ideas to the people, and it may be, when they are praying, they feel a breath of Paradise fanning them. If we could only see any good effects in their daily life, we might deem it an excellent thing to be able to find incense and a prayer always ascending, to which every individual may join his own. I really wonder that the Catholics are not better men and women.[9]

Rose, of course, saw Italy through the eyes of her parents and older brother and sister, but she was presumably less dominated by New England culture than they. Una writes of "the idolatrous mummeries of the Catholic church" and the "miserable Romish religion."[10] But in 1897 Rose writes in *Memories of Hawthorne:*

> Through the streets of Rome trotted in brown garb and great unloveliness a frequent monk, brave and true; and each of these, I was led by the feminine members of the family, to regard as a probable demon, eager for my intellectual blood. A fairer sight were the Penitents, in neat buff clothes of monastic outline, their faces covered with their hoods, whose points rose overhead like church steeples, two holes permitting the eyes to peep with beetle glistenings upon you. They went hurryingly along, called from their worldly affairs; and my mother imparted to me her belief that they were somewhat free of superstition because undoubtedly clean. Sometimes processions of them chanting, came slowly through the city, bearing the dead to burial. I did not know then, that the chanting was the voicing of good, honest, Bible-derived prayers; I thought it was child's play, useless and fascinating. In the churches the chanting monks and boys impressed me differently. Who does not feel, without a word to reveal the fact, the wondrous virtue of Catholic religious observance in the churches? The holiness of these regions sent through me waves of peace (376–77).

Rose's memories of Italy were not all pleasant, but the villa of Montauto in Florence leased to the family by a slightly impoverished count, stirred her imagination with its gloomy staircases and the chapel where the servant girl prayed before a crucifix—while Rose tried to distract her. Her recollections are fused in her writing with subsequent values, as are all memories, but her descriptions provide extraordinary glimpses into a world not easily imaginable. They reveal also what most American visitors to Italy experience: a sense of time and tradition that can make American culture look truncated by contrast. Here we read of her memory of Robert Browning, who with Elizabeth and their son Penini lived just a few short blocks from the Hawthornes' first residence in Florence.

> I had learned to be grateful for art and ruins, if only they were superlative of their kind. I put away a store of such in my

fancy, but Mr. Browning was a perfection which *looked at me,* and moved vigorously! For many years he associated himself in my mind with the blessed visions that had enriched my soul in Italy, and continued to give it sustenance in the loneliness of my days when we again threw ourselves upon the inartistic mercies of a New England village. He grouped himself with a lovely Diana at the Vatican, with some of Raphael's Madonnas and the statue of Perseus, with Beatrice Cenci and the wildflowers of our journeys by *vettura,* besides a few other faultless treasures deeply appreciated by me (404–405).

In 1860 when Rose was ten years old, the Hawthornes returned to Concord, to their former home, Wayside, which now needed renovation and new additions. With three children, a relatively new house, and his consulate position at an end, Hawthorne needed money. But the Civil War was beginning and, worse yet, his health was failing dangerously. Rose records her own initial unhappiness upon returning to New England. It seemed a drab place indeed after the Continent, and her father's changed aspect affected the whole family, she was to write later "like the first notes of a requiem." Julian was enrolled at the famous Sanborn coeducational school in Cambridge, Massachusetts, and later went to Harvard (with indifferent success). The girls remained at home, or in Una's case, with Aunt Elizabeth Hawthorne. Sophia thoroughly disapproved of coeducation.[11]

In 1864, the day before Rose's thirteenth birthday, Hawthorne died of the unknown illness which had depleted him gradually since the family's return from the Continent. Three years later Rose began attending schools sporadically, first at the Dio Lewis School in Lexington, which seems to have been well known for its emphasis on physical education, at another in Lee, Massachusetts, at a third in Salem, run by Miss Jane Phillips. The family was in very straitened financial circumstances, not only because of a bank failure, but because royalties from Hawthorne's books were not coming through adequately. Rose's tuition was paid by a friend, Mary (Mrs. George B.) Loring who was fond enough of Rose to want her company while the younger girl attended classes in Salem. Sophia writes to her sister Elizabeth, "Rose is now in clover, and Mary Loring's aid in this important matter has relieved me of a great anxiety and trouble. For Rose is hungry to learn and it seemed cruel not to give her a chance."[12] Sophia was fiercely intent upon getting the money owed to her and equally intent upon conserving frugally what money she had. Servants were dismissed; Rose and

Una entered much more into the housework and sewing of the now diminished family. Sophia wrote to her sister Elizabeth that "Rose also has painted things which Childs and Jenks sell for her, and she has bought materials for a bonnet and made it herself."[13]

When Rose was away at school, her letters to Una testify to the fairly typical efforts of an adolescent girl to deal with her moods and her untried virtue: "I see how good mama is, but it don't make me good," she writes. And then about one of her schoolteachers at the Dio Lewis School who had criticized her: "If he pricks me any more, he will be unpleasantly surprised for I will nock him over. He regards me with sublime pity."[14] One does not get the impression that Rose had developed that serenity of disposition her parents had always desired for her. Her father was not there to admonish his little "Pessima," but letters from Sophia in 1868 give us insight into the extraordinary spiritual direction Rose's mother was capable of offering her young daughter:

My darling sweet briar Rose—

I suppose you observe that though the sweet briar Rose has the most thorns of any rose, it is also the sweetest of all Roses. And so I think with you it will prove that the thorns will only defend you from harm and finally will not wound anyone. My dearest love I did not know you had any danger from the failing of vanity. I thought always you were not vain. But the simple reflection that all our natural advantages are given us by our Heavenly Father for our own and others' advantage, take away the possibility of being vain of such advantages. And a lofty ideal keeps us humble because we never quite reach it, and so preserve a sense of shortcoming, which guards us from boasting and pride. Read a sentence of Thomas a Kempis every morning—for he has the very soul of humility with the utmost nobleness also. Una has read me the two last Sundays, each day a very graced sermon of Jeremy Taylor. Perhaps Aunt Mary has Jeremy Taylor's sermons. I should like to have you reading the same as we do so as to be sympathetic with and edified with us.[15]

On Rose's sixteenth birthday Sophia wrote the following extraordinarily nuanced greeting: It should be read against Rose's November 4, 1866 letter to her mother.

May 20th, 1868

My own darling—I am very lazy today—whether from my

six calls yesterday or the continued foul weather, I cannot tell. But I began to fear I was to be disappointed in writing today, the happy day when you came down from God, to make us happier than we were before. I do not know as there is yet any language in which I can convey to you an adequate idea of how I love you and have loved you since I first saw your tiny form, wrapped up in fine linen and saxony flannel, the softest little bundle that was ever laid in a mother's arms. Your baby-hood was most lovely and sunny. Grandpapa used to declare that you did not know how to cry. You showed the most philosophical patience about attaining your ends. If one way failed, you tried another way, and all in perfect quiet and repose. And you had an uncommon insight into the most probable ways, as well as into all things about you, aided by those unwinking eyes of which you have so often heard. This calm, intent outlook which you maintained, before you could speak, won for you the title of Lord Chancellor the Dispenser of Equity. You were extremely fastidious in respect of your acquaintances; and when you could walk, you would never come within a circle described in your thought towards a stranger, until you had settled clearly whether you liked the person. Life is "in circles." You were very critical in your observations, and one day, when you did not fancy the appearance of Grandpapa, he could not induce you to pass over the described line, till he took out his watch, when with a protesting, dignified air, you condescended to approach. I think you inherited from Papa this immitigable demand for beauty and order and right, though in the course of your development, it has made you sometimes pettish and unreasonable. I always was glad you had it, because I know the impatience and crossness it often caused, would prove a transient phase. I knew that religious principle and sentiment would surely render you at last gentle and charitable to the shortcomings of your fellow mortals, while would remain forever this demand. And this will lead you to the heights of being at last. Whereas if you were easy and indifferent, you might deteriorate, and lack the exquisite felicity which comes with the exquisite pain of a noble fastidiousness. I never doubted your most profound and tender love and devotion to me, in the worst paroxysms of your impatience—and so my heart was never seriously wounded, though sometimes hard hit. But I should never have minded the hit, if I should always been in strong spirits. We have had shadowed times together, but do not recur to them, since your love did not fail. I ascribe everything of that kind to a vivid temperament, and close packed brain, which overcame your patience in its rapid development. I see it as the temperament often united with a creative element. You have to suffer because GOD has given you the perilous gift of genius. With it you are to become greater and lovelier than your less gifted fellow beings. It has come down to you from that wonderful father, who has not been surpassed among men for character or intellect or imagination. In your childhood you showed the deepest generosity and magnanimity of soul, and though you think you have grown selfish, I do not see it. The wants you have, and the interests in providing them in your girlhood, when the fancy for ornament and silk attire always culminate, these are no proof of selfishness. And if you go into your heart, I am sure you will find there as single and sincere a desire to make others happy as you used to have when you were more unconscious of failures, because too young to question yourself. To see an error in an ingenuous person is to abandon it. When we know ourselves, we can be kinder to ourselves, as well as more severe. I have always felt that it was most important for such a mind and character as yours that you should be truly religious. GOD alone can rule in your heart. Where He does, all other influence will be harmless. But you must have the highest motives for action, for no others will move you, except to scorn. It was a profound intuition that *man needs superstitions* in the course of his progress before he is possessed of the Pearl of Price, Truth itself. Forms must stand till substance be found. And it is a singular thing that when substance is found, Form becomes more beautiful and is transparent, not smothering, but clothing substance. This is one of the circles returning into itself, the true emblem of eternity. I believe as much in a past eternity as in a future one—for I conceive that there can be no beginning, in the nature of things. This is the secret of my burrowing into the earth to find proofs of immemorial civilization. In studying the oldest polities [polity means principle of government] I have tried to discover why the most refined and high manners and perfection of art could not preserve the nations—But that they have been wiped off the earth, one after another, mostly with their marvellous works—as if they encumbered the ground. And not even broken columns and pottery were allowed to remain of the wicked cities of Sodom and Gomorrah, but they were utterly swallowed up, while over them seethes and swelters forevermore the oily abomination of a sea in which no creature can live. But I see why this is, and though I always feel a sharp anguish at the thought of any elaborate work of art being destroyed, I understand the justice and necessity of it. It is; I think because until Christ came, Love to our brother man was never made the whole Law. We find dim gleams of this everlasting light in the mosaic dispensation, as well as in the divine Plato, and far back in the Sanscrit sages—such as he who wrote the Bhagavad Gita, for he almost uses the very words of Christ. But Christ alone preached and acted that great redeeming truth. In old civilizations, all men were chattels who were beneath princes. Thousands of human beings would be harried to death and worked out of life—for the sake of erecting a pyramid or a temple. The works of art, over whose destruction the lover of beauty mourns, were brought into being by the agony and oppression of millions of captives. For whenever a conqueror subdued a nation, all whom he did not massacre he made slaves to his will. Artists of the highest order, and artisans of highest skill were subject to his pleasures, and he obliged them to build his vast walls, to erect his palaces and temples, and to cover them all over with sculpture and painting. And nothing was returned to them for their pains—nothing but contumely and wrong. So all those works which would have been immortal in their strength were by human hands demolished. For Time could have had no power upon many of them. They were truly accursed. The nations who lived and flourished and became luxurious through the toil and misery of men, had to be swept into the tombs and their signs obliterated. Many illustrious cities are only grass fields now—The places that knew them know them no more. Without Love nothing can endure. This grand and awful lesson taught us by Past History, we can bring down to the small plane of daily life,—Even in the circle, smallest of all,—yet, as you say, still containing the three hundred and sixty-five degrees, the circle of home—the sublime affirmation [command] holds— "Love one another, as I have loved you!" Darling, just take the Bible on Sunday, and read those chapters of John, beginning at the 14th "Let not your hearts be troubled." As I go on in life, those words seem to increase in power and unspeakable pathos.

So I will end my letter with that tender assurance, most hope inspiring: "Be of good cheer. I have overcome the world."

Your happiest, lovingest mamma.

P.S. The sacred day. 19th yesterday, I had no time hardly to myself for the first time. Hitherto, we have been together, and I hope the next anniversary it will be so again.

When I know anything definite about the house I shall tell you.

Did you receive the letter enclosing one dollar? Today one went, enclosing five dollars.

This nice paper was only seven cents a quire. I can get some like it for you at Mel——'s when you have used up the quire you bought at West Street for 25 cts.

Oh, I am so sorry you will only find a scratch with a pencil in your box of paper today, instead of the letter I wished to write. Love to Cousin Mary.[16]

Rose's letters in the sixties express not only her fears of vanity—to which her mother alludes—and lack of virtue, but her impatience with church attendance and particularly with the preaching, which she described as "vile." She confessed to boredom, characterizing the Unitarian church as "uninstructive." This dissatisfaction with church worship continued into the beginning of her adult life, as her diary in 1870 indicates: "I went to the English Church with Mama. I did not enjoy the service—there was no sermon."[17]

In 1868 Sophia decided, for economic reasons in particular, to move the family to Dresden, Germany—the scene of the above-mentioned liturgical ennui. Both Julian and Una needed to get away from broken love relationships; and although some money was coming in from book royalties, life in Germany would save the Hawthornes some living expenses. The Wayside was sold. Rose was assigned to a private school in Dresden where she was apparently unhappy. She did not get along with her schoolmates, presumably because they were jealous of some of her privileges. She seems to have withdrawn considerably and attracted few friends. When Sophia and Una left Dresden for travel in England, her loneliness was exacerbated. Her letters from Dresden indicate that she spent most of her time practicing music and learning to paint, although it is clear now that she was never to succeed particularly well at either effort. But Dresden was to be an important turning point in her life. The young George Parsons Lathrop and his mother were living in the city at the time, and George was deeply attracted to Rose. She does not reveal her feelings in her diary, but one entry in 1870 reads interestingly: "George L. had a spree and a supper."[18]

When the Franco-Prussian War was about to make life in Germany too dangerous, London became the next residence for Sophia and her daughters. Mrs. Lathrop also moved to London and the women remained friends. Rose's letters imply a mild preoccupation with news of George who had returned to the United States. They had much in common: his father was serving as an American consul in Honolulu; his brother Francis was studying painting under Whistler, and George was already writing articles on events in the art world, as well as poems and stories for publication. Rose was continuing her own studies at the Kensington Art School. It was in London that Sophia died of typhoid pneumonia in 1871, and in London seven months later that George and Rose married. He was nineteen, and she, twenty years old. Francis Lathrop and Lucy Madox Brown were witnesses to the marriage performed in St. Luke's Anglican Church in Chelsea, but Una was not present. She was seriously ill, never having completely recovered from the Roman fever of her girlhood days, or at least from the quinine treatment which had brought about her recovery. There is some indication also that she did not want to suggest to the family that she approved of the marriage. Most commentators, including the family, believed that the marriage itself brought on Una's illness. She was hospitalized briefly in an asylum and her illness was described in subsequent family correspondence as "insanity."[19] The original plan for the two sisters, designed by Julian, then in America, was that George would accompany both girls back to the United States. When Rose married and Una elected to stay in England, Julian's anger was both understandable and unconcealed. In fact, no one in the Hawthorne family made much of an effort to disguise their shock at Rose's impulsiveness. Her married life began under a cloud that was rarely to dissipate. As Julian was to write later, ". . . it was an error not to be repaired."[20]

But she, at least, was happy, even if no one but George was happy with her, and her letters in the early months of their marriage are appropriately rhapsodic. Only later do the shadows appear.

MARRIAGE AND CONVERSION: 1871–1898

Rose and George sailed to America on the *Oceanic,* the trip launching Rose into her adult letter-writing career. A violent storm at sea inspired a long, witty letter to Una, filled with vivid descriptions of a sea rescue, a pitching boat, indisposition, New Year's Eve bells that they interpreted as alarms, a German woman putting on two pairs of stockings and a coat "so that she could drown warmly," and she, the young bride, "clinging to George and screaming idiotically."[21]

Arriving at New York, the couple stayed six months with George's mother at 29 Washington Square until George joined the staff at the *Atlantic Monthly,* edited at that time by William Dean Howells. The couple moved to Cambridge. Among the advantages of the move for Rose was distance from her mother-in-law who was no more enamored, at least initially, of her new daughter-in-law than the Hawthornes were of George. By 1874, Rose's letters start to indicate trouble. Una was informed before her visit to Cambridge that some family difficulties were being healed and that she was not to bring up unpleasant matters. Aunt Ebie (Nathaniel Hawthorne's sister Elizabeth) received a note that read in part: "Your severe criticism of my husband hung like chains about my hands, and I could not bring myself to write to you. Your sweet letter has made me feel more than ever how much happiness is lost by family dissensions."[22]

In 1876, Rose and George's first and only child Francis was born, but the addition of a new member to the family did not alleviate the problems that were piling up on the young couple. Rose was ill and depressed after the birth of "Francie," and required hospitalization for puerperal fever.[23] A letter from George dated December 20, 1876, implies that he had to communicate with her through the attending physician at McLean Asylum in Somerville: "I am anxious to have Mrs. Lathrop know how well we are all getting on here at home . . . She herself will know how much this absence in search of health will increase (if that were possible) the happiness of having her with me, when she recovers."[24]

On January 1, he writes directly to her:

> *January 1, 1877*
> *Toward evening*

My Dearest Rösl,

This is only a brief messenger to remind you how soon I am to be with you again, and to counsel you to keep as cheerful as when I left you, until we meet on Wednesday. Do not think again of that dilemma which you had imagined, that it might be too much for you to come back, and at the same time too trying to remain at Somerville. The coming back will be the happiest, most quieting thing in the world, I think. When it comes, and that will be very soon—I think quite likely within a few days, instead of two weeks. Therefore, my precious wife, be cheerful and busy for one day, till I see you again early on Wednesday; and sleep peacefully for baby's and my sake. All is going well, and *will* do so for the brief time until you come. Remember how I have had to wonder every hour just how you might be feeling, and wishing that I could be with you to ensure your good cheer and happiness. Not to be with you all the time has—do believe this—been as hard for me as your absence from the little boy to you; for you are more to me than my child, and as I am not a mother but only a father, the baby's presence has only made me miss you more. But I knew that I *must* be brave and try to be thankful for all that there was to give thanks for. Very very soon to meet, yours wholly,

George.

Other problems were added to that of sickness and postpartum depression. Chief among these was debt. George was simply not making enough money by writing despite his obvious competence, if not genius, and despite continuous effort. Records and letters indicate Rose's rather desperate attempts to find a place to live in the Boston area that they could afford. Eventually they purchased the Wayside in Concord where they lived during the summer months. In the meantime, George resigned—apparently in a huff—from the *Atlantic* and began looking for another position, and Rose learned that her sister Una had died in England. The consistently unfortunate Una, who had experienced at least two broken love affairs, had converted to the Anglican Church and had been working at the Industrial Orphanage Home and School near London as an assistant to the superintendent. She had not only contributed her money to the institution but used her influence as a Hawthorne to solicit money by means of at least one letter to the London *Times*. It was a model that Rose was later to find useful. Una had journeyed to a Protestant convent to inquire about joining the Sisterhood when she became dangerously ill. When Julian arrived at the convent in the small town of Clewer near Windsor after hearing about her collapse, she was already dead. Una was buried next to Sophia in Kensal Green where she herself had planted a hawthorne tree near the headstone six years earlier.

As if illness, death in the family, George's professional troubles, and debt were not enough, Rose's endurance was strained by continual conflict between George and her brother Julian. The latter was angered when George not only wrote the first book-length literary critique of Hawthorne, but obtained the rights to edit the Riverside edition of Hawthorne's works. Marriage to Rose had worked to his literary advantage. Julian had publicly criticized George Lathrop's work and betrayed his resentment that George had somehow insinuated himself into the Hawthorne literary heritage. Critics generally sided with George in the controversy. He was considered a better writer and a more skillful and responsible editor, even if marriage to Rose had indeed worked to his literary advantage.

But marriage to George had worked no advantage to Rose, either emotionally or economically. When four-year-old Francie died suddenly of diphtheria in 1881, Rose's one hope for joy and solace seemed extinguished. She and her husband left the Wayside, incapable of dealing with their sorrows in that house. That was the reason offered to the public to explain the move. The more fundamental reason was that George could not keep up payments on the house. Julian's wife and family occupied the family home during the following winter.

Rose's effort to escape took her to London where Julian was living and where she could be distracted. George was writing a travel book about Spain, and the young husband and wife were only intermittently together. By 1882 Rose and George were back in the United States and a new quarrel started between Rose and Julian, who announced without any warning to his sister that he was about to publish a late Hawthorne manuscript, *Dr. Grimshawe's Secret.* Rose, who knew nothing about the manuscript and assumed that she was aware of all posthumous Hawthorne works, publicly disavowed Julian's claim, implying in an August 16, 1882, letter to the New York *Daily Tribune* that the manuscript was a forgery. Julian, who offered proof in his father's handwriting that the text was no forgery, attempted and achieved reconciliation very shortly with his sister. Theodore Maynard, who describes the controversy, notes that Rose alludes to her father's penmanship in *Dr. Grimshawe's Secret* in *Memories of Hawthorne,* clearly in an effort not only to set the record straight, but to confirm the reconciliation.[25] Rose, moreover, did not have the kind of temperament that permitted long-term hostility.[26]

When the Lathrops returned to New York, they entered into a busy social and literary life as George cultivated his career. He was a prolific and facile writer, though by no means an extraordinarily gifted one. The society the still very young couple frequented in New York was by all accounts the most sophisticated that America had to offer. Rose and George became close friends of Richard Watson Gilder and his wife Helena de Kay, whose salon attracted artists, musicians, social workers, and writers of every persuasion and talent. The social pressures became intense. George was often traveling while she was alone or traveling herself, or trying her own hand at professional writing, both her husband and Julian having assured her that she had talent. She had begun to write seriously as early as the 1870s, managing to publish short articles and stories in *Appleton's Journal, St. Nicholas,* and *The American.* In 1882 she published a short story in *Harper's Weekly,* entitled "Huff and Tiff" (September 2, 1882:554). The following year *Harper's New Monthly Magazine* published her "Prisoners!" These stories are not memorable. Her heroines are either admired extravagantly or abused. They are all extraordinarily beautiful with bountiful wardrobes, which are always described in the tone and terms of a fashion conscious young woman writer. Her male characters are either worshipful or cunning. The crucial problem is how to *know* if one is loved, and when love is expressed, problems are resolved. In "The Love of an American Girl," published in *The Ladies' Home Journal* (February, 1892), the heroine, who is beautiful and virtuous and who is dazzling London society, discovers her *real* lover in Mark White, a gentle young man from her "native village" in America. In choosing him she escapes from the financial clutches of "Hazleton," who says he loves her but has embezzled her fortune. Rose's poetry is better, but not much more in touch with reality than her prose. Of her book of poems *Along the Shore,* one reviewer wrote: "Mrs. Lathrop's poetical talent is like the orchid. Its roots are in the air."[27]

Her grief over the death of Francie in 1881 was overwhelming, but the poems in which she tries to express that grief are not so much efforts to write poetry as efforts to moralize about the loss. "I am glad I lavished my worthiest," she concludes in her poem "Francie," "to fashion his greater worth; | since he will live in heaven | I shall lie content in the earth." The verse is clearly forced, and the idea obscure. Only her piety is evident. There is no clue in this poem or others of any fundamental discontent with the ways of God. What we detect in this poem and others is sorrow and loneliness that occasionally resembles gothic melancholy. Reviewers refer to her, typically, as a "female poet." The volume of verse is described quite often as "dainty." A little less dainty, however, than most of her poems is one entitled "The Violin."

Touch gently, friend, and slow, the violin,
    So sweet and low,
That my dreaming senses may be beckoned so
Into a rest as deep as the long past "years ago!"

And ever gently touch the violin,
Until an impulse grows of a sudden, like the wind
On the brow of the earth,
And the voice of your violin shows its wide-swung
    girth

With a crash of the strings and a medley of rage
    and mirth;
And my rested senses spring
Like juice from a broken rind,
And the joys that your melodies bring
I know worth a life-time to win,
As you waken to love and this hour your violin.

A poem entitled "Life's Burying-Ground" is curiously ambiguous. A catalogue of injuries is described as "buried." And yet the narrator visits these buried griefs "every day."

My graveyard holds no once-loved human forms,
    Grown hideous and forgotten, left alone,
    But every agony my heart has known,—
The new-born trusts that died, the drift of storms.

I visit every day the shadowy grove;
    I bury there my outraged tender thought;
    I bring the insult for the love I sought,
And my contempt, where I had tried to love.

In another, entitled "God-Made," the narrator asserts her "worth" and in an apostrophe asks her "jewel,"—her "worth" to "light my love's eyes to read my soul." In "Grace," she speaks of an "ill-wrought life." In "The Clock's Song," someone named "Eileen" lives long enough to pass from being "Untouched by sorrow's treacherous kiss" to "Mourning her dreams in queenly state." Most of the poems are about love and sorrow, disillusionment, death. The dedication is to G.P.L. who is greeted as "best friend," whose "unexcelled protection" is won with "wild flowers of love." The collection, published by Ticknor and Co., has more mood than thought. And the mood, which is relatively uninteresting, isn't redeemed by any particular technical competence. Publishers never knew quite what to say about her work, except to suggest that she send them "something else."

Why anybody would keep rejection slips for years defies explanation, but Rose Hawthorne Lathrop seems to have kept every comment on her poetry ever expressed. Along with her letters and mementos— which she carried around and stored in breadboxes—are all her rejection notices, most of which are kind, probably because of the personal friendship she entertained with the editors. At the same time, it is clear that editors of the more prominent literary journals consistently refused her material. A letter from the reader at *Century Magazine* says, "I have read, re-read, and read again and for the life and death of me I can't make it out."[28] But she tried and tried again, sending much of her material to Thomas Bailey Aldrich, editor of *The Atlantic Monthly.* His responses are equally firm. "It would be so nice to find something which you approved of. . . ." she wrote on one occasion, sending him another cache of verses.[29]

If her poetry is any indication of her mood, Rose was not usually in a happy frame of mind during these years of her marriage. The effects of a decade of economic and marital stress began to accumulate. Rose had to deal with a relationship that was at best a loving but increasingly distasteful incompatibility. George and Rose loved each other. There are too many letters, mementos, diary entries, and common projects to suggest that the marriage was a complete fiasco. What eroded the relationship was in part—perhaps for the most part— George's "illness," one of the symptoms of which was severe gastrointestinal distress. Maynard, her principal biographer, believed him to be an alcoholic. Friends sometimes described George as nervous. His letters, as well as reports about him suggest that he was bright, handsome, hard working, likable, and vain. He seems to have been somewhat pompous, if not arrogant, on more than one occasion, shallower than Rose, excessively quick to defend himself, promote himself, but somehow recognizing that he would never quite measure up to his own projected self-image: scarcely a personality type that is easy to live with, especially if the one trying to live with him is equally, if not far more intelligent, quick to perceive, interpret, and judge: a young woman who as a child, at least, never distinguished herself by her ability to exercise restraint. "I will nock him over," she had written of the teacher she disliked. We can speculate on what kind of conversational pitch, or at least emotional stress, Rose and George may sometimes have reached in their domestic privacy.

In 1883 Rose separated from George, offering in her letters very little by way of explanation. "My affairs are in a revolutionary state," she writes to her cousin Richard Manning, "and I do not expect to return to Mr. Lathrop's care."[30] In a second letter the following week she adds:

> I have had long consideration before coming to the conclusion I have done, and in which I am supported by Julian and my aunts and intimate friends; but hope that for the sake of much mutual happiness in the past, Mr. Lathrop and I can hold a more gentle relationship in seperation than such proceedings would warrant. If I had more courage at present in throwing off my despondency I would go to visit you and your wife as you have been so good as to suggest, but I am not yet able.[31]

In October of that same year, she writes from 8 Chestnut Street in Boston:

> ... I have been so heavy of heart from my changed circumstances of which I spoke to you in the Spring. I have been able to accept no invitations and have barely returned calls made by intimate friends. The thought of going either to Salem or Concord has been very painful. I am now settled for the Winter at the above address, my aunt Mrs. Nath'l Peabody and her daughter being on this same floor, which is a very pleasant arrangement for me.

After describing Julian's literary activities, she concludes:

> Every renewal of intercourse with my best friends has caused me to realize more keenly the change in my life from old times, and my summer has been hard to bear in the most prosaic conditions which I could arrange to help me to forget

my loss and the absence of my husband. I am not sure what
the future will develop for me in regards to him.[32]

In 1883 the Wayside was sold to Daniel Lothrop, who had married
Margaret Stone, the "Margaret Sidney" of the *Five Little Peppers*
fame. In a letter to Thomas Bailey Aldridge, George states that he gave
$1000.00 from the purchase to his wife, although "her lawyers admit-
ted that her dower right was worth nothing."[33] But in the summer of
1884 Rose and George were again living together in New York on East
55th Street.

Two years later George became the literary editor of the New York
Sunday Star. He was beginning, however, to experience more serious
health problems, and according to a letter from Rose to her cousin
Rebecca Manning, his doctor ordered him to stop working and to leave
New York. In 1887 they moved to New London, Connecticut, where
they built a house—designed somewhat unconventionally by Rose
herself—at 27 Post Hill Place, naming it Overdale. They were not so far
away, however, as to lose important contacts with the literary world.
George proceeded to turn out novels, plays, and articles, and to give a
prodigious amount of time to getting an effective copyright law enacted
in the United States. This law may have been his single most important
accomplishment.

Religious Conversion

The Lathrops had not been a conspicuously religious couple; in
fact they were so inconspicuously religious that George had to write a
defense of beliefs held prior to their conversion, bristling a bit at the
charge in the New York *Independent* that they had been agnostic before becoming Catholic. Arguing that Mrs. Lathrop had been brought
up as a Unitarian, George Lathrop noted that both Nathaniel and
Sophia had been "full of reverence for Christ, little differing in devout-
ness from that paid to him as the Son of God, one with the Trinity." As
for himself, he had been once a baptized Episcopalian and "never" an
unbeliever.[34] The private reasons for the conversion of George Lathrop
and Rose Hawthorne Lathrop are difficult to probe. No document
presently available describes any spiritual hunger or prolonged intellectual search comparable to what we find, for example, in the diary of
Isaac Hecker or the letters and writings of Orestes Brownson. Neither
of the Lathrops composed the kind of spiritual autobiography that
converts often undertake.[35] Suddenly, without warning, we see the un-
affiliated but not unreligious Lathrops, converting to Roman Catholi-

cism with an energy that can only be described as astonishing. This was a wholehearted profoundly personal commitment undertaken against social and familial dismay, if not professional risk. The swirl of journalistic controversy surrounding the conversion testifies to the religious and ecclesiastical tumult of the period, much of which Rose and her husband had already experienced at first hand.

The Religious Heritage

The Hawthornes had lived for generations under the famous curse of an innocent woman burned as a witch in the presence of Judge Hathorne of Salem. Nathaniel, his descendant, had never quite accommodated himself to the pseudo-spectral implications of the prediction of Sarah Good, "If you take my life, God will give you blood to drink," and his dissociation from ecclesiastical fidelities may be linked in part to his discomfiture with public allegiance to any version of religion.[36] His biographers suggest that he believed deeply in Providence, however, and was almost Neoplatonic in his idealism, however convinced he was also of the shadow that seemed to be cast across nature and the human condition. Julian once wrote of him: "He had deep and reverent religious faith, though of what precise purport I am unable to say."[37] Sophia was much more at ease with religious pieties, especially since at the time of their marriage religious philosophies were exciting the liberal intellectuals of New England, generating a flood of sermons, searches, lectures, debates and communitarian experiences. She attended the sermons and lectures, read deeply in the classic religious texts recommended by her Unitarian and Transcendental neighbors and friends and exemplified a goodness and piety that could scarcely be rivaled, least of all by her voluble sister Elizabeth.[38] The Transcendentalist descendants of Unitarian traditions, opposed to the Lockean epistemology of Unitarianism, were drawn to the romanticism they read about in the flood of English writings arriving regularly, but their romanticism had its own native roots. Their piety was related to the mystic potential in dissenting Puritanism, the divine and supernatural light described by Jonathan Edwards.[39] Insofar as the Transcendentalist movement was romantic, it was also almost prophetically individualistic and democratic. Interest in mysticism led Transcendentalists to examine Roman Catholicism with some degree of sympathy, despite their resistance to its authoritarian structure. The Brook Farm experimenters, especially, found it congenial in many ways to their own ideals. George Ripley's wife Sophia, and his niece, Sarah Stearns, eventually converted to Catholicism as did George Leach, Isaac Hecker, and James Kay, Jr. Others such as Frederick Henry Hedge and James Freeman Clarke often demonstrated considerable interest in the writings of the church fathers as well as the Catholic mystical tradition.[40]

Rose had lived among heirs to the Transcendentalist movement and former Brook Farmers, although the movement had died out when she was still a little girl. She had heard theological conversations and listened to numerous sermons and lectures. She was quite aware of the religious issues of the day, but she was not drawn to speculative thought and seemed unmoved by most of the sermons she heard. Only her mother's constant example of faith in an all-loving, all-caring divinity seemed to have touched her mind and shaped her soul for a life of religious faith. Letters to her girlhood friends suggest that she could be intensely affected by the music and art of a Catholicism whose institutional character and doctrinal assertions her family rejected completely. Her long letter to Martha Stearns from Dresden describes how overwhelming was her emotional reaction to a performance of the "Stabat Mater." Unitarian lectures, theories of human goodness, and social causes, of and by themselves, did not stir her heart. But suffering did, especially the suffering of the innocent. It would be a long time, however, before that instinct in her would find expression.

The Catholic Church Mrs. Lathrop and her husband joined in 1891 was a divided ecclesiastical body, torn between "Traditionalists" and "Americanists." During the same years when New England intellectuals were moving away from Puritan theocracies to psychological theodicies shaped in part by the tide of English and German romanticism, Roman Catholicism was trying to find a home in a young nation scarcely sympathetic to its foreign fidelities, cloudy political history and its sovereign theological and religious claims. Its collective personality in the New World had been formed initially by Bishop John Carroll of Baltimore, cultured, eloquent and a master of what we would today call a gracious and tactful ecumenism.[41] A devout man, he recognized his historical situation clearly and began to shape an American Catholicism that could blend into the new society without losing its distinctive identity. But in the middle of the nineteenth century that unobtrusive blend of American culture and Catholicism was to be shattered by a wave of immigrants whose religious allegiances as well as foreign origins set them apart from the mass of Protestant Americans, and who clung to those allegiances with a tenacity explained in part by their desperate need for identity and survival. If these Italians and Germans, Irish and eastern Europeans were often seen as aliens, foreigners, subverters of the commonweal, they saw themselves surrounded by a wealthier entrenched class of traditional religious enemies who denied the true church and who were trapped in their iniquitous errors. How were these people, now separated from their traditional religious heritage, to survive in a land that had generated its own religious environment, one that did not include papists and popery? Theology, ecclesiology, homiletics, evangelization, politics, culture— everything was at stake. The careers and convictions of bishops and religious superiors were on the line. The fate of seminaries, universities, unions, and parochial schools would be shaped by the tensions of this church that began to collide with itself in its struggle to find its identity in an environment it had never before experienced.

In 1852, the year after Rose was born, the First Plenary Council of Baltimore had been convened to legislate about parochial schools, church administration, and uniformity of belief and worship in the American Catholic context. The attention of the bishops was directed entirely to internal church problems and to the immense task of organizing the diverse ethnic groups that found themselves struggling, not only for economic and religious survival in a religiously unfriendly environment, but for national identity. Ten days after the council, the Democrats came to the same city to nominate Franklin Pierce, Nathaniel Hawthorne's old friend and classmate. Ostensibly those two conventions had very little to do with one another, but both gatherings were inaugural: the American church and the American nation were both to face decades of internal conflict. Catholics were urged to be patriotic, to show what good citizens they could be and were. But as historians have noted, the most serious moral problem of the western hemisphere— human slavery—was not a matter for discussion among the gathered bishops. They were far more concerned about unifying a church that could fragment along ethnic lines, or possibly along a perceived fault called American democracy.[42]

The Second Plenary Council of Baltimore in 1866 found the bishops of the New World still immensely preoocupied with church organizational problems. Later, to their credit, the American hierarchy at the Vatican Council of 1870 evidenced their profound pastoral concern for the American people, their democratic traditions, and their preference for clarity and practicality over European ecclesiological theory. As the Catholic population continued to expand on their own shores, their problems had very little to do with European theology. In 1871 there were over four million Catholics in America; nine years later there were two million more, and by 1910 the Catholic population had reached 16,336,000. Archbishop John Ireland preached at the Third Plenary Council in 1884, urging lay people "to dedicate themselves to making America Catholic and establishing, once and for all, the profound compatibility of American and Catholic ideals."[43]

Among those who preached and evangelized, the problem was whether to preach a theology of isolation and confrontation with Protestantism or to find some kind of intellectual and religious accommodation. Bishops were divided in their understanding of whether Roman Catholicism could ever accommodate itself to the apparently irremediable religious hostility of American society. In this divided ecclesiastical setting, there was no more powerful spokesman for the possibility of fusing American culture with Catholic belief than Isaac Hecker, former Brook Farmer, who had found his way to the Roman Catholic Church, to the Redemptorist Order and to priesthood, and who finally became the founder of the Society of St. Paul. His successor and biographer, Walter Elliott, and the next generation of Paulists were among the most articulate voices in the struggle to bring Catholicism into the mainstream of American society. These Paulists were often the instructors and the spiritual directors of American converts to Catholicism. Many of the Paulists were themselves converts and could speak to potential adherents in their own religious tongue. At the same time, most of them believed that pressing on in an accommodating rather than confrontational mode would bring all of America eventually to the Roman Church. It was an optimistic strategy that contained within itself its own impossibilities, but it was not without immense significance to those who were influenced by their publications and evangelizing efforts.

One of the most conspicuous examples of the evangelizing technique of the Paulists was described in an 1889 article in *The Catholic World*. The author, Alfred Young, C.S.P., who two years later was to be Rose and George's instructor in the faith, argued that those instructing or evangelizing potential converts should be aware of the mutual misunderstanding and prejudice that centuries of religious conflict had engendered and, despite everything, to allow for good will and charity on the part of Protestants who knew nothing of the church but what hostile preachers had painted.

> We may go as we are, armed with our old-fashioned reaping-hook, spying around the borders of the Protestant harvest, and may glean a few handfuls here and there; but he who would cut a wide swath a-field must go equipped with a sickle

of a fashion to suit the grain *as it is* and *as it now stands,* and not as controversial painters have pictured it.[44]

Young urged an attitude of charity and openness, writing of the Protestants *in perfectly good faith* who sincerely sought the truths of religion.

> Take their so-called "Holy Communion," for instance. Who can doubt that they obtain much merit from all their devout prayers, and acts of spiritual communion made with Jesus Christ as the Son of God and Redeemer, made by them in that service, erroneous in form and false in doctrine though it be? (359)
>
> It must be evident to my readers that I look upon the spiritual state of Protestants generally as a peculiar one, almost entirely out of reach of judgment upon technical points of law. The problem of their reconciliation with the visible church (alas! that it has to be called a problem at this late day) is to my mind a practical rather than a theoretical one (359).

If this tone seems condescending to a more pluralist generation, it needs to be compared to the more acrimonious denunciations of other Catholic preachers of the time. Young's approach was amiable indeed and thoroughly in keeping with the Paulist project. Walter Elliott, his religious mentor, had been influential in developing the earliest Redemptorist model of the parish mission into a pattern for missions to non-Catholics. The missionary strategy he urged was eventually codified in the Paulist documents *Non-Catholic Missions* and *Manual of Missions.*[45]

Judging from Alfred Young's published convictions, when Mr. and Mrs. Lathrop sought admission into the church, their conversion experience may well have been perceived by both of them as part of a continuum: affiliation with Catholicism, however dismaying to their friends, must not have seemed to them, at least, dramatically discontinuous with their past. They found in the church, moreover, a devotional life that seemed to reach beyond institutional forms and to satisfy in Rose, especially, an emotional hunger that her previous experiences with religion had not offered. Alfred Young's approach to the spiritual life, his intelligence, and tempered view of Protestant-Catholic disagreements was the ideal channel for Rose and George's entry into their new religion. It is not surprising that we detect so little personal anguish in their transition to new doctrinal positions and to a

new ecclesiastical fidelity. The Paulist approach worked particularly
well with middle-class well educated potential adherents. Christine
Bochen notes that converts to Catholicism in St. Paul's parish, where
George and Rose were instructed, totalled 1675 between 1860 and
1900, and that thirty–five percent of the converts were former
Episcopalians.[46]

But the Isaac Hecker, Walter Elliot, Alfred Young view of Protestant-Catholic relations was not shared by all clerics. Indicative of a
more conservative view of attracting converts was Augustine Hewit,
himself a convert, who eventually became the Paulist Superior General. His article in *The American Catholic Quarterly Review* analyzed
the dangers of an "accommodating" Catholicism and argued for an
insistence on its distinctiveness.

> There are three essential elements which are the constituent
> principles of the Catholic religion: Dogma, Authority, Wor-
> ship, which cluster around the great central Act of Worship,
> branching out and blooming into ritual and all the rich and
> variegated flowers of architecture, sculpture, painting, and
> music. These are what have attracted the intelligent and edu-
> cated converts, who have tried the Lutheran and Anglican
> forms of Protestantism, one or both, and finding the Mene-
> Tekel written on their walls, have sought for certainty and
> completeness of faith, for divine authority in lawgiving and
> government, for a worship worthy of God and a pure foun-
> tain of grace in the Catholic Church.[47]

Hewit's view corresponds very much to the dynamism of Rose's
inner conversion, especially in her attraction to Catholic culture, and
her love for the mass and the eucharist—all of which appealed to her
sense of beauty and her need to be grounded in visible symbols of love
and sacrifice.

Among the prelates the most conservative spokesmen for the
church were Archbishop Michael Corrigan of New York and Bishop
McQuaid of Rochester, who could see no way to deal with the
surrounding Protestant culture, except to struggle against it on every
front. They were opposed by the "Americanists," Bishop John Keane,
rector of the Catholic University of America, described by historians as
Hecker's spiritual heir;[48] Archbishop John Ireland of St. Paul, and
Denis O'Connell, rector of the American College in Rome. Typical of
the kind of problem on which Traditionalists and Americanists clashed

was the proposed World Parliament of Religions to be held in Chicago in 1893. It was to follow the Catholic Columbian Congress held in conjunction with the World's Columbian Exposition. The Columbian Congress, designed primarily for lay participation, was itself controversial, but less so than Catholic participation in the World Parliament. Conservatives considered any participation of Catholics in the World Parliament as yielding to pluralistic anarchy, a concession to the possibility that Catholicism was "just another kind of religion." The true church would not gain from such a concession. Americanists saw the World Parliament as an opportunity to evangelize, to proclaim the messsage, and to demonstrate the willingness of Catholics to argue and defend their cause in any forum. That Rose and George both participated in the Columbian Congress as speakers within two years of their conversion is an indication of their association with the intellectual and moderately progressive wing of Catholicism which, given their limited experience with the church, they may have perceived as the norm. Archbishop Corrigan attended the Columbian Congress, along with Bishop Francesco Satolli, the papal delegate.[49]

The clashes between Americanists and conservatives, or among evangelists, did not ordinarily make a difference, however, in the private pieties of believers. Those practices were very much the same for most Catholics, and Rose and George, as new converts, found these practices appealing. The Lathrops' discovery of the devotional life of Catholics may have been as simple as observing the religious behavior of their Irish servant girls. The Lathrop servants found Rose loving and affectionate and their memories of her were tender. Rose kept a number of letters from a certain Nellie Sullivan until her death. The letters of this faithful servant are filled with simple expressions of endearment and utterly sincere references to her Catholic faith. Rose kept them, along with every other note from her friends, in the breadbox filing system.

Maynard suggests that John Boyle O'Reilly, poet and journalist, editor of the Boston *Pilot,* was influential in George's attraction to Catholicism. The immediate influence seemed to be Alfred Chappell and his wife Adelaide (Huntington) Chappell, whom the Lathrops met in New London and whose company they enjoyed. Chappell was an accomplished organist, and he and his wife used to entertain somewhat lavishly. Chappell had been first a Congregationalist, then an Episcopalian, and eventually a Catholic. He had studied for the ministry once and was quite knowledgeable about religious doctrine. An extant letter from him to Rose suggests that she had been looking for a book by Isaac Hecker to read, knowing that he had once been at Brook Farm,

although not at the same time as her father, and she had surely heard
much about him from her spiritual director.

The disturbed course of the Lathrop marriage suggests that both
Rose and George needed deeper fidelities than what their life to that
point had provided. Whatever the immediate reasons for their seeking
instructions, in public George's explanation of their conversion was
strictly intellectual. His published text follows the argument of the
Isaac Hecker apologetic tradition that American culture and Roman
Catholicism constituted a happy union. His remarks about papal infal-
libility are temperate and constitute a response to attacks against him.

The Conversion Experience

It was George, apparently, who had initiated the faith search. He
brought home Cardinal Gibbons' *The Faith of Our Fathers* one day,
and gave it to Rose. Together the couple read also Monsignor Capel's
The Faith of Catholics and Cardinal Wiseman's *Lectures on Doctrines
of the Church.* Subsequently they called on Father Young at the
Church of St. Paul in New York. After a course of instructions they
were received into the Catholic Church March 19, 1891. Two days
later they were confirmed by Archbishop Corrigan.[50] News of their
entry into the Catholic Church was published in newspapers throughout the country, engendering mild debate, some acerbic observations
about George's sincerity and a vigorous (and very competent) apologia
by George. The Catholic press exulted. The Protestant press sulked.

The Boston *Pilot* (April 4, 1891) published the news of the conversion, along with a letter from George describing something of his intellectual journey. In the letter he says nothing about his wife's intellectual journey. Either he thought he was speaking for her as well as for
himself, or he did not consider her motives sufficiently pertinent to be
included. The letter is directed to John Jeffrey Roche, the editor who
succeeded O'Reilly, and reads, in part:

New London, Conn., March 24.

My Dear Mr. Roche:—

No one ever suggested my becoming a Catholic, or tried
to persuade me; although a number of my friends were Catholics. The attempt to inform myself about the Church began
with the same impartiality, the same candor and receptive-
ness that I should use towards any other subject upon which I
honestly desired to form a just conclusion. Notwithstanding
that my education had surrounded me with prejudice, my

mind was convinced as to the truth, the validity and supremacy of the Roman Catholic Church, by the clear and comprehensive reasoning upon which it is based. And while the reasoning of other religious organizations continually shifts and wavers, leaving their adherents—as we now see almost every day—to fall into rationalism and agnostic denial, the reasoning of the Church, I found, led directly into sublime and inspiring faith. This union of solid reasoning and luminous faith I cannot discover elsewhere.[51]

The explanation ends with a surprisingly lengthy comment on the consolations offered by the doctrine of the communion of saints:

Moreover, the present active and incessant spirituality of the church does not stop short with this life or end in that pagan acceptance of death as an impassable barrier, which one meets with in Protestant denominations. It links together the religious souls of all periods, whether now on earth or in the world beyond. . . .

Subsequently the Boston *Pilot* of April 4, 1891 reported:

The interest in the conversion to the Catholic faith of George Parsons Lathrop and his wife, Rose Hawthorne Lathrop, is widespread, as both are authors of international reputation. Mrs. Lathrop, as our readers know, is the daughter of Nathaniel Hawthorne. Everyone remembers the attraction to the Catholic faith manifested by Hawthorne in "The Marble Faun," especially in those chapters, "Altars of Incense" and "The World's Cathedral." All that Hawthorne felt of St. Peter's his daughter learned of the Universal Church. "There was room for all nations; there was access to the Divine Grace for every Christian soul; there was an ear for what the overburdened heart might have told." These famous passages from the father's pen, by their insight into the divine character of the Church and its tender, indispensable helpfulness to humanity—helped, incidentally, to guide the daughter into the full light of faith. We have in literary history a parallel case for Hawthorne and his daughter, in Sir Walter Scott and his sympathy with Catholicity, and the subsequent conversion of his daughter, the wife of Scott's biographer, J.G. Lockhart.

Other Catholic papers reported the Boston *Pilot* story, printed the letter, and added their own comments: The *Colorado Catholic* of April 4, 1891, luxuriated: "The understanding and beauty of the dogma, hidden from those outside the church arose on the horizon of Mr. Lathrop's intelligence, and lo! all the world of the True Church opened its spreading beauty to him. He, seeing, entered upon its delights." *The Knickerbocker* of Albany, New York (March 30, 1891) commented innocently, "Protestants and Catholics alike will listen to this neophyte and endeavor to learn some grace from the lips that are freshly aglow with the fire of faith."

But the New York *Independent,* a fiercely partisan Protestant newspaper, was not about to give much credit to George for theological astuteness. After conceding that joining the Roman church was slightly better than remaining "in the camp of unbelief," and that the Catholic Church was admitted to be a Christian church, the writer implies that Mr. Lathrop had offered no compelling reasons to justify his decision. That charge moved George to write an extensive apologia which, given his neophyte status in the church was exceptionally well written. Opposing the *Independent's* arguments that the Catholic Church called for *unreasoning* obedience, he cites *Critères Théologiques* on the relationship between reason and belief. "Mr. Edison," he continued in an interesting allusion, "has said that we do not yet know what electricity is. Does he therefore doubt its existence, or its immense importance? Or do any of us doubt it? Not at all."[52] In a further argument for doctrinal submission and the principle of papal authority in matters of faith and morals, George Lathrop uses the United States Supreme Court as his model: "We Americans all bow to decrees of the Supreme Court and submit to proclamations by the President, even when those decrees and proclamations run counter to our individual wishes or opinions. But no one is so fatuous as to argue that, because we do this, we are the slaves of an "unreasoning obedience." And since the *Independent,* by citing Pius IX's bitter attack on the invaders of Rome, had disputed George's claim that the Catholic doctrine presented to him impressed him as remarkably calm, thorough, [and] free from malice and abuse, the Apologia argued,

> The logic and calmness and spirituality of Catholic doctrinal expositions are in no way impaired by the severity of those epithets attributed to Pius IX, in speaking of Italian Liberals, viz., "wolves," "thieves," "liars," "monsters of Hell," etc. Those were not used in a discussion of revealed truth, but in rebuke of rebellious children of the faith or of inimical skep-

tics; types of that class whom our Lord himself, as *The Independent* is aware, denounced as "fools," "hypocrites," "blind guides," "whited sepulchres," "serpents," and "vipers."

There is nothing in private correspondence to suggest how much or what kind of help George may have received in composing this very long essay, but the rebuttal is skilled and represents the kind of polemic Catholic and Protestant thinkers engaged in at the time. It does not seem that George's arguments persuaded anyone, but at least he vindicated his (and Rose's) decision.

While George was struggling to defend the conversion, a laconic observation appeared in the Boston *Beacon* (April 4, 1891):

> Considerable publicity has been given to the fact that an author of limited importance has joined a certain church. . . It is certainly contrary to the dictates of good taste, to say nothing of common sense, that so much fuss should be made about so very simple a matter. Hundreds of persons join a church every week, and none of them consider it necessary to proclaim the fact to the world.

By April 30, however, the *Independent* was inveighing against the New York Protestant Episcopal Church, especially its seminary, and its fatal "high church" tendencies: "The shower becomes a downpour," the writer declared. "First, we had the report of the conversion to Rome of Mr. and Mrs. Lathrop, then of Father Ignatius' fifty nuns, and now it is announced that two of the students in the Episcopal General Theological Seminary in this city have gone over to the Catholic Church." So, perhaps only for the reason that George had been a baptized Episcopalian, he and Rose became linked to internecine Protestant debate.

But there is no indication in the public records of Rose's feelings about any of these issues, about her own presumably intellectual search or her own emotions. George carried on the public debate, although Rose speculated on whether or not she should enter into it. She considered writing an article entitled, "The Way as I Found it," but never did so. Only private letters imply that she discussed her obligations with her spiritual director, Father Young. She was concerned about her presumed obligation to write on "religious subjects," although her debts motivated her to continue publishing in secular magazines. He prudently suggested that she avoid scrupulosity and direct her energies to "the daily needs of her household."[53]

Other letters suggest a certain surprise on the part of her friends and family about the decision. Aunt Mary Peabody wrote from Boston in a less than successful effort to extend understanding and affection:

Dear Rose,

I must confess to being a good deal taken aback at the news of your change of faith, not having a suspicion of there being a tendency in that direction and still more surprised, when I think of the pure and beautiful religious faith in which you were born and reared . . . I do not wish to judge or criticize anyone for joining a particular sect as long as I feel they are honest and true in their convictions, no matter how much I wish they had not done so. . . . If you and George are the happier for your "new light"—I am sure we are glad.[54]

The letters were not unfriendly. Some, in fact, especially from Rose's close women friends, were loving. These letters reveal, moreover, how close her friendships were.

The new converts undertook several joint projects: the first, a Catholic Summer School in New London; the second, a collaborative effort to write *A Story of Courage: The History of the Georgetown Visitation Convent.* The Summer School was a conjunction of the John Boyle O'Reilly Reading Circle of Boston and the Catholic Educational Union of Youngstown, Ohio. The concept of a Catholic Summer School had first been formulated by Warren B. Mosher of Youngstown, who had worked for fourteen years promoting the project. The first session of the Summer School was held in New London, and it was there that Rose and George Lathrop became involved. The model was the Chautauqua Assembly begun by the Methodists who sought some means to provide more education and culture to their adherents. The idea of the Catholic Summer School was "to have the most prominent Catholics in the country and such foreign Catholics as might be available to lecture from the Catholic point of view on all the issues of the day in history, in literature, in political science, upon the economic problems that are agitating the world, upon the relation between science and religion . . . to remove false assumptions and correct false statements; to pursue the calumnies and slanders uttered against our Creed and Church to their last lurking place."[55]

James J. Walsh, in the Jubilee booklet describing the origins of the Catholic Summer School, offers some astute observations on its necessity in 1892:

The aim of the movement was to bring the Catholics of America into joint action on the intellectual side. The parochial idea had done its noble work and had proved its value; but it also threatened to keep the Catholic mind parochial, to divert its attention from the great enterprises necessary to the general welfare. In 1892 the Catholic press was as parochial as the church administration, the Apostolic Delegation had not been established, nor did the Archbishops meet to consult for the general welfare, the Catholic University was only beginning its career, and Catholic Church extension had merely been dreamed of; therefore the Catholic Summer School may safely lay claim to the honor of innovation. . . .[56]

Archbishop Corrigan, influenced by Father Walter Elliott, had established a reading circle apostolate in the New York archdiocese for the purpose of converting and instructing potential Catholics and new converts. The reading circles had been initiated by Elliott's fellow Paulist, Father Thomas McMillan. The Lathrops contributed their efforts to joining the several reading groups and forming the Catholic Summer School. The effort proved so remarkably successful that the program was eventually transferred to Plattsburg, New York, where Father McMillan took complete charge, after which, because of the distance, the Lathrops participated minimally. But both new converts lent their influence and talent to various Catholic causes. Rose accompanied George on a lecture tour in 1892 when he gave literary talks for various charities, and in the following year George and Rose were working together on the history of the Visitation Convent in Washington, D.C. A diary kept by Rose gives us important details about the relationship between her and her husband during that period and the intensity which she brought to her newfound religion. Father Alfred Young can be credited for giving her sound spiritual direction, as well as a model of the spiritual life. His influence is evident throughout the early years of her conversion, although it is doubtful that he encouraged her to take on every pious practice she discovered.[57]

The 1893 diary is especially revelatory of Rose's devotional life in those years when she was exploring Catholic life and culture. The book itself was the typical microscopic calendarized notebook that allowed only telegraphic entries. Rose wrote her name as Rose H. Hildegarde Lathrop, and began her tiny record keeping January 1. She continued making entries—many of them simple notations about shopping and household tasks—until September 9. The following excerpts are indicative of some of her preoccupations.

January 1893

Sun. 1 Thursday. Mild Weather. Cloudy
The Circumcision. Went to Communion. Read Fenelon's
Letters/Women. Read Miss Dorsey's Catholic Midshipman
Bob. Read in Prayerbook. Wrote to Sisters of Charity at
Loda, Ill. and sent sketch of life, and story for their paper
called Sunball. Gave Mary Fiske book to read. Wrote letters
to Ida.
Mon. 2 Wrote to Mother Leocadia.[58] Sent cards of happy
New Year to Alice, [Alice Wheeler] Mrs. Sonther, and Mrs.
Janvier.
Wrote on visit to Visitation Convent all afternoon.
Worked at houseplans in evening.
Finest moonlight nights and frosty.
Letter from Minne asking help about Consulate.[59]
Tues. 3 Mr. Cole came and there was great talk about house
plans and estimates. Note from Alice. Wrote note to her. Got
George oysters for lunch. After lunch went to house lot.
Called on Mrs. Thomas—not in. Mrs. Latham, Sr. and Mrs.
Latham Jr. called while I was out. Wrote several hours on
Convent visit.

. . . .

Thurs. 5 George ill, Doctor called to inject morphine.
Washed and ironed window curtains, and helped clean windows. Such a storm. Mrs. Amelung did not come as she had
planned.[60] Lovely letter from Henry Amelung.[61] A present of
beautiful pearl knives from Mother, and lovely little scarf
pins. Went to Confession, but the priest had forgotten "A."
Read in "Messengers."[62]
Fri. 6 Epiphany. Made Spiritual Communion. Served. Wrote
to Cleveland and Mrs. Gilder for Minne.
Wrote to Minne and Gwendolyn.[63] Sent Even jacket I made.
Letter from Mrs. Janvier. Invitation to go to Starks and recep-
tion in p.m., went.
Provoked with servant twice.
Sat. 7 Mrs. Thomas called early. Helped her with advice and

encouragement. Wrote to Augusta St. Gaudens.[64] To Mrs. Janvier, Mrs. J. Boyle O'Reilly.

Went on house errands for George to Mr. Bishop.

Took long street car ride.

Wrote on visit to Convent.

Mr. Bishop called to express interest further. Read most interesting Catholic faith and history in Mil.Citizen.

Began new afghan.

Sun. 8 To High Mass. Wrote to Mrs. Mary Cronyn.

Finished Miss Dorsey's "Mid. Bob."

Began "Wild Birds" by Mulholland.

Mr. Cole called about house.

Provoked at unkind words.

Mon. 9 Letter from Lena Gilder, Kind but cannot ask Cleveland favor (of course).

George starts for New York, to S.S. Meeting.

Servant gone, and am enjoying (mildly) a quiet house.

Began Novena to Virgin, in thanksgiving for George's relief while in pain. Lovely air that blessed one on going out. Read the [illegible] of the Convent.

Engaged girl.

. . . .

Wed. 11 Wrote to George and Minne.

Called on Mrs. Thomas. She said how much I helped her.

Took present chocolate pot to Katie Sullivan for work done last summer, for which she would take no money.

George returned in evening.

Painted on present for Sister Seraphina.

. . . .

Sat. 14 Girl came.

Began again Novena to Blessed Virgin for George's relief in pain.

Letter from Sisters at Loda, thanking me for my story and autobiographical sketch and saying they pray for me, and their pastor remembers me at Mass on 19th. God be praised!

Asked at the Memorare that my life be made a willing sacrifice

Mrs. Thomas sent for me. Lovely call.

Sun. 15 Went to Church at 1/2 past 10

Read Little Pilgrim of Our Lady of Martyrs, about Sodality of Bl. Virgin in Spain (Wonderful) and Missionary letter.

Wrote to Mrs. Thomas and sent her two Agnus Deis and leaflets.

Wrote to Sisters at Loda, Ill.

Began to read Christian Symbols in Art.

Painted a little.

Brighter day.

George read me fine sketch he had written.

Mon. 16 Housework. Read in Christian Symbols

Wrote long letter to Beatrix about Niagara.[65] Wrote to Independent, with Miss Benjamin poem.

Called on Miss Benjamin.

Did house errands for George.

Frank sent us the photo of St. Paul in fine frame.[66] George angry and [illegible] about servant, and I was in despair for awhile.

Tues. 17 Began Novena to Blessed Virgin again . . . [illegible] I can't remember whether I said the Litany yesterday. Began again to St. Anthony, as I find certain other prayers must go with that for the Tuesday.

Sent gift to Sister Seraphina; it looked very pretty.

Sent Beatrix cats mounted on rough paper and fixed with ribbon to hang up. Very pretty.

Letter from Mrs. Janvier.

Wrote to Augusta.

Letter from Mrs. O'Reilly asking for visit.

Read Papa's Niagara.[67]

Wed. 18 Went out in morning. Met Mrs. Thomas in street who had been to Church in thanksgiving as her husband had written her his business trouble was over, and he wanted her to come and *help him to be thankful.* The very thought I had in praying for his relief.

Sent for 6 *Pilots* with articles about the Pope in them and wrote at same time Miss Conway. Read in "Grandmother's Chair."

Thanksgiving prayer to Blessed St. Anthony.

....

Sat. 21 George very restless last night.
Prayed beside him for an hour and he was much better and slept. Read at his request from the Bona Mors prayers. Went sleighriding with George in afternoon. Very pleasant.
Saw Brown and Denison, builders for George, in evening. Their price for house lower. Letter from Minne.

....

Sun. 29 To half past ten church. George read and called very fine my experimental opening to the Annals of the Visitation. Wrote to Mrs. Thomas.
Read story in *Pilot* by Rosa Mulholland.
Happy day.

....

February
Sun. 5 1/2 past 10 Church.
Began Novena for Mother's conversion.
Wrote Mary Peabody.
Very tired.
We got two blessed candles. I used one for evening prayers. It burns as steadily as True Faith
Read aloud to George.

....

Shrove Tuesday. 14 To 8 o'clock Mass.
Called on Sister M. Xavier. She gave me her own beads of the Seven Dolours. Gave her $2.00 for thanksgiving in connection with Novena.
Wed. 15 To Mass. Began Novena for Mr. Thomas' conversion, also for Mr. Goddard, Sr. and Kitty Goddard.
Our Lady of Good Counsel, with blessed candles, and Litany of Loretto. Sister M. Xavier gave me beads for my cook.

Sat. 18 Confession.

Letter saying I was taken by the Sisters of Visitation Convent in Brooklyn into Pious Union of O.L. of Good Counsel.

Sent three dollars for three candles on altar on Tuesday, for the three Conversions.

Happy Day

....

March 1 Special prayers to St. Joseph this month. His litany everyday.

Fri. 3 Una's birthday

Sent Nellie Moran picture of Our Lady of Perpetual Help.

Took communion in honor of Sacred Heart

Wed. 8 Using holy water at home

Blessed candle during Novena prayers

....

Tues. 14 Ended Novena of 9 Tuesdays to St. Anthony. Went to 8 o'clock Mass and took Communion. Father O'Connell then invested me with Scapular of Mt. Carmel, using one given me by Father Young. A lovely Spring Day.

Wed. 15 George begins to ask about St. Anthony to use his book of life and prayers and to feel his influence.

....

April 1 Moved into our new home at 8 Broad St. Charmed with it.

April 7 Went to Mass and Communion at 7 at Convent. Began Novena of first Fridays for "nobility of life" for us both. George's increasing liveliness is almost astonishing.

April 8 . . .

60.00 from BOK for story[68]

....

July 23 Began Novena to Our Lady of Perpetual Help for George's recovery

....

July 24 Communion of Reparation

....

August 4 [No entry but a sketched cross]
Tues. 15 Novena to St. Anthony-first day for success of *Annals*

....

September 1 Forgot to begin first Friday and must begin Novena of First Fridays again.

This record of Rose's new devotional life exemplifies what was typical of Catholic piety of the period, although some passages suggest an intensity that was probably not typical. The January 14 Memorare petition, especially, goes beyond the usual requests of pious Catholics, even in a petitioning age. The *Bona Mors* devotion was a series of prayers for a "happy death" which included meditation on the passion and death of Jesus, the suffering of his mother, and the five wounds.[69] The "Agnus Deis" referred to in the January 15th and subsequent entries was a small cake of virgin wax stamped on one side with an image of the "Lamb of God immolated for us on the altar of the Cross." It was usually blessed by the pope and worn on the person. Ann Taves notes that prayers to be recited daily by its wearers often appeared in prayerbooks after 1840.[70]

Rose had clearly accepted every recommendation. She was trying to be attentive to the calendar of the saints, the appropriate devotions of the month, and she believed deeply in the power of novenas. If there was any discontinuity in her conversion, it would be in her cheerful adaptation of a system of prayer that Protestants despised. These were the daily acknowledgements that Catholics were different from Protestants, that Catholic culture had links to the whole world. Displaced Europeans still had St. Anthony and the Sacred Heart, and faithful Catholics could be identified anywhere by a rosary in a purse or back pocket, or a medal around the neck. Because this accumulation of prayers and sacramentals were the recommended forms of prayer to all

Catholics, from bishops to servant girls, it would be surprising if Rose and her husband had not embraced these universal customs whole-heartedly. The concentrated effort Rose's diary reveals suggests not only that she was pleased to take on a daily schedule of prayers, but that she needed such a method to give form to her emotional and spiritual life. Her poetry, "with its roots in the air" clearly had not been a medium for emotional discipline.

What we see less of in her recorded devotional life during this particular year is what at that point in Catholic cultural history was not urged, namely frequent reading of the scriptures. Her 1898 diary suggests more attention to biblical reflection. The most prominent reference to scripture in her subsequent publications is a reprint of a letter from President Theodore Roosevelt to a Methodist gathering in New York in 1902. In that letter Roosevelt responded to the question of what kind of men and women the world needed. Answering that the world needed more people who read and revered the Bible, Roosevelt concluded, "If we read the Bible aright we read a book which teaches us to go forth and do the work of the Lord; to do the work of the Lord in this world as we find it; to try to make things better in this world, even if only a little better, because we have lived in it. . . . We plead for a closer and wider and deeper study of the Bible, so that our people may be in fact as well as in theory 'doers of the word and not hearers only.' "[71] By 1902 nothing could have been closer to Rose's own convictions, especially when expressed by one of her favorite people. Protestant believers had made biblical study their domain. To counteract that emphasis on the triumphantly beautiful King James translation, the Roman Church called its adherents to devotion to Jesus in the blessed sacrament.

Eucharistic devotion emerged most powerfully during the years that Rose was learning about Catholicism, and especially during the first decades of the twentieth century when she was entering more and more deeply into the life of the church. Five National Eucharistic Congresses were held between 1895 and 1911, at one of which her own spiritual director was a principal homilist.[72] Rose's devotion to the eucharist, which had clearly been urged upon her from the beginning, was never to diminish. All things distinctively Catholic she embraced without hesitation, and gradually that most distinctive life of all began to attract her: the visible presence of women consecrated publicly to the service of the church.[73]

Her first reaction to nuns was breathlessly idealistic, as letters and essays indicate. What is surprising is how quickly realistic and practical she became when her own opportunity to profess vows eventually became possible.

In 1893 Rose and her husband were asked to assist in the composition of a history of the Visitation Convent in Washington, the convent referred to in her diary. Since, by her own account, Rose wrote the Introduction to *A Story of Courage,* the chapter is interesting to examine for its defense of religious life in general, as well as its function as a Foreword to the history of the Georgetown Visitation Convent. Her style in this account is recognizable. The chapter is entitled (in retrospect, interestingly) "On the Threshold." We read:

> The religious celibate cheers other human creatures, but never relies upon being cheered by them; she brightens the lives of others, but she never throws aside her solemn adoration of Christ. She smiles, it is true, and even turns a happy phrase, or jokes daintily, with a laugh of genuine mirth; but her eyes are calm, the while. Always there is something that tells of the heart once and forever pierced with the sword; the peaceful dwelling of a nature which has been touched and tamed by God. This seriousness strikes cold through one's less pure and generous nature; the whole aspect of the convent is too sudden a contrast from luxury and confusion to spare one a gasp of dread.[74]

In the next chapter we read of George and Rose being given a tour of the convent and grounds which included a new graveyard where one of the sisters, Rose writes, "a cherished friend, the niece of Ralph Waldo Emerson, and formerly an intimate visitor in the household of Nathaniel Hawthorne, is buried."[75] The sister was Sister Jane Frances, formerly Phoebe Ripley, who had once been Rose and Una's music teacher in Concord.

In February, 1893, *The Ladies' Home Journal* published an interview with Mrs. Lathrop as part of a series entitled (unfortunately) "Clever Daughters of Clever Men." The style of the interview by Lillie Hamilton French is in the purring tone adopted by women's publications of the period and contains no real insights into Rose's own thinking. It focuses, rather, on Rose's interest in art and her years of study in Dresden and Kensington. Only the final paragraph offers a glimpse into her personality and the impression she made on the writer: "Mrs. Lathrop has no pose nor is she content to assume one for you. She is, moreover, constantly leading you away from herself, suggesting to you other pictures she has seen, till for the time being, you forget even the woman before you in your own delight at seeing with her eyes."[76] A letter from the writer in the Rosary Hill archives testifies more directly to the impression Mrs. Lathrop made: "I never knew," she wrote to Rose, "how hard it was to write of anyone of whom you were fond. You want to tell the world how nice and how lovely and how charming they are and you do not want to overstep the bounds of delicacy when you do so."[77]

Rose was gaining attention. In 1893 when she was one of the speakers at the Catholic Congress held in conjunction with the World's Columbian Exposition at Chicago, her speech was a startling announcement. However idealized, her image of woman constituted a rejection of the merely decorative use of women for whatever purpose and their exploitation as objects of admiration:

> Is she who is the mother of all perfect impulses, to be represented anywhere forever as the adorer of vanity? Is she always anywhere to appear laden with jewels, like a jeweler's showcase . . . ? O woman, the hour has struck when you are to arise and defend your rights, your abilities for competition with men in intellectual and professional endurance, the hour when you are to prove that purity and generosity are for the nation as well as for the home. . . .[78]

This was not a new Rose Lathrop talking, but it was a new *public* Rose Lathrop. The sentiment alerts us to what was ahead in her life, as well as to the then current controversies on woman suffrage. She seems not to be in agreement with either John Boyle O'Reilly or his eventual successor to the editorship of the Boston *Pilot,* Katherine Conway, both of whom were opposed to woman suffrage.[79] Nor do her words bear much resemblance to what was being taught and preached from the pulpits and lecterns in the American Catholic world. Not even the most liberal American bishops in that decade believed that women should have the vote, let alone careers.[80] In 1900 only six Catholic clergymen are reported to have supported woman suffrage.[81] The *Catholic Encyclopedia* had stated that the "female sex is in some respects inferior to the male sex as regards body and soul," and the bishop of Fall River, Massachusetts, had pointed out bluntly that "smartness is not becoming to women."[82] Rose Hawthorne Lathrop was to suffer more than once from comparable affronts to her understanding.

It was at this same Congress that the Catholic feminist movement had its most conspicuous inauguration. It was there that Alice T. Toomy founded a national league of Catholic women modeled on the Women's Christian Temperance Union; and there that Eliza Allen Starr declared that women who declined to contribute to the social good 'in the cloister or under the protection of the religious habit' had a duty to move out into the world."[83] This gathering of Catholic women could not have left Mrs. Lathrop unaffected.

The debate on the role of women continued in the liberal Catholic publication, *The Catholic World,* where the views of three influential Catholic women were presented under the title "The Woman Question among Catholics." Flanking Eleanor C. Donnelly's "The Home is Woman's Sphere" and Katherine Conway's "Woman Has No Vocation to Public Life" was Alice Toomy's "There Is a Public Sphere for Catholic Women." Here the writer argued:

> Tens of thousands of our ablest Catholic women are working with the W.C.T.U. and other non-Catholic philanthropies, because they find no organization in their own church as a field for their activities. Every Catholic woman who has had much association outside the church is frequently met with the question, Why don't you Catholics take care of your own poor, and not leave so much work for other churches to do for you? The truth is that ours is the church of the poor, and manifold as is the charity work of the religious and the benevolent societies, a vast amount has to go undone because there is no one to attend to it.[84]

It would be surprising if Rose Lathrop, herself a delegate to the Congress, had not read the debate in this prominent Catholic journal. It is clear where her sympathies were directing her.

In public Mr. and Mrs. Lathrop were the ideal couple, their home, by all accounts a bright and welcoming center of hospitality, their friends cordial, their faith earnest. Private letters indicate, however, that close friends and family knew of domestic problems, although the precise nature of those problems is never identified. Rose Lathrop revealed very little of her particular difficulties. Even the diary, which she must have seen as a record, rather than a means of self-expression is of little help. But something extraordinary was happening to her interiorly. The diary gives us only the traces: "Asked at the Memorare," she had noted, "that my life might be made a willing sacrifice."

Rose Lathrop was becoming deeply interested in social concerns and charitable works. In 1892 the same year that several of Rose's

poems had been published in *Scribner's Monthly,* a series of articles
entitled "The Poor in Great Cities" had appeared. These included one
by Jacob Riis—"The Children of the Poor," and another, especially
pertinent, entitled "Life in New York Tenement Houses, As Seen by a
City Missionary," by William T. Elsing. Among the suggestions for
reducing the extent of suffering in New York's lower East Side is an
increase of trained nurses for the sick. "Anyone who desires to relieve
the suffering poor in the most direct and effective way can do it through
a trained nurse," says the missionary.[85] Rose would in a few short years
write her own description of such tenements and her 1897 article is not
unlike the account in the June, 1892, issue of *Scribner's.*

Maynard notes that Rose gave a talk at the New England
Women's Press Association, probably in 1894, on Catholic works of
charity, a topic she selected herself and which may have startled her
literary audience. She had heard from Father Young about the charitable works of Father John C. Drumgoole, founder of the Mission of the
Immaculate Virgin for the care of orphaned children.[86] In the same
year Father Young told her of a seamstress sent to Blackwell's Island to
die of cancer because there was no one to care for her. By 1895 she had
sought and received permission to separate permanently from her husband. When George's operatic version of *The Scarlet Letter* opened in
March, 1896, Rose, escorted by a friend, sat in the balcony, hoping not
to be noticed.

Separation and Service

The sequence of events can be traced in part from her letters to a
close friend addressed as "Mattie," presumably Martha Stearns, an old
school friend.[87] In 1894 or 1895 she made a retreat under the direction
of Sister Mary Bernard Stuart of the (Halifax, N.S.) Sisters of Charity at
the Academy of the Assumption in Wellesley Hills. Her old friend from
childhood days, Alice Wheeler, offered her hospitality. An undated
letter in the Berg Collection to a Miss Charlotte Holloway says:

> Your dear letter was a great source of pleasure to me, and you
> were a good girl (do not wince at the accusation) to write to
> me now, when I am so in need of [illegible, possibly *friends*]
> and sympathy.
>   But in the last few days I have been a great deal stronger,
> and almost wholly free from disagreeable aches, and so I am
> full of hope and gratitude.
>   I write especially now to thank you, because I am going

into "retreat" with the Sisters of Charity here, for ten days, and I shall remember you, dear, and all yours, and I want you to say a prayer for me that I may become less stupid and more useful.

During the retreat she learned of St. Vincent de Paul's motto, "I am for God and the poor." We know also from her subsequent writings how deeply Father Young's story of the impoverished seamstress had touched her.

In 1895, Rose took a trip to Jamaica to visit Julian and his family and left Jamaica in May of that year, planning to spend the winter and summer with the Grey Nuns of Montreal where she would participate in the prayer life of the community and study nursing. "My hope has long been," she wrote to Mattie, "to learn *nursing,* and the way has at last been opened and granted to me." Her plans are surprisingly clear at this point:

After I have learned this blessed art to some extent, and also become familiar with devotional exercises, and the care of the *souls* of the sick and dying, so that I can *intelligently* teach the poor who are ignorant of God the wonders of His love, or fulfil for the devout the exercises they long for in their distress, I shall expect to come from Montreal to work in New York. But I do not trouble my little head with much thought of the far future; I lean so wholly upon our Lord that I am sure He will feel my appeal, and lead me on, where I can serve Him best. I feel very weak and stupid just at the entrance to my work; but I know this is actually the way, for Mr. Satan knows when to attack better than any General. . . .

Two letters written the following summer to Henry Oscar Houghton from Montreal, recommending her nephew Henry Hawthorne for a position in the publishing firm, are signed Rose Hawthorne. She was later to be consistent in retaining the name Lathrop. A February 7th letter from Wellesley Hills to her cousin Richard says, "I am, alas, separated from my husband, and of course sanctioned in this step by my Church. This will show you how wise the step was. I will explain to your sisters about it when I see them. I have the greatest admiration for Mr. Lathrop's powers, and hope for his complete sanctification for which I pray lovingly."[88]

In the summer of 1896, within a year of her separation from her husband, she studied nursing at the New York Cancer Hospital at

106th Street and 8th Avenue. Her letters abound in good spirits and she seemed gratified that the patients considered her especially kind. She describes a drop-in visit from Archer Huntington, the heir of the millionaire railroad magnate and warned him that when he or his mother would come they could expect her to beg. There were too many patients being turned away because they could not afford hospital care. In September of that year she set out to provide nursing care for the cancerous poor. Her first letters are addressed from 5 East 12th Street. The day after settling in she wrote to her friend Mattie again, describing how her bag "with some of my very precious Catholic objects and prayer books, and my *mother's watch*" was stolen in the hall of her lodging on the very day of her arrival. "Fortunately I was spared the worst distress," she comments, "by not being at all cross myself, and by feeling strongly that here was another step towards the absolute poverty which is growing so dear to me."[89]

George, however, was not yet reconciled to her change of status. A letter dated October 31, 1896, from an official in the Chancery of the New York Archdiocese says rather cryptically: "Mr. Lathrop has been in to see me. We have had a very practical and sensible talk. I think you will find him much improved in kindness and in other things."[90] But by then the separation was complete and Rose had begun a new kind of life. A transformation had been effected that was as startling in its own way as her marriage to George had been. But this change of status was to be permanent.

After completing her course work in nursing cancerous patients, Rose Hawthorne Lathrop began what was to be her most demanding life project: providing nursing care to those cancer-afflicted people who could not afford care and who, because of an exaggerated fear of contagion were treated as the outcasts of society. She had failed as an artist, and achieved only minimal success as a writer. Her marriage had faltered, her only child had died. At the age of 45, she began a new commitment. The diary and journal she kept during this extraordinary period in her life testify to a resolution that was both practical and idealistic. In the months she spent at the New York Cancer Hospital she had become convinced of the necessity of the work she was about to undertake, the way she would begin, and the principles that would guide her. She was fortunate in the spiritual direction she was receiving at this time from Father Fidelis Stone, whom she described as "her chief adviser" and who had written her to say he wanted "to have a talk such as we have not had before." She adds, "He is so kind in his expression of respect for me that I am really quite encouraged."[91]

The initial task was to find space to establish her particular kind of service. She rented two rooms on Scammel Street and began her ministry and within two months she was ill. A Thanksgiving letter to Mattie mentions the companionship of Mary Mahoney, a mutual friend, and her "patient," who would have been Mrs. Watson, whom she first cared for at the Cancer Hospital. She notes that she has to be cautious because of her illness:

> I used to receive the sick and sore-beset at 8 a.m.—then go out till 1 p.m. on sick calls; then more patients came to be "dressed" and to get advice and at 5:30 p.m. I started out for my visits to dress wounds etc., with my heavy basket of medicines and salves, etc., on my arm, and fortunate to be able to return at 9 p.m.[92]

She knew that she was going to need more space, additional co-workers, and money: "Even I . . . would not have believed the dearth of help and remembrance and kindness were so great and pervasive. It must not be—this politic, business-like rejection of responsibility and godly love." She wanted to achieve all of these goals and obtain at the same time the blessing of the church—in her case, the New York Archdiocese—on her efforts. The obstacles to these purposes were formidable. Her next move, in the Spring of 1897, was to 668 Water Street where she now had four rooms instead of two, as well as two additional live-in patients.

Few of those who joined her in those first few years could stay with the project she envisioned. And those who stayed could not always refrain from describing their fatigue, discouragement, and occasional disgust at the searing hardships they endured. From Rose's pen we read only of the needs: the need to go on, the need to beg for money, the need to provide care for more and more suffering people.

The document describing Rose Lathrop's first venture into the project which was to consume her mind and soul and energies for the rest of her life is as compelling and powerful as it is simple. The spiritual maturity she had reached, to judge by the level of compassion her journal reveals, is extraordinary. To convert publicly to religion is not rare; to practice the works of charity is not rare; "to declare I wanted to be *of* the poor as well as among them . . ." is the beginning of heroism. The 1897–98 diary entries show a woman consumed with her work, her prayer, her concern for the cause she had undertaken. She describes without undue comment two visions of Christ during this year, but does not dwell on the experiences.

Her description of the death of her husband (April 19, 1897) in the April 21 entry suggests a love and respect and tenderness that never died. What is perhaps even more revealing is her reference to his soul, which "came, I am sure, to console me, in his loveliest way of forgiveness." There is not a hint in the diary of any suffering she may have endured in her years of marriage. She also records in a subsequent entry that on April 19 she and her companions began to pray for a new house for their work. It is evident that she did very little looking back. To Mattie she wrote:

I was crushed by George's death, not ever having dreamed that I could bear his death at all, if it came before he had accepted my work as a wise measure, and helped in it, and raised our lives to a high united service of God. My heart was filled with love and misery. . . . How well I knew that I loved him, and that the shadows were not to live, but the beauty and joy of the past. But I could not bear to live and work with George dead, and no goodbye. But I heard lovely things of what he had said . . . about me lately; and the morning after his death he seemed to come to me and say in his most enchanting mood of boyish tenderness, that of course he loved me, and of course we never could have any real misunderstanding of each other.[93]

FOUNDRESS: 1898–1926

If we compare her writing style, her preoccupations, the impression Rose Hawthorne Lathrop made on others during the years between 1871 and 1897, we should not be surprised at evidences of her transition from being a (very) young woman filled with her own sense of happiness and presumably romantic good fortune, a little flushed with her newfound intellectual companionship and social successes to a gracious, self-effacing, and mature heiress to the Peabody-Hawthorne connection. We hear in the 1870s and 1880s of her exuberant decorating tastes, her continuous efforts to write in the style appropriate to the popular journals of the day, of extensive travel, correspondence, dinners, visits to conversational salons. And we read in the available records of an increasing interest in charitable works, in historic convents, in the role of women in public life, in prayer and spiritual reading. She remained on affectionate terms with her family, despite misunder-standing, disagreements, hurt, and marital conflict. She yielded to rec-onciliation and urged others not to stir up disagreeable memories.

Between 1871 and 1897 Rose Hawthorne Lathrop became a ma-ture and unusually virtuous woman. She had always been beautiful. By 1897 her beauty was touched with the signs of both suffering and deter-mination. A comparison of two photographs taken in these years is especially revealing. In the second, the last taken before she assumed a religious dress, we detect not only sorrow, but strength. The prettiness has left, but something else has affected her features. It is not fatigue, but longing. How much she would yet do was not clear; how much she would try to do is transparent.

In the spring of 1897, Rose rented four rooms on Water Street, as more and more patients began to seek her services. Some of Rose's former friends, and even her nieces, attempted to help her in the work, but they all found it too difficult to sustain on a regular basis. Volun-teers came and went, nurses daunted by the sacrifices involved in such a project gave what they had strength to give, but none could imagine such ministry to the suffering poor as a lifetime commitment. The diary tells of her prayers for coworkers who could see her vision and stay with the possibilities. On December 15, 1897, those prayers were answered.

Alice Huber

The young woman who was to join Rose Hawthorne Lathrop in her project and to become a cofounder of the Servants of Relief was to remember every detail of that first visit to Water Street on a cold De-cember afternoon. Later she was to describe in her own memoirs the first conversation, all of her initial misgivings, and her own gradual realization that this perfect work of charity was to be her own life's calling.

She had been born in Jasper, Indiana, and had grown up in Louis-ville, Kentucky, where she attended school at Holy Rosary Academy and St. Catherine's Academy in Springfield. Both schools were oper-ated by the Dominican Sisters, and Alice had considered joining their community. But instead, she postponed a decision to enter religious life and began studying art in Cincinnati at the Academy of Fine Arts. After returning to St. Catherine's to teach art, she had eventually con-tinued her studies in Baltimore, Springfield, Illinois, and finally New York City—all the while reflecting on what kind of religious commit-ment she would undertake. Early in November, 1897, one of Rose's numerous letters to the New York *Times* attracted her attention. It read in part:

> Let the poor, the patient, the destitute, and hopeless receive from our compassion what we would give to our own families if we were really generous to them. Let the woman who begs for care have comfort and bestow upon this representative of Christ a little gentle attention until she dies. This is all. Yet it requires the sacrifice of your life. But that is why Christ asked it and blesses with unending reward the simple choice.[94]

Alice Huber had once heard of Rose Hawthorne Lathrop through her spiritual director, the same Father Fidelis Stone whom Rose knew. Now she wrote to him in Rome and asked for a letter of introduction. Several weeks later with the letter in hand she came to 668 Water Street. After her first conversation with Rose, she agreed to return and work one afternoon a week. On March 24, 1898 (a few weeks before George Lathrop's death) she joined Rose, the first coworker to assist in the project and to remain for the rest of her life. The initiation into the work, and the deprivations it called for were so overwhelming that she was to write later: "I became extremely homesick and shed so many tears then that I have not been able to shed any since."[95] Rose had recorded in her own diary on January 4, underlining the sentence emphatically, "*Alice Huber decided to give her life to the work.*"

After George's death Rose knew she was free to declare her religious commitment more conspicuously. With Alice looking on with surprise and grief, she cut off her hair and put on a quasi-religious habit, modeled after that of the Sisters of Charity. Like the Charity Sisters, she put on a little cap instead of a veil. Alice also adopted the mode of dress (refusing the hair cutting suggestion) and together they approached Archbishop Corrigan for permission to wear it. The Archbishop was apparently startled, his manner so abrupt that Rose's eyes filled with tears. The dress was too "religious." He was not as gratified by this enterprise as they had expected and, in fact, recommended that Rose join another community of pious women, founded especially for widows, dedicated also to the care of cancer patients. Rose in the spirit of obedience agreed to be interviewed by the foundress of the "Women of Calvary."[96] Alice, when queried about what she would do—not being a widow and thus ineligible—replied that she would "go back to Water Street." Subsequently Rose, after one conversation, was rather perfunctorily dismissed by the foundress of the Women of Calvary who observed that the two projects had nothing in common with each other. But apparently threatened by the work proposed by Rose Lathrop, the same woman requested that the Archbishop terminate Rose's work. This he refused to do.[97]

In the following year the number of patients had increased to such an extent that larger quarters were required. The records indicate that as many as three hundred people a month were seeking help. Rose had attracted the sympathy and attention of enough influential people to purchase with their initial donations a three-story building at 426 Cherry Street which the now-christened "Servants of Relief" were to call "St Rose's Free Home for Incurable Cancer." The name of the home was decided, after three days of prayer, by drawing from a list of possible saintly patrons. St. Rose of Lima was an appropriate designation. The statue of Rose's patron saint was conspicuous in the quarters she had used since the inception of the work. Among the contributors to the Cherry Street Home were J. Warren Greene, Nathanael Whitman, Theodore B. Starr, John D. Crimmins, and Mrs. Frances A. Moulton.[98]

Just prior to the move to Cherry Street a young Dominican priest had stopped into the Water Street home to thank Rose and her co-workers for their assistance in caring for a parishioner from St. Vincent Ferrer Church on Lexington Avenue. He had noticed the statue of St. Rose of Lima and suggested somewhat casually that given such devotion to the saint, perhaps the women should join the Third Order of St. Dominic. They would need the graces and support such affiliation would provide. The priest was Father Clement M. Thuente, then an assistant at the parish, eventually to become one of the lifelong supporters of Rose's work.[99] He was planning to establish a local chapter of Dominican tertiaries at his parish, and in August, 1899, he visited Rose and her small community again, this time, with an invitation to become Third Order Dominicans. Archbishop Corrigan authorized the affiliation in September with the admonition, "I think it would be well if you and your companions would join the Chapter and thus have a share in the spiritual benefits and helps. With regard to the Religious costume, it is not to be worn in public, but if you call on Father Thuente some arrangement could be devised, suitable for your work, and at the same time, according to the Rule of the Chapter."[100]

Rose and Alice Huber were entering at this point into what may be called the visible mission of the church; they were no longer private individuals embarked on private works of charity, but were linking their work to the life of the Catholic Church in the United States, and to the Archdiocese of New York in particular. It would be safe to observe that until this point in her life Rose's experience with that church was still somewhat limited. She had been received into it only eight years before and knew of the church only through private instruction and spiritual direction; and in retrospect, it is clear that she had some of the most brilliant and broadminded directors in the American church as her spiritual advisors. She had never had occasion to work with church officials or hierarchy. She had begun to meet prominent lay Catholics, but there is no reason to believe she had any understanding in depth of local church history or the then current and immensely important sequence of events involving her archbishop.

The Servants of Relief and the Church

Rose Hawthorne Lathrop and her husband George had been confirmed in 1891 by Archbishop Michael Corrigan, whose approval she now depended upon completely. He was the third bishop of New York, described by a contemporary scholar as the "pivotal conservative in the key American diocese . . ." whose "conservative, authoritarian, monolithic stance . . . became the dominant one in the American Church in the first half of the twentieth century."[101] Consecrated bishop of the New York Archdiocese in 1886, Michael Corrigan had been enmeshed in ecclesiastical controversy from his first years in New York as coadjutor under Cardinal McCloskey. He had opposed the establishment of the Catholic University in Washington (clearly preferring a New York provenance), he had fought Archbishop John Ireland on the proposal to have released time religious education instead of a parochial school system financed completely by Catholics, and his long battle with the political and social activist Father Edward McGlynn had devoured his energies for years. In 1892 Archbishop Francesco Satolli was appointed apostolic delegate to the United States in a Roman effort to oversee American affairs. This was the same Satolli who had supported American liberal bishops in every cause that Corrigan opposed. Corrigan's political fortunes were at a low ebb. Subsequent events, however, determined that the American church would take the direction that Michael Corrigan envisioned. Pope Leo XIII condemned participation in parliaments of religion or interfaith assemblies; the liberal Denis O'Connell was forced to resign as rector of the North American College in Rome, and John Keane as rector of The Catholic University in Washington. Archbishop Corrigan got the auxiliary bishop he wanted— John Farley—and in 1896 he opened a new seminary, St. Joseph's at Dunwoodie, New York. In 1898 Corrigan celebrated his Silver Jubilee; the Spanish-American War began and America was bathed in a sea of wild patriotism. One year later Pope Leo XIII, partly in response to the slanted interpretation given the French translation of Elliott's *Life of Isaac Hecker,* issued the notorious *Testem Benevolentiae,* the condemnation of "Americanism," a "phantom heresy" that no single group of Americans was known to have believed or preached. But Archbishop Corrigan praised and thanked the pope for his "infallible teaching." His enemies were overthrown and he, the most powerful—but perhaps among his episcopal peers, the least liked bishop in America. No one ever questioned his personal piety, but as Robert Emmett Curran has remarked, he seemed unable to translate private piety into public probity."[102]

A convert from Unitarian New England, the daughter of Emerson-inspired Sophia Hawthorne, was in no position historically or culturally to assess the political situation or the internal problems of the church she had joined. But there were many, especially in the New York archdiocese. She was not always to understand how the innumerable problems of that situation were to impinge on her own hopes and needs, but she and her companions were to suffer from the clerics of the church as often as she was helped by them. Archbishop Corrigan was one of the more supportive prelates in Rose's life. It was he who authorized the small community of Dominican tertiaries in 1900 to wear the Dominican habit, and he who allowed them to profess public vows and to assume religious names. Rose's memories of his support became very much a part of the history of the community.[103] Several issues of the community publication contain tributes to him, and upon his death (1902), we read an especially revealing comment:

> The loss of His Grace, Archbishop Corrigan, is deeply felt by the Sisters of this charity. Although His Grace had many years ago adopted the proposed work of the Women of Calvary, for cancer, as the diocesan activity in this direction, he believed that a different method of caring for such sick poor was also useful and worthy of encouragement. No one has felt the gentle courtesy of the Archbishop more completely than the Servants of Relief, who have received his guidance, finally sanctioning the admitting of them to the Dominican Order, (when maligned and opposed in some quarters) with a cordial respect and mercy that was sufficient to soothe the pain of trial, such as all effort for the general good is certain to encounter.[104]

This is one of several references to harsh opposition to the Servants of Relief, even at the beginning of their project, and the parenthesis seems to suggest that the opposition came from within clerical circles. No motive for this opposition can be determined.

Clement Thuente, the liaison between the archbishop and his struggling little group of tertiaries, was to experience problems of his own, for the New York Dominicans could not always agree on the directions their lives and ministry were to assume; and not all the members of the order were to give Rose the affection and support a fledgling Dominican community needed. But those experiences for both of them were yet ahead. For the moment Rose, Alice, and another coworker who had joined them—known in the records as "Miss Higley"—were in the first phase of achieving full status as a canonically approved religious congregation in the American church.

Rose does not seem to have consciously planned to found a religious congregation, but so many were being established at the time that the possibility must always have been before her. The nineteenth century saw 119 religious foundations established in the United States, of which twenty-eight were of American origin. Fifty-nine of these congregations were established in the last third of the century. Whatever her specific desires, her spirituality dictated only that she keep the vision of her proposed ministry clear and that she remain faithful to the principles she knew to be essential to her work. Her diary indicates that every crisis was met by prayer, usually by a novena—sometimes several novenas.

In the decade in which she was beginning her nursing ministry, lay women as well as religious communities were launching projects. This was an age when many women wanted to be "useful." If Catholic girls became nuns, Protestant women became missionaries, suffragettes, deaconesses, temperance reformers, and social workers. Day nurseries, homes for working girls, training schools, homes for friendless women, homes for convalescents, bureaus for settling the thousands of arriving immigrants, maternity hospitals, hospitals for "consumptives," training hospitals for nurses—all were part of the vast charitable works begun at the end of the century.

In the New York archdiocese, as in church organizations and social service agencies, these undertakings required some kind of managerial attention and eventual approval, especially if organizers of the charity were to receive or solicit funds. It is not surprising that Rose and Alice were sometimes given brusque advice to join one of the existing charities, or to modify their position that charitable donations were to fund all of the work, or even to expand their field of work so that the sisters who joined them in the future "would have enough to do." After one of the innumerable meetings with prelates and priests that their work required, Alice, later to be known as Sister Rose, remarked in her *Memoirs:* "In these early days we rather looked for kindness, now we are philosophical enough to be satisfied with ordinary politeness." The observation is an indication of how wearying the task of obtaining approval for every step of the way was starting to become and how overbearing their clerical superiors could be.

But in 1899 Rose and her companions were preoccupied with immediate needs: getting bandages, beds, salves, medicine, food, pharmaceuticals, money. At the same time, they needed to establish a rule of sorts that would guarantee some community stability and a common life of prayer. For two years her spiritual director had been Father Charles Parks, who had drawn up a rule of life for her to follow and recommended the classical spiritual books of the period for her to read: Faber's *Growth in Holiness, Spiritual Conferences, The Light of the Conscience.* When in September, 1899, they became members of the Third Order of St. Dominic, or chapter tertiaries, they were not yet permitted to wear the Dominican habit, because the community was still officially a lay community, like many comparable groups attached to major religious orders who entered into the spirit of such orders but did not join them by public vows. But they did adopt a Rule of Life which more closely approximated the life of canonically established religious congregations. The Little Office of the Blessed Virgin became the community prayer, and mass was offered in their quarters on Sundays and feastdays, although it was originally not permitted until two representatives from the Chancery came to check on whether or not the women had appropriate vestments for the celebrant and adequate facilities. It was not until November, 1900, that Archbishop Corrigan allowed the tertiaries to assume the black and white Dominican habit and to make public profession of vows. The delay had been a source of disappointment to Rose, but the ceremony of profession, December 8, was an important milestone. The Servants of Relief would date the founding of their community to that event. Father Thuente received their vows, and the three women adopted new religious names—Rose becoming Sister Alphonsa, Alice taking the name Sister Rose and Cecelia Higley, Sister Mary Magdalen. The only invited guest was Father Charles Parks. The Columbus Dominicans, stationed at St. Vincent Ferrer Church, lent the three new sisters the rule and constitutions of their own congregation, and the Servants of Relief entered into a new phase of spirituality and public ministry.

With this small but important initial step taken toward establishing continuity in their work, the clearest ministerial need was (again) for larger quarters. For one thing, the sisters were not adequately equipped to provide a home for the numerous men who sought help. The usual recourse in pastoral need was to pray. The sisters prayed. The patients prayed. The novenas began. If their prayers were not answered at the end of the first novena, a second novena was begun. At the end of the second novena, patients and sisters looked about for results. The number of times these insistent novenas were answered is almost disconcerting. On the last day of a second novena to the Sacred Heart, when the community was about to start Novena Number Three, Father I.M. Cothonay of a community of French Dominicans living in what was then known as Sherman Park arrived at St. Rose's Home, requesting to see the superior. He had heard that the sisters were looking for a larger place. These Dominicans had been in the United States for only six years, having been driven out of France when their property was confiscated. But tensions were easing in France, and the property, once the Tecumseh Hotel, was no longer needed. Price: $28,000.00. Size: Sixty rooms of house and nine acres of land. The Servants of Relief had $1000.00. Archbishop Corrigan authorized the purchase, forbade the sisters to "seek alms," and expressed the hope that they would be able to pay for the property by means of donations.[105]

Efforts to Expand

On June 1, 1901, Mother Alphonsa and the postulants moved out of the city to Sherman Park where the railroad station was marked Unionville and the Post Office, Neperan. And in that year the twenty-five-year correspondence between Mother Alphonsa and Sister Rose began. Sister Rose remained in the New York house, and the two women who had formed such an instantaneous affection and respect for each other were never again to live together. Their correspondence, however, is a signal indication of the love that enables human beings to sustain great work when every sacrifice is needed and gratification is minimal.

From Rosary Hill, the name orginally given to the monastery and now retained, Mother Alphonsa was to direct the life of the community, raise money, stabilize the ministry and shape its spirituality. Sister Rose would be her confidante, her assistant, advisor, cofoundress and eventual successor. The two women were very different, but one wonders if the project could have survived without their combined gifts, as well as their mutual love. Rose Hawthorne had never relished being alone, neither as a child, nor a young woman. If her mother had not died, would she have married George so precipitously? That Alice

Huber entered her life at such a critical juncture, that Rose was to be wonderfully consoled by her friendship and support, that her buoyancy never seemed diminished once some purpose to her life was found and she had a companion with whom to share that life—all of these events must have seemed to the new "Mother" (another irony of grace) such an extraordinary turn of events in so few years that her subsequent intensity becomes more understandable. The public would never again see a written expression from her, poetic or otherwise, of meandering emotion and ill-defined purpose. She knew where her real genius lay and had found her real love. In 1901 she began her first new sustained writing project on behalf of her work, a pamphlet called *Christ's Poor.* In it the ideals she set herself and laid before the public are forcefully articulated.

The most fundamental element of the ministry of the Servants of Relief was that only the poor would be admitted to their "homes." (The term "hospital" was excluded as a definition of what kind of service they were providing.) They were not to accept money from their patients, nor were they to accept money from relatives of their patients. Beds were to be *free.* Further—and this condition was absolute: there were to be no medical experiments or operations on the patients. The patients the community accepted were those classified as "incurable," although this term was subsequently abandoned because of its possible discouraging effect on those who came for help. Money to support the charity was to be sought from those who could afford to give freely. No money was to be accepted from government sources or even from official church resources. The money was not to be banked for the purpose of accumulating interest, nor was it to be invested. It was to be spent completely on the suffering poor who sought help. If donors attached conditions to the money they contributed (such as assigning the money only to the care of Christians) the money was returned. It was no wonder that the small corporation experienced some initial difficulty acquiring a lay treasurer. In one of the early "Reports" issued by the Servants of Relief, Mother Alphonsa was to write:

> The Sisters do not ask for State aid. The charity is in the State, but not of it, simply because charity is not yet a strong point with the State, although it is trying for that distinction; and all parts of the country are steadily laboring to find some means by which to snatch the poor in durance of the law or of disease from the grasp of sad conditions as they now are. The Sisters do not wish to have each sufferer "committed" by the State to

the Cancer-Homes. Is there anyone who would like to be "committed"?[106]

Another concept essential to the work of the sisters was the insistence that cancer was not contagious. The public and the patients themselves were to be so persuaded. Alice Huber was reprimanded very early in her own days of service when she put aside a glass for her own use. Rubber gloves were not to be used. The sisters were never to indicate that they considered the illness contagious, and equally essential to their mode of service was that they were in no way to suggest that the appearance of the patients or their odor, which was sometimes suffocating, was in any way disagreeable. Father Thuente, himself a courageous and charitable man, became almost uncontrollably faint and ill the first time he distributed communion to the patients, so the requirement that no slightest expression of repugnance be manifest on the part of those nursing was itself a call for unusual restraint. Finally, and most important, all of the nursing was to be done by the sisters. There was to be no hired help.[107]

When Rose wrote in her diary that she wanted to be *of* the poor, she knew what that desire would imply. Her original concept of the ministry was one that the sisters were never to change. They were to be "servants" with all that the concept necessitated. In one of her newspaper appeals, she was to write:

> I am trying to serve the poor as a servant. I wish to serve the cancerous poor because they are more avoided than any other class of sufferers; and I wish to go to them as a poor creature myself. . . . In order to accomplish anything that will be lasting, women must be called who are capable of renouncing ease and pastime, for the sake of that true love of God which shares the sufferings of Christ in a mode of life which He recommended and lived.[108]

It is clear from this excerpt that the small community and their foundress were struggling on several fronts simultaneously. They wanted to provide an authentic Christian work of mercy, approved and thus spiritually supported by the church. They needed money for more space, and they needed women to join them in the work, especially so that it could be stabilized and continued. The kind of woman who could sustain such a commitment was rare. To make matters worse, some of the earliest members of the community died early deaths, several because of tuberculosis. Mother Alphonsa was, moreover, very particular about the quality of applicants. She knew the work was too difficult and too important to be entrusted to anyone insufficiently generous or ill-adapted to life in a small community. But her high standards were sometimes the occasion of quiet advice on the part of Father Thuente who reminded her that the dismissal or departure of too many women would damage the reputation of the community. As early as 1901 he admonished her for assigning penances that were too severe: "I think bread and water for a day is simply awful," he wrote. "It is certainly considered a severe punishment. Do not punish the novices in presence of the postulants. Give them little prayers to say. Deprive them of . . . sugar for a day. Make them kneel for a few minutes in the refectory, and do not make them fast too much. Your days are long and your work is hard and the body demands its food. Be not too strict."

After the move to Rosary Hill, Mother Alphonsa was officially the Superior of the Congregation, and Sister Rose Huber, the novice mistress, but since the postulants and novices lived at Rosary Hill, Mother Alphonsa had much to do with their formation. Sister Rose met them once a week. Such an arrangement was possible before the promulgation of the 1917 Canon Law for Religious. Mother Alphonsa's strictness must have seemed harsh, on occasion, but the annals of the community indicate that she sought forgiveness from the sisters if, upon reflection, her words or actions seemed to her too severe. She was not easy on herself. Her room was spartan, consisting of a bed, stools, and few books. It was less adequately furnished than the rooms of the other sisters. She never permitted any of the sisters to lean on their arms when praying. She herself always prayed in an upright position, and the same austerity was required of others. When she had time, she did mending for others, and continued to do so, as she became older, especially when physical labor became more difficult. An undated note, obviously written hastily (in pencil) contains the following reflections: "Necessity of rather frequent interims of two days, or three, that the Sisters may receive fresh air, and break the monotony of distressing conditions, in order to have more strength and spirit for the work." After a break in the page, she writes:

> We should be exact about the perfection of our own work, but as the work done in the Home cannot be in itself of much value to God, no matter how charitable, and useful to the poor, we must not spend time and strength in worrying over confusion and poor work by anyone else, especially the— [illegible, possibly *rougher*] class of workers. Life can be con-

sumed in these regrets and arraignments. A good example of work is all we need give, from ourselves, not others.

Censoriousness is a great evil, and as we cannot find anything human that is perfect, it is foolish to begin to criticize at all. The Superioress has great responsibilities, and must keep people around her up to the mark or be guilty of their shortcomings, but she cannot force anyone to be good, and must take pattern by our Lord who never coerced free will. Penances must be given for wilful failures, as they are inflicted by God; but after this the matter becomes one of grace, and the disturbance of mind we feel over the faults of the rest must be recognized as malicious and selfish.

Mother Alphonsa's private letters to Sister Rose often discuss the applicants to the community or their capacities as postulants and novices. Both women were extremely concerned about the quality of women who came to them and their letters discuss these concerns frankly. If there was any suspicion of emotional imbalance, laziness, frivolity or self-indulgence, the candidates would be asked to leave. Mother Alphonsa's constant prayers and appeals for women to join her in the work suggest her conviction that many more could have done so. At the same time, the letters suggest her frequent disappointment with some of the women who did volunteer. Evident in her notes and letters is a private struggle to work with women who did not, probably could not, meet her expectations. An isolated comment in her random notes says simply: "A Philistine by any other name is quite as hollow—even a religious name." And one of the essays in *Christ's Poor* deals frankly with the fact that God can use quite mediocre people to do his work. The essay suggests that she did not come to this conclusion easily. (See "For the Poor, By the Poor," January, 1902).

A curious reflection is included on the third page of the penciled notes. It represents one of the few times Mother Alphonsa talks about Catholicism almost as an outsider. She does not usually evidence her "convert status," but convent conversations apparently surprised her more than once.

The way people take the Catholic religion, it seems to kill a great many of them. For instance, a Sister expressed what I have often heard from such minds that it was useless to try to do a thing unless you had a vocation to it,—a young girl was saying she was too fond of icecream and dancing to be a nun.

So. It is the cause of Catholic women often doing the most selfish thing, because they pretend they are not called to anything better. So, in many ways, the mechanism, and secondary effect, of our religon is made the idol, and the real generosity and sacrifice of it are coolly shifted. I am astonished to find how the truth, long lying in human hands, can so universally be turned to brass, as far as the intelligence of the ordinary creature can see, so that to these unheroic minds holy matters are roughly referred to, and the undying Faith is more like trumpery than those religious sects that are scarred by this phenomenon. It is an everlasting wonder that the holiest possibilities given to us are by the will turned into the basest self-complacence, because the most ignorant, that I have ever known: that Catholicity, able to give us heaven, can by us be made to destroy all liberty and perception by its letter and chance of corruption and laxity. God give us all the necessary light and courage!

This reflection is followed by a milder view:

Our Lord teaching in the Temple, the wisest minds among the perverted. So we must realize that all the wisdom we need to receive is that childlike humility and obedience and courage which a noble child can teach; so that, as St. Catherine of Siena taught, the eloquence and learning of the greatest soul sums up nothing greater than fraternal love in God's love, leading to purity and loving labors, reliance upon God's will, and universal forgiveness. The intricacies of the Old Law and Scriptures were clear to the Child of the Cross because a child may learn how to please God.

In 1904 Mother Alphonsa and Sister Rose renewed their vows for five years. In that same year the daughter of Nathaniel Hawthorne received an invitation from Mrs. Daniel Lothrop, the author of *The Five Little Peppers,* to return to the Wayside in Concord for the Centennial celebration in honor of her father. She was asked to present a paper. Only nine years had passed since she had left the house in New London to begin a new life, and in those nine years she had found a new identity. Mother Alphonsa knew she was free to go and, in fact, was probably encouraged to do so, but she declined. In a formal letter read to the assembled Hawthorne devotees, she wrote:

I have tried very hard for a couple of years to leave my work among the poor, to go to Concord or its neighborhood, but have been prevented very imperatively. This is usually because taking care of the dying, and few of our patients living beyond expectation for some months or years, we are constantly thrown into extremely arduous situations, when everyone must join in watching, laying out the dead, and seeing to the last rites; and too, new patients are to be received, which entails much preliminary work, until they are refreshed and settled.

In a modest conclusion she added:

I am so glad that my brother will be present, and I wish with all my heart that I could be, and could add any words of interest to the commemoration. That, however, I could not do, as I am not used to addresses, such as will be given. But I am, I think, a good listener, and grieve that I must lose the interesting experience.[109]

In a subsequent letter for the same occasion she had written to Mrs. Lothrop, ". . . the women attending the twenty-five cancer cases whom we harbor in the Country Home are too few to allow any of us to fall out of line for a day."[110]

A 1908 letter to Sister Rose Huber suggests the discouragement Mother Alphonsa often experienced in organizing a small, fragile community: "Father Thuente will, I do hope, come to visit us here, and he will know how to help us in the Community, if we can be helped. In his May letter, he says: 'You need help; intelligent, practical religious women.' But he wants us to stop sending people away, no matter what they are, because it frightens women and their confessors, as well as the other Sisters, to see Sisters hurtling through the air. So we must indeed pray for intelligent pious women."[111]

The two foundresses made final profession of vows in 1909. As usual there was little time to celebrate. St. Rose's Home on Jackson Street could scarcely handle the stream of patients that sought help, and the problem of paying for the support of two homes was formidable. If Mother Alphonsa was strict with the sisters, she would never scrimp with the patients. Sister Rose Huber was better at balancing the books and paying the bills. A number of letters from Mother Alphonsa to her express regret for bouncing another check. She certainly hadn't *intended* to do so. We read of Mother Alphonsa's buying a dog for one of the men patients, dainty tea cups for women who were not used to institutional cookware, having summer houses built, even buying tobacco and cigarettes for those used to smoking. But the records were scrupulously kept and published in regular Reports to the public and to the Trustees. A 1903 Report, for example, lists $3.50 for ice cream (May–August); $4.71 for grape juice (August); $4.85 for shoeing horses (July); $200.00 for plumbing and an interesting $25.00 for Lessons in singing for Sisters. (The latter was no doubt a stipend for assistance in chanting liturgical prayers.) The Reports continually list the needs of the patients: bandages, linens, flannel robes, rocking chairs, breakfast foods, claret, sherry, oranges, jams. If nursing care was to be given lovingly, another strict principle of the homes was that the meals should not be *mean.* Liturgies and feastdays were to be as festive as possible. The 1914 Report describes "quantities of blackberry vines and every wild flower, with branches of flowering trees" sent from Rosary Hill to St. Rose's Home in the city for a Corpus Christi Procession. Story after story is told in *Christ's Poor* of individual patients who received help, some of them virtually unknown and abandoned, some who may have been criminals once, of others inarticulate and almost dead on arrival, of indescribable sufferers with faces almost eaten away by cancer, of the despairing and hope-filled, mostly the aged, but some children—all of them requiring constant, unremitting attention. From 1901 to 1914 a total of 580 people had been cared for at the Rosary Hill Home and 850 at St. Rose's Home. There were fewer than ten sisters at each residence.

One of the reasons Mother Alphonsa was able to accomplish so much with so few sisters and so little in the bank was the zeal she aroused in others to assist in the work. One of the earliest benefactors was a pharmacist named Henry Reel who often did not charge the very poor for prescriptions and for the work of the Servants of Relief he organized a 600-member auxiliary for drugs, each member contributing $1.00 a year for medicines. He eventually became a member of the Board of Trustees and continued to provide services long after his retirement. James J. Walsh, physician and author, gave benefit lectures. George M. Cohan gave a benefit performance. The second St. Rose's Home, built in 1912 on Jackson Street not far from the first home, was begun with the initial contributions of Edward J. Smith and Cornelius F. Cronin who each donated $25,000 to the project. John D. Crimmins, prominent New York banker and influential lay Catholic, raised $43,000 more.[112]

In addition to these major contributions as well as legacies, a host of small donors and auxiliaries gave money and service to the charity.

Everyone's contributions were scrupulously acknowledged with gratitude, for Mother Alphonsa knew she could not succeed without extensive support. Part of her genius consisted in eliciting and sustaining support from every quarter she could think of. She even wrote Mark Twain on one occasion and requested an article for her little publication. She didn't succeed in obtaining the article but his daughter left a financial donation to the work in her will, and Samuel Clemens wrote a letter to her which she was able to use later. Among the list of donors in the 1902 issue of *Christ's Poor,* $100.00 was given by someone identified only as "Heretic." J. Warren Greene contributed substantially every month, and numerous small donations arrived faithfully as a result of her constant promulgation of needs, not only in her own publication, but in the New York papers, both secular and Catholic.

One hope of Sister Alphonsa that was never satisfied was to encourage a group of devoted *men* to assist her in caring for male patients. She could never understand why men would not take on the kind of nursing that at least some women were willing to assume. In a dream that was at best a wild hope, she started to correspond with Brother Joseph Dutton of Molokai, thinking that perhaps she could persuade him to join her in *her* work. She had heard of him and the illustrious Father Damien long before beginning her ministry and confessed more than once that their devotion to lepers had been a powerful example to her. He was not one to write at any great length, but he was touched enough by her letters to sustain contact with her and her community until his death in 1931. He clearly had no intention of ever leaving his own work, but his notes suggest his deep respect for her efforts. "Your unanswered letters," he once wrote her, "are among my treasures."

Stabilizing the Work

These years of founding and sustaining a work of charity by establishing a religious community are extraordinary in the life of the American church. In the New York area alone, more than sixteen communities of religious women, most from European congregations, had started foundations between 1885 and 1905. Dominican Sisters from Ratisbon, Germany had arrived in what is now Brooklyn (then Williamsburgh) in 1853. By 1881 they had moved to Amityville and started foundations in Newburgh and in Caldwell, New Jersey—where in 1900 Rose, on retreat, first experienced Dominican community life. Mother Seton's Sisters of Charity had already divided into two groups, one of which stayed in New York to adapt to the necessity of teaching boys as well as girls. John Talbot Smith in an early history of the New

York archdiocese describes their American flexibility as a model. With 930 members they were the largest religious order in the United States in the 1880's. But other communities were eager to open houses in New York, knowing that the abundance of possible religious vocations in that diocese would help their expansion. The Sisters of Mercy, the Sisters of Notre Dame, Ursulines, the Sacred Heart Sisters, the Sisters of the Poor of St. Francis, Marianite Sisters, the Sisters of Christian Charity—all had begun to educate and to serve the growing population of New York City. By the time Mrs. George Lathrop arrived on the scene with yet another work to do, another community to establish, the diocese was beginning to experience what authorities began to see as a kind of maximum density. "The increase of female communities," writes John Talbot Smith, a contemporary of the scene, "surpassed all expectation, and at one time threatened to outstrip the demand for them."[113]

The problem of regulating the communities was in itself a large task, especially since Canon Law for religious was something of a labyrinth before 1917.[114] Mother Alphonsa's struggles to get a constitution for her own community was affected by this disarray, as well as by her own inexperience in designing a structure that would work for many different kinds of women, not all of whom could match her asceticism, even if they shared her zeal.

She sought help from all designated ecclesiastical superiors in the guidance and management of two homes and the religious community. Not everyone was equally supportive, and she was not one to submit easily in the event of disagreement. Both she and Sister Rose Huber had difficulty with chaplains and clergy. One priest in a fit of pique left St. Rose's Home and took the blessed sacrament with him, depriving both sisters and patients of the sacraments for several months. Sister Rose finally sought help from diocesan authorities at which time (1914) Bishop Thomas Cusack, Archbishop Farley's auxiliary, was appointed the Ecclesiastical Protector of the Congregation.[115] Until 1900 most religious congregations of women were subject to an Ecclesiastical Superior appointed by the local bishop. The office of a priest-superior had been abolished in 1900, but the concept of a "Protector" remained. This Protector functioned as a religious and financial advisor. Archbishop Farley, who had succeeded Michael Corrigan, discovered to his surprise that the Servants of Relief had had no such designated episcopal authority, although Father Thuente had been appointed to receive their first vows and had been advised by Archbishop Corrigan to give them the habit. But Archbishop Corrigan had thought it prudent not to acknowledge officially the existence of the community until he was persuaded that it would survive. He and other New York diocesan authorities were generally otherwise encouraging. These included Archbishop John Farley, Msgr. James McGean and Msgr. James Flood—all on Archbishop Farley's Council, and later Msgr. James T. McEntyre, who for years was Sister Rose Huber's advisor, as well as chaplain, until his appointment to the rectorship of St. Joseph's Seminary in Dunwoodie. He eventually succeeded Bishop Cusack as Ecclesiastical Protector.

Mother Alphonsa expected more support from the American Dominican authorities than she ever received, and had to break off her relationship with the remaining members of the French Province after a series of disagreements. But several Dominican priests were exceptionally helpful. Father James A. Daly of St. Vincent Ferrer Church was a confessor and spiritual director to the community when they first moved to Sherman Park. An early letter of his urges Mother Alphonsa not to lose heart: hers is a "necessary charity." But she could not always follow his advice, since he thought their ministry was a little too focused on one charitable need. His letters suggest that he had very serious and probably reasonable doubts about their status. Father Eugene A. Wilson, also a confessor in both homes for several years, was always supportive. Among other benefactions, he supplied Christmas dinner for nuns and patients for years. Father Thuente remained loyal to the end, constantly offering what can still be recognized as clear-sighted, prudent, and realistic counsel. He dedicated a book of spiritual conferences to Mother Alphonsa and her companions and wrote a tribute to her in the Dominican publication, *The Torch,* after her death.[116]

As a young priest, Father James T. McNicholas—eventually to become Bishop of Duluth, Minnesota and Archbishop of Cincinnati—was assigned to hear confessions and to assist the congregation, but it is clear from Mother Alphonsa's letters to Sister Rose that she considered him no blessing. There is some evidence that he was influential in persuading novices to leave and that he effected the transfer of a few sisters to other congregations that were more permanently established. Although it is known that he offered similar advice to sisters in other struggling young Dominican communities, he had, nevertheless, been instrumental in securing the affiliation to the Dominican Order of the Sisters of the Sick Poor at a time in the history of their community when it was extremely fragile. He also urged the affiliation of the Maryknoll Sisters to the order. They were to be known officially as the Foreign Mission Sisters of St. Dominic and were so designated under the Master-General, Louis Theissling. One of Father McNicholas' dreams was to unite all the Dominican Sisters' congregations into one large American order.[117] Whether or not his occasional efforts to effect transfers or his conflict with Mother Alphonsa had anything to do with this dream is impossible now to determine. What we do know is that when he was transferred from St. Vincent Ferrer's to Rome in 1916, Mother Alphonsa was relieved, referring to him in a letter to Sister Rose as the overlauded Father McNicholas. She was not convinced that he had helped her at all. When she learned that priests, especially Dominican priests, sometimes advised women not to join her congregation because of its presumably impermanent status, her grief was difficult to restrain. Given the intensity of her zeal, this questioning of the long-range possibilities of her work was a searing frustration.

She did, however, have friends among the many religious orders in New York, religious who, like Brother Dutton, recognized how radical was her commitment to "God and the poor," and who loved and respected her for that commitment. These included the founders of Maryknoll—Mary Rogers, James Anthony Walsh, and Thomas Frederick Price—who began their own project in Hawthorne before purchasing property in Ossining, and who formed with the first Servants of Relief a communal affection that would last beyond all of their lifetimes. When the Theresians, as the Maryknoll Sisters were called at the time, left Hawthorne for Ossining, Mary Rogers wrote Mother Alphonsa:

> You, of course, will never know how good you have been to us, for a truly generous heart never counts its gifts. If you could only peep into our hearts you would find how much they love you—how sorely grieved they are to go out from the shelter of your wing. You have made us feel that no matter how great our need is we may call on you, assured of sympathy and help, and as we enter upon our work—unprepared spiritually—having only our desire to do this well and a constant prayer for guidance and perseverance on our lips—you can readily appreciate how we shall miss you and the great silent example of heroic self-sacrifice that your house affords.[118]

Mother Alphonsa is reported to have said after a visit to Ossining: "I love Maryknoll from top to toe!"

One of the most difficult responsibilities Mother Alphonsa had to take on, especially after the 1918 revision of canon law, was the composition and approval of a constitution for the congregation. Her letters in 1920 and 1921 indicate how preoccupied she was with this task, and how many disagreements she had with clergy who were advising her. Fathers Charles Callan and John McHugh, Dominicans living in nearby Holy Rosary parish and professors at the Maryknoll seminary, were the chief writers of the first constitution. For whatever reason, her collisions with Father Callan gave her considerable grief, and some of her bitterest observations about the clergy focus on her conflicts with him. A 1920 letter reports a visit from Msgr. Flood who wished to assist Mother Alphonsa in settling the troubling business of the rule. "I am to try to get the *St. Catherine's Rule,*" she writes to Sister Rose Huber, referring to the rule approved for the Dominican Sisters of St. Catherine, Kentucky, where Sister Rose herself had once gone to school. "Mgr. Flood and Father saw the Provincial (I think on Thursday) and he was (of course) very flattering all around, and he is very much in admiration of the St. Catherine's Rule." She notes that Msgr. Flood indicated that approval would take at least five years. "But," argued Mother Alphonsa, according to her account, "I cited the Maryknoll Rule put into Mgr. Bonzano's hands, which took only 5 months to settle, and I said probably his Grace would get an even prompter answer." But the letter continues, "Both of our Superiors wanted us to keep in fair fettle with these dreadful Fathers, at least until the questions about their Rule and payment was settled—till the Autumn."[119]

Her November 27th, 1921 letter to Sister Rose Huber describes her reaction to a proposed model for her own constitution that had been designed for another community. Clearly Mother Alphonsa had strong convictions about what was appropriate to the work her Sisters would be doing and the spirituality she wanted to encourage:

I fancy he [the priest adviser] wrote the Rule himself. It has been approved by the Archbishop. Well, *lawks,* it is almost the worst I have seen! It is awful in essential parts, and the diction is repetition and verbosity gone mad. In regard to the Novitiate, it is for two years; the Mother General is elected for only 3 years, with a limit of 3 years more! Two months are required for police investigation before a postulant is accepted, and the *Ordinary* must be notified that long before she is allowed to enter. The Mistress of Clothing has to make a written list of all that goes into the wash; and three departments are needed for Professed, Novices, and postulants. And the Novices have no work, not even study or painting, in their first year, but are to pray all the time; and recreations are to be from one and a half to two hours at midday, and an hour and a half in the evening. . . . Today I wrote him how that St.

Catherine's Rule had twice been approved at Rome, once for Kentucky and lately for Maryknoll. He seemed thoroughly interested in us, and thought our total of women splendid; and he told me to write to him as often as I wished about points; and he would even come to talk matters over if I needed it. . . . Of course I do not know what is in store for us. I thought the Archbishop had a decided flush of disappointment in his eyes, when he found I was not booked for Boston by the next train, and the Rule which we cannot, and who could? follow, may be a tripping stone. In that case, I shall step into a volume of St. Thomas à Kempis, and admit that one must not trust to human beings.[120]

The Constitution for the Servants of Relief was not finally approved until 1927 after Mother Alphonsa's death. But all the time she was worrying about that problem, when she was now over seventy years old and perhaps well entitled to give over most of the work to someone else, she took on yet a new project. The original building, the old resort hotel and former priory, was less than safe. Rosary Hill is very much a hill, where winds can blow with unusual strength and where a fire in a wooden building was an ever present danger. When in 1922 a small but potentially dangerous fire did break out, Mother Alphonsa knew that a new building had to go up and that a fireproof annex for the most helpless patients had to be constructed as soon as possible. She needed $200,000 for the project, which was to be her last great effort, for the time and energy she spent on it took the last of her heart's strength. To begin, she herself designed the kind of structure she wanted and then launched another begging campaign. It was then that Clifford Smyth, who had married Julian's daughter Beatrix, came to her aid. He had long admired his Aunt Rose, and as editor of the *New York Times Book Review and Magazine* used his influence to get publicity for her cause. Maurice Francis Egan, a friend from the days of the Catholic Summer School in New London, agreed to write an article about her work. It was published in the *Times Magazine* April 16, 1922. Donations began to arrive. Her pleas continued unremittingly in letters to the Catholic Press, to New York newspapers, to her traditional donors. In 1926 she had in her fund $150,000.00, and excavation for the new building began.

In the meantime her life achievements had not gone unnoticed. Bowdoin College offered her an honorary degree in memory of her alumnus father and in recognition of her charitable work. In April, 1926, the New York Rotary Club presented her with a medal for outstanding service to humanity. She was clearly deeply moved by this visible acknowledgement of her efforts, turning to her nephew when the time came for her to speak and she could not. "Clifford! Speak for me," she said. A picture was taken of her with the group on this occasion, the only picture the congregation has of her in the religious habit. She had never allowed any to be taken since the day she had cut her hair and put on the first black dress and cap which she and Alice had modeled for Archbishop Corrigan in 1898. Three months after this occasion on the anniversary of her parents' marriage, Mother Alphonsa died in her sleep of the heart ailment that had troubled her for years.

Father James A. Walsh, the cofounder of Maryknoll, preached the funeral sermon, and Msgr. James McEntyre celebrated the mass. A little known detail of that event is that the pallbearers were six local merchants that Mother Alphonsa had dealt with through the years. She had specifically requested that these men perform that function.

The community and the work went on. Sister Rose Huber succeeded her closest friend to the governance of the congregation, and in her lifetime—she lived until 1941—founded four more homes for the care of the cancerous poor. Today there are seven foundations in six states, and the work is as demanding—and as necessary—as ever.

The Spiritual Heritage

Rose Hawthorne Lathrop lived during a sea-change in American religious and social thought. Her parents, like most of the New England literati had rejected their Calvinist ancestry, if not their Puritan culture. Although her father's religious convictions remained darkly ambivalent, her mother had adopted the Unitarian optimism of Channing and Emerson. But Rose, judging from Sophia's pleading with her, had never liked Unitarian services or Unitarian preaching. She had been married in an Anglican church, but never adopted George's religion. It may have been too English for her taste. She had mentioned in a letter to Una, as if in response to Una's conversion to Anglicanism, that when she and George returned to the United States she was determined to love America.

The Calvinist strain, however, that never quite evaporated from New England religion, may account for her persistent need to be "useful." The word appears often enough in her letters to be taken seriously as a driving impulse in her life. Part of her dissatisfaction with her marriage was the sense that she was of no real use to anyone—even George, and her restlessness, about which family members often com-

plained privately, stemmed as much from the boredom and tedious-
ness of her wifely duties, as with George's fitful career. Rose was not
totally satisfied with a round of social obligations and salon conversations, but for much of her life she had no way to focus her energies.
Augustine Hewit had written that Protestants were attracted to Catholicism on the basis of dogma, authority, and worship. Of the three, it was
clearly worship that drew Rose to the heart of Catholicism. She never
had a quarrel with dogma, and her disputes with authority had nothing
to do with Rome. If anything she was completely submissive intellectually and consistently expressed reverence for the popes of her era and
the bishops to whom she was responsible. But she was not an ultramon-
tane. When it came to governance she was as attracted to Teddy Roosevelt as to her ecclesiastical superiors, and occasionally inserted curious
fillers in *Christ's Poor* that betrayed her political and patriotic prefer-
ences. Worship was the most powerful religious change that her conversion entailed—worship and the pious traditions of Catholic religious life.

The aspect of New England liberalism that affected her most profoundly was not speculation but the current of social reform that characterized the ethic of many of her relatives and acquaintances. She
must have known of the work of George Ripley's wife, Sophia, and
their niece Sarah Stearns with the Good Shepherd Sisters in the rehabili-
tation of prostitutes and wayward girls. She knew of Una's settlement
work in England, of Aunt Lizzie Peabody's multiple causes, of Horace
Mann's achievements. She knew Emma Lazarus and had met some of
the great women reformers of the century. Her place in the history of
American spirituality can be traced, at least by contrast, through Unitarian theology, most of which she rejected, Emersonian optimism,
which shaped her early years, and social reform, which was the cry of
the century. She is best seen against the history of nineteenth century
conversions and the impulse to usefulness, especially among women.
But her personal vocation was unique.

Although it is impossible to identify all the influences that finally
persuaded both George and her of the value of conversion to Roman
Catholicism, it is certain that when she converted, she was intellectually and emotionally rooted, once for all. Judging from how little she
looked back, it can be suggested that she interiorly rejected what she
may have perceived as the the religious vagaries of her New England
relatives and forebears. Other than her attachment to her mother, she
did not express in her later life any particular allegiance to Concord
culture or New England religious beliefs. After her conversion she was
particularly fortunate in the quality of instruction and spiritual direc-

tion she received, especially from the Paulists. It could be argued that she was equally fortunate in the instruction she did not receive, since she was spared by her heritage and the independence of her congregation from some of the European or Irish versions of piety that could have distorted her distinctly American religious vision. Her sense of the universality of poverty prevented her from focusing on service primarily to Catholics or to a single ethnic group, and the religion or race of her patients was never a factor to be considered in any relief of suffering she could provide.

She had adopted with alacrity the devotional life and practices that characterized American Catholic piety in the nineteenth century, and in this she was no different from all the Catholics she knew and admired who were themselves caught up in multiple appeals to Christ and Mary under various titles, as well as to favorite saints, whose intercession promised affection, companionship, and sympathy. In fact, it was the doctrine of the communion of saints that seemed to offer the greatest appeal to George, apart from a certain intellectual surety that Catholic doctrine provided for him. Judging from her diary and her letters, Rose was eclectic in her devotion to the saints. She took the name Alphonsa in religion—which Alice Huber didn't care much for —almost casually, arguing for Alice's benefit that St. Alphonsus' piety attracted her. If this seems surprising in an age when St. Alphonsus' prayers with their excessive emotionalism have lost favor, it should be noted that St. Alphonsus, along with Frederick William Faber were both extremely popular in the nineteenth century. The influence of St. Alphonsus was felt not only in his numerous devotional works, but especially in the handbook used by Redemptorists and others to conduct parish missions.[121]

The spirituality of St. Alphonsus describes much of Mother Alphonsa's own spirituality, especially his emphasis on the prayer of petition and the appeal to the intercession of saints. Clearly, Mother Alphonsa resorted to this intercessory prayer in her needs. She placed a petition in the hands of the statue of St. Joseph when she needed property. The paper is still in the archives: "Glorious St. Joseph, please give to the Servants of Relief, a house in which they can take care of many sick in safety for many years." She buried a medal of the Blessed Virgin in a vacant lot she wanted to buy for the new St. Rose's Home on Jackson Street. (They eventually secured the property.) She buried another medal on the land where she wanted to build the new Rosary Hill Home. She prayed to the Sacred Heart, to Our Lady of Perpetual Help, to the Infant of Prague, and especially to Our Lady of Good Counsel, for she often accused herself of "stupidity." On the finger of the statue of the Infant of Prague, she put her engagement and wedding rings. In one letter to Sister Rose Huber, she urged her to continue to pray for a particular need, then added abruptly, "What prayers are you saying?" Recent studies on the devotional practices of late nineteenth century America have noted how extensively the prayer of petition was fostered in the prayer books and manuals of the period, and how suspect was the mysticism associated with pre-Reformation spirituality. "Prayer and charity opened the treasury of Christ and the saints to believers," writes Joseph Chinicci in an examination of the relationship between capitalism and the spiritual life, and this sense of divine response elicited by relentless request continued well into the twentieth century, influencing the prayer life of Catholics for at least three generations.[122]

The most interesting prayer to be found in her papers is one to George Washington. It testifies to her undisguised patriotism and appears in the May, 1904, issue of *Christ's Poor,* along with a full page photograph of the equestrian statue of Washington, presented to France by American women, in response to the statue of Lafayette, presented by France to America. She gives no source for the following petition:

> Father of our country, whose piety appealed to God before every action, and who in peace calmly obeyed Him, it is our prayer to our Creator that piety may imbue the thought of men and women for whom you gave your genius and your possessions. May we uplift to Christ the swords of our endeavor, and leave our native land more like your hope for it, when we die; and win still greater love for it from aliens who, joining hands with us, make the blood of other nations mingle with ours for a common righteousness. Washington, friend of Catholicity and holy freedom, may the home which you adopted humbly and defended magnificently be worthy of your heart and unbending honor!

Given the ecclesiastical politics of the time, it is unlikely that she found this in a Catholic prayer book—or at least one approved of in Rome—but it says much about her eclectic love of the "saints" and her intense love of country. There was a dark side to these endless prayers of petition—the sense that somehow God's blessings were only to be wrenched from heaven by vocal persistence, but these were the prayers of the Roman church and especially the American church of Rose's moment in history. Designed in part to foster docility and fidelity in the faithful, these prayers could sustain the faithful indefinitely because

of the sense of familiarity and tenderness they elicited.[123] Such a prayer
life corresponded to Rose's own deep sense of dependency, both emotionally and, in the practical order, financially. Very much alone in
many ways after the death of her child and during the last years of her
marriage, she turned to constant prayer for the support she needed.
Given the extraordinary sense of service her life manifested, this attachment to novenas, litanies, prayers of petition, and medals was a
structure through which her self-offering found its articulation. She
was not at the business of gathering indulgences, but of emptying herself, of offering her life as "a willing sacrifice." So complete is her sense
of dependence on God as revealed in her devotional life that the bold-
ness and independence expressed in her essays and articles come as
something of a literary shock. Hers was not a submissive, docile, dependent personality except when she was before God and in need.

Among the devotional works in Mother Alphonsa's small personal library is a copy of *The Following of Christ,* with her name and
date written on the flyleaf (July 15th, 1897) and a short inscription: "I
have prevented them with blessings of My sweetness." To which she
had added, "May Thy blessings prevent me from offence, oh my God."
In the same library is a set of seven short meditation books by Frederick William Faber. Judging from marginal markings, one of them,
entitled *All Men Have a Special Vocation* was read closely, as was
Faber's *Maxims and Sayings,* with other sections marked in pencil
along the sides of the text. The passages to which Mother Alphonsa was
attracted refer almost invariably to the mystery and uncertainty of
God's will and the imperative to seek and follow it. Another book with
numerous passages underlined is *Henry Drummond's Addresses* (Phila-
delphia: Henry Altemos, 1893). The chapter she seemed to have studied most closely was one entitled "How to Learn How," which deals
with doubt in the spiritual life. Katherine Conway had given her
Thoughts of the Curé of Ars and several of her own small books.

Mother Alphonsa was not one to call attention in letters or even a
personal diary to any wordless religious or mystical experience, although there are hints of such moments. Julian had written of Rose's
uncontrolled imagination as a young girl, how she had endowed people
"with virtues which they lacked or with faults of which they were innocent; vehemently repenting afterward, her errors of judgement, but
prone as ever to repeat them."[124] But in her later years, he wrote, "she
had abundant common sense . . . she was resolved that her regeneration should be unfaltering and permanent." He notes, in a presumable
reference to her spiritual life: "She did not beguile herself with ecstatic

emotions."[125] Despite his limited capacity to appraise her spiritual life, in this he was undoubtedly correct.

Mother Alphonsa's prayers were usually described as being offered before the blessed sacrament. The presence of the eucharist was extremely important to both foundresses. They longed for the day mass could be celebrated in their home, and Sister Rose Huber recorded in her own *Memoirs* how cruelly she suffered when her chaplain deprived the community of the sacraments, especially the eucharist. In her private retelling of the early days to the sisters, she is reported to have described that period as the darkest of her life. Sister Alphonsa constantly mentions in her letters the occasions when benediction of the blessed sacrament was permitted, what kind of flowers were on the altar, and what the singing was like. Such attention to liturgical detail typified the piety of the era, and yet Mother Alphonsa does not seem to be as bogged down in such detail as many of her contemporaries. She described one visiting priest as covered with scruples like "burrs." Her devotional life never manifested the morbid fixation on personal sin or minutiae that was so often the overflow of post-Reformation spirituality.

Because she was especially concerned after her conversion about usefulness, apparently feeling that after twenty years of marriage, she had accomplished very little, work was for her an exceptionally important value. Not only did she write several essays praising her father's work habits, but in her community direction she was insistent that, if health and strength permitted, time must be used well. Her spiritual life translated itself into a driving sense of service. This intensity was a result both of her childhood education and, we can assume, a personal reaction to twenty years of something less than domestic bliss and achievement. She was not unlike a whole cluster of nineteenth century women profoundly convinced of the need to consecrate their lives to usefulness, as Carolyn de Swarte Gifford has written.[126] The young Mrs. Lathrop was not known to have been conspicuously preoccupied by the public dimensions of the developing feminist movement such as temperance, women's suffrage—a cause to which few Catholic women gave themselves—, or other social reform efforts, but like many of the feminists of her era, she had been clearly restive with the role assigned her by marriage. Her earliest letters as a young wife testify to the tensions she was beginning to experience in this shadowed role as George's wife. She had not only her Aunt Lizzie as a model of feminist vigor, but her sister Una, and Emma Lazarus, who was not merely a rich young poet, but a social reformer deeply committed to relieving the suffering of Jewish refugees in America. Rose's speech at the World Columbian Expositions in 1893 was one of the first indications of her own new feminist spirit. She notes in her 1897–98 diary the "stalwart women" who were already working in settlement houses in her area of New York.

Women of every religious persuasion were taking up social causes at the end of the century. In the New York area, settlement houses were beginning in the eighties, working girls' clubs in the nineties. Hospitals and charitable institutions were springing up so rapidly that the church organizations could scarcely handle the vast administrative structure that such enterprises necessitated. Rose was in her forties before she herself was gripped by the urgency of the problems. When she turned to them, however, she did so with such intensity that her zeal was difficult to match. It suffused the religious life of her community.

Sister Joseph describes the daily routine in the first years: The sisters rose at 4:30 a.m. and assembled as soon as possible in chapel for prime and meditation. (In most religious orders, twenty minutes were allowed for dressing and appearing in chapel). At 6:00 the angelus rang, and mass was celebrated. After mass, the sisters went immediately to their assignments—taking care of the sick, cooking and serving breakfast, milking the cows. Breakfast was served to the patients on trays, handed along in relays like a bucket brigade. After breakfast, there was a visit to chapel before returning to tend the patients. At 11:00 a bell rang five times to commemorate the five wounds of our Lord, and an hour of silence followed. In addition to the recitation of the Little Office of the Blessed Virgin, late in the afternoon, psalms were recited before and after meals. Community recreation was after supper. The horarium was not unlike that of most communities of religious women, and fidelity to religious observance was always a matter of conscience, although Dominican tradition was insistent that the rule did not bind under pain of sin. In the days of minute classification of sins and their degrees, this distinction was always considered freeing.

The constitution that was eventually approved (after her death) contains a section that is clearly indicative of Mother Alphonsa's theology of ministry. The second of three parts of that document is entitled "The Patients." Article 162 reasserts the absolute independence of the work from the money or influence of patients or their relatives:

> When a person who brings in a patient says, "You will not receive money, but I will make it all right," the person must understand that the work is only for the poor, that if the person is in a position to make things all right, the patient is

not a subject for our work, for when once such persons come
in, the work is in more or less danger, and persons who can
well afford to pay elsewhere will take the place of the poor.

Similarly, that the foundation remain faithful to the original charism of
Rose herself, the following passage is especially telling: "When new
foundations are opened, they must begin in poverty and in a poor part
of the city. Until the foundation is secure, the Mother House must
supply all that is needed" (Article 170); and, "Probably in poor foundations, the Sisters may come into close contact with the female patients;
they should not shrink from doing so" (Article 181). Such insistence
that the congregation never fail in its absolute option for the poor was
unusual for its time, since the spirituality of the American church of
the latter part of the century was curiously ambivalent about "identify-
ing" with the poor. Indeed this late nineteenth century spirituality has
correctly been described as "capitalistic," and not only in its devotional
life. Church architecture, liturgies, vestments, the life-styles of high
ranking prelates often reflected the energies of a self-conscious and
slightly embarrassed people to rival their wealthier, more politically
powerful fellow citizens in other churches. The object of much Catholic education was to fit the young first or second generation immigrant
to rise in American society, to make a place or a fortune and so (eventually) to bring the American church into a more powerful political position. Political pragmatism was at the root of many of the endeavors of
the American church for the simple reason that the faith itself was
often dismissed because its adherents were poor and frequently uneducated. Archbishop Ireland had urged Catholics to stop considering
money as evil and to set about getting some. "It is energy and enterprise that wins everywhere; . . . in the church, . . . in the state, . . . in
business." Cardinal Gibbons had praised Andrew Carnegie's theory of
the Gospel of Wealth published in the June, 1889, issue of the *North
American Review,* an article that argued, in part, that those "worthy of
assistance, except in rare cases, seldom require assistance." Carnegie
believed that almsgiving rewarded vice rather than virtue and that the
greatest service to the poor was to provide libraries, schools, parks, and
museums, which would provide them with the means to rise from
poverty. Not least among the energetic voices urging Catholics to accumulate money so that they could be better providers for the people of
the church was Mary Theresa Alter whose journalistic efforts in *The
Catholic World* argued that the three men Christ restored to life were
all men of wealth. Arguing that Catholics should be taught how to
make money honestly so that they could contribute philanthropically

to the church, the writer argues feistily: "Art is a power, literature is a power, oratory is a power; but what is their power compared to the power of money? And it is a demonstrable pity that our practical Catholics hold and wield so little of that power."[127] M.T. Elder, as she signed herself, argued that more of the monies of the church should go to eliminate the causes of poverty, and less to the hopeless cases, who should be turned over to the state. Mother Alphonsa's insistence, therefore, that the sisters were to identify with and serve only the poor and, in fact, to turn away any others was not the norm. In fact, the tension between luring philanthropists to her cause and excoriating the miserliness with which many of the rich parceled out their money to charity was a tightrope she walked constantly. She had no use for cautious economy when it came to assisting the helpless poor.

Mother Alphonsa's wit, her extraordinary capacity for loving and her habit of self-deprecation kept what has been called her "capacity for scorn" in check. She had a powerful will and quick, verbal intelligence, together with administrative acumen. That flaring up of anger which had once evoked her father's admonitions, and her fury at a male schoolteacher—and presumably not a few arguments with George—never quite disappeared into the baptismal waters of 1891. It would be surprising indeed if those qualities did not evoke conflict with anyone who was in a position to obstruct the work she had undertaken. "I have a faggot of bones to pick with Father Z—," she wrote once before closing one of her letters to Sister Rose. She was independent enough to reject advice that conflicted with her aims or compromised the integrity of the congregation, and never hesitated to disagree with the powerful if the powerful tried to dissuade her of what she believed in as essential to her work. She did not always have nice things to say about the rich, about doctors and clergy, or even architects; but once, after a vigorous dispute with an architect who was not about to go along with her ideas, she wrote to Sister Rose Huber: "Well, I finally had to get off my high horse and ride a Shetland pony!" She could deal with her limitations in amused self-awareness. To Father Thuente in a 1911 letter, she remarked: "I am sick often, Father, to forget for a moment how easily I might die: but I do enjoy everything very much and am rather too frolicksome, as you may know, when I feel better. I will do my best, both to be a good mother and to live until I need a cane. You will say that it would be dangerous to give me such a thing."[128]

Her piety was completely dominated by her concern for the work to be done: the needs of the patients, the needs that she did not yet have the resources to meet, the need to direct the community of sisters prudently so that their own work would be effective. She valued intelligence and refinement, and she recognized appropriate counsel when she received it. She knew her own competence, but recognized that competence was not enough. Her devotion to Our Lady of Good Counsel was an authentic recognition of the limits of both intelligence and competence, and an acknowledgment of her own need for good judgement. And she knew the importance of the word: the preached word, the published word, the private word of advice, the word that is proclaimed in every act of mercy. She knew also that proclamation of God's love could not take place without human love. She herself was a lover, of George, of her patients, her community, of her beloved Alice Huber.

The importance of her love for Alice cannot be overemphasized, and best understood when seen within a whole culture that encouraged homosocial bonding. Carroll Smith-Rosenberg's study of female friendship in the eighteenth and nineteenth centuries offers ample evidence of the intensity of love and the abundant expressions of love that characterized correspondence between women in an age when heterosexual companionship was discouraged. Rose's letters to her schoolgirl friends, and her correspondence with her own mother, reveal how common and how expected were tender expressions of affection. In fact, her letters to George are affected and a little coy by contrast. If her love for Alice seems unusually passionate by contemporary standards, we need only sample the letters of other equally prominent women who poured out their hearts and secrets and emotions to one another in a world that separated men's and women's spheres more than is the case in the present culture.[129] What is unique in the letters between Rose and Alice is the religious status of the two women. Neither of them, fortunately, had been through the standard novitiate training of another religious community where the prohibition against apparently exclusive friendships would probably have inhibited their love. Alice was the companion Rose needed, more perhaps than she herself realized.

But Rose was not fully who she could be until her capacity for love was stretched beyond her own life and strength. The night before she died, she wrote a number of letters, including one to the editor of the *New York Times* that read in part: "Many people know nothing of our work for the cancerous poor, and if accosted by a person asking for a donation would give a sum out of politeness, mentally asking, 'What unheard of thing is this?' We are practical enough to want everyone to know what it is and to give a bit because their hearts are touched, to help us build this house of mercy." Rose Hawthorne Lathrop succeeded in building her house of mercy, not only because she herself was a merciful woman, but because she preached mercy vigorously, calling others to the most fundamental Christian responsibility: care for the weakest and most abandoned of human society.

NOTES

1. See Hubert H. Hoeltje, *Inward Sky, The Mind and Heart of Nathaniel Hawthorne* (Durham, N.C.: Duke University Press, 1962), 145–46.

2. Ralph Waldo Emerson's grandfather built this clapboard house in 1770. As every tourist to Concord knows, it is a field away from the North Bridge and the graves of the three British soldiers killed in 1775 by New England farmers turned minutemen. The Hawthornes rented the house from Samuel Ripley, Emerson's step-uncle.

3. Nathaniel and Sophia Hawthorne, *Journal Dated 1842–1854.* Mss. The Pierpont Morgan Library. New York, MA 580, vol. 2. Sophia was more prophetic than she realized. Determination and love would mark the personality of this child throughout her life. She would scold and comfort many in her days.

4. Rose Hawthorne Lathrop, *Memories of Hawthorne* (Boston and New York: Houghton Mifflin, 1897), 212. This book was completed during the first months of Rose's efforts to serve the poor, just after she moved to the Lower East Side in New York City. Earlier versions of four chapters had appeared in the *Atlantic Monthly,* 77 (Feb., March, April, May, 1896) in four installments, under the general title, "Some Memories of Hawthorne." Subsequent references to the book will be indicated in the text.

5. Edward Wagenknecht, *Nathaniel Hawthorne: Man and Writer* (New York: Oxford University Press, 1961), 155–56.

6. Cited in Julian Hawthorne, *Hawthorne and His Wife,* 2 vols. (Boston and New York: Houghton Mifflin, 1884), 2:352–53.

7. Ibid., 82.

8. See Julian Hawthorne, *Hawthorne and His Wife,* vol. 2.

9. Nathaniel Hawthorne, *French and Italian Notebooks,* ed. Thomas Woodson, Centenary Edition 14 (Columbus, Ohio: Ohio State University Press, 1980), 357.

10. Una Hawthorne to Cousin Richard [Manning], December 2, 1859, Essex Institute. Una converted to the Anglican Church in 1864.

11. The Hawthornes were advised by friends to allow Una, at least, to attend school. Una was so disturbed by the refusal that she became

violent. She was then given "electrotherapeutic" treatment. For a further discussion of Hawthorne's relation to Una, see especially, T. Walter Herbert, Jr., "Nathaniel Hawthorne, Una Hawthorne, and *The Scarlet Letter:* Interactive Selfhoods and the Cultural Construction of Gender," PMLA 103 (May, 1988):285–297.

12. Sophia Hawthorne to Elizabeth [Peabody], May 10, 1868. Essex Institute.

13. Cited in Theodore Maynard, *A Fire Was Lighted, The Life of Rose Hawthorne Lathrop* (Milwaukee: Bruce Publishing Co.), 136.

14. Ibid., 139.

15. Sophia Hawthorne to Rose, [April] 1868, Archives, Rosary Hill Home, Hawthorne, New York.

16. Sophia Hawthorne to Rose, May 20, 1868, MA 3400, The Pierpont Morgan Library.

17. Rose Hawthorne, unpublished diary, 1870. Archives, Rosary Hill Home.

18. Ibid.

19. See Raymona E. Hull, "Una Hawthorne: A Biographical Sketch," *The Nathaniel Hawthorne Journal* (1976): 87–119.

20. Julian Hawthorne, "A Daughter of Hawthorne," *Atlantic Monthly,* 142 (Sept., 1928): 372–77. This observation needs to be seen in the context of the ill will that pervaded the relationship between the two men.

21. Rose Hawthorne Lathrop to Una, [On board] *Oceanic,* January 8, 1872. Berg Collection, New York Public Library.

22. Cited in Maynard, 175.

23. A letter from Elizabeth Peabody to Ellen D. Conway (Mrs. Moncure Conway) dated November 21, 1876, describes Rose's condition with its attendant period of irrational suspicions and her own indignation that she was not permitted to see Rose. She seemed equally indignant that the baby was not to be named "Hawthorne." George was adamantly opposed to such a suggestion. See *Letters of Elizabeth Palmer Peabody: American Renaissance Woman,* ed. with Introduction by Bruce A. Ronda (Middletown, Conn.: Wesleyan University Press, 1984), 378.

24. George Parsons Lathrop to Dr. Jelly, December 20, 1876, Rosary Hill Home.

25. See the chapter "The Artist at Work," in *Memories.* See also Edward Davidson, ed., *Dr. Grimshawe's Secret* (Cambridge, Mass.: Harvard University Press, 1954). According to Davidson, Julian did, in fact, piece together fragments of his father's writing to shape the newly discovered "novel."

26. In 1913, as Mother Alphonsa, Rose went to Washington for a possible interview with President Woodrow Wilson in an effort to save her brother from a long prison term. Julian, always desperate for money, had used his name and influence to solicit investments in what was, in fact, a land fraud scheme. She succeeded in talking to the President's Secretary, Joseph P. Tumulty, who assured her, after consulting personally with President Wilson, that there was no reason to exonerate Julian or to offer an early parole. Mother Alphonsa's dramatic attempt to help her brother tells us something about her subsequent trust in him and the lengths to which she would go to assist him. Her claim that he was only "technically guilty," since he really believed the scheme was honest, was disallowed. There seems to be little doubt, however, that he was quite guilty. See Vernon Loggins, *The Hawthornes* (New York: Columbia University Press, 1951), 331.

27. *Epoch,* 8, in Private Papers of Rose Hawthorne Lathrop, Rosary Hill Home.

28. K.W.G. to Rose Hawthorne Lathrop, March 12, 1889, Rosary Hill Home.

29. There are sixteen letters to Thomas Bailey Aldrich and his wife in the Houghton Library, Harvard University. This line is from a note dated June 16, [1883].

30. Rose Hawthorne Lathrop to Cousin Richard [Manning], April 28th [n.d.] from 7 James Street. Essex Institute.

31. Rose Hawthorne Lathrop to Cousin Richard Manning, May 7 [n.d.] from The Parker House, Boston. Essex Institute.

32. Rose Hawthorne Lathrop to Cousin Richard Manning, October 10th [n.d.]. Essex Institute.

33. George Parsons Lathrop to Thomas Bailey Aldrich, January 28, 1884. Houghton Library, Harvard University.

34. Maynard, 231

35. See Christine Bochen, *The Journey to Rome: Conversion Literature by Nineteenth Century Catholics* (New York: Garland, 1988). Bochen notes that the narratives of converts deliberately accent the differences between conversions as experienced by evangelical Protestants and conversion to Roman Catholicism. Converts to Catholicism emphasize in their spiritual autobiographies intellectual *process* rather than emotional *event.* Motives for writing often dictated an apologetic approach. The conversion literature of the nineteenth century, however, reveals that the journey to Catholicism was always and also a matter of the heart as well as mind.

36. This prediction was uttered by Sarah Good to Reverend Nicholas Noyes in the presence of Judge Hathorne. It is often attributed to

Rebecca Nurse who is said to have cursed Hathorne. See Vernon Loggins (note 26), 133.

37. Julian Hawthorne, "Hawthorne's Last Years," *The Hawthorne Centenary Celebration at the Wayside* (Boston: Houghton Mifflin, 1905), 105–118, at 114.

38. Elizabeth, however, was far more engaged in the great social issues of the day, especially abolition, than was Sophia, and the energy she gave to these causes was unrelenting.

39. See the Introduction of Bruce A. Ronda to *Letters of Elizabeth Palmer Peabody,* 24 (note 23).

40. See John Farina, ed. *Isaac T. Hecker, The Diary: Romantic Religion in Ante-Bellum America* (New York: Paulist Press, 1988).

41. See Joseph P. Chinnici, O.F.M., *Living Stones. The History and Structure of Catholic Spiritual Life in the United States* (New York: MacMillan, 1989).

42. See especially James Hennesey, *American Catholics: A History of the Roman Catholic Community in the United States* (New York: Oxford University Press, 1981), 114–115.

43. See John Tracy Ellis, ed., *Documents of American Catholic History* (Milwaukee: Bruce Publishing Co., 1956).

44. Alfred Young, "A Plea for Erring Brethren," *The Catholic World* 50 (December, 1889):351–66.

45. A description of Walter Elliott's life and work is included in Thomas J. Jonas, *The Divided Mind: American Catholic Evangelists in the 1890's* (New York: Garland, 1988).

46. Bochen, p. 66.

47. Augustine F. Hewit, "Pure vs. Undiluted Catholicism," *American Catholic Quarterly Review* 20 (July 1895):460–80.

48. James Hennesey, S.J., *American Catholics: A History of the Roman Catholic Community in the United States* (New York: Oxford University Press, 1981), 198.

49. In his remarks acknowledging the greeting extended to him, Corrigan used the opportunity to urge his own agenda. Referring to the Columbian celebration in New York, he argued in the inflated prose so characteristic of 19th century ceremonial occasions:

> After the parade of the public school children then the Catholic children of our free schools followed, and according to the testimony of our secular press, by their neatness, their proficiency in drill, their manly appearance, they undoubtedly carried off the palm. A similar scene was displayed in the long line of our 30,000 young men attached to various re-

ligious or literary societies. I had the honor that evening of being seated near the Vice-President of the United States, as well as our own Chief Executive, His Excellency Governor Flower. Both were most favorably impressed by the numerical strength and bearing of our societies, and they added that young men so carefully nurtured by the conservative spirit of the Church could not fail to be patriotic and sterling citizens. (See *The World's Columbian Catholic Congresses and Educational Exhibit* [Chicago: J.S. Hyland and Co., 1893], 69.)

50. Sister M. Joseph, O.P., *Out of Many Hearts* (Hawthorne, New York: The Servants of Relief for Incurable Cancer, 1965), 11.

51. This letter and subsequent newspaper references are in the Archives of Rosary Hill Home.

52. George Lathrop had already begun a collaboration with Thomas Edison on a science-fiction novel, a project that engaged his interest for several years, but was never completed.

53. Maynard, 240.

54. Mary Peabody to Rose Hawthorne Lathrop, April 13, 1891, Rosary Hill Home. Mary Peabody was the wife of Nathaniel Cranch Peabody, Sophia's brother.

55. James J. Walsh, "The Intellectual Life at Cliff Haven," *The Catholic Summer School of America, 1892–1916,* ed. John J. Donlan. Walsh is here quoting Brother Azarias, one of the founders of the Catholic Summer School.

56. Walsh, 23.

57. Alfred Young, C.S.P., was born in England and was brought to the United States as an infant. He graduated with honors from Princeton [College] and studied medicine at New York University. He attributed his eventual conversion to an early experience in the Catholic chapel at Princeton which he entered once out of curiosity. When he was received into the church in the old St. Mary's on Grand Street in New York, his godfather was John Drumgoole, the sexton, later to be known as the American Don Bosco, the founder of the Immaculate Conception Mission for newsboys and orphans. (It was this John Drumgoole, whose story so intrigued Rose Lathrop that she gave a talk about his work to the New England Press Association.) Alfred Young entered the St. Sulpice Seminary in Paris, joined the Newark diocese, served as vice-president of Seton Hall College, and was pastor at Princeton when the Paulists gave a mission there. He subsequently joined the congregation. A musician, he made efforts to restore traditional church music to the parishes. He wrote extensively, often publishing in the

Catholic World. In the 1890's he was in failing health and died April 4, 1900.

58. Mother Leocadia was the superior of the Georgetown Visitation Convent.

59. Julian Hawthorne wanted President Grover Cleveland to appoint him to the Consulate at Kingston, Jamaica, in the British West Indies. This effort failed, but the Hawthornes went to Jamaica anyway and lived there about three years. Rose was to visit them shortly after her separation from George in 1894.

60. Julian was married to Minne Amelung. This, however, could not have been her mother, who had died in 1887.

61. Julian and Minne's third child.

62. *The Messenger of the Sacred Heart,* A Jesuit publication. This is generally considered the conservative Catholic magazine of the era, reflective of popular piety. The Paulist publication, *The Catholic World,* was conspicuously more intellectual and liberal.

63. Julian and Minne's fourth child.

64. Wife of the American sculptor Augustus St. Gaudens. The marriage was notoriously unhappy. He was not conspicuous for fidelity, nor she for an even temper. Cf. Mother Alphonsa's last letter to Sister Rose Huber (July 8, 1926).

65. Rose had gone to Buffalo with George in 1892 where he was giving a lecture. At that time she visited the Loretto Convent in Niagara Falls. Beatrix was Julian and Minne's fifth child.

66. George's brother Francis had become well known as an artist and was then living in New York.

67. Rose is referring to Hawthorne's "My visit to Niagara," an early essay first published in *New-England Magazine,* 8 (February 1835):91–96. It was reprinted in *Tales, Sketches, and Other Papers,* ed. George Parsons Lathrop (Boston and New York: Houghton Mifflin, 1883), where Rose probably read it. It is included in the *The Snow Image, and Uncollected Tales,* Centenary Edition XI (Columbus, Ohio: The Ohio State University Press), 281–88.

68. This reference is presumably to Edward Bok, editor of *Ladies Home Journal.* He had published in February, 1892, her short story, "The Love of an American Girl."

69. For a study of Catholic devotional life of mid-nineteenth century America, see Ann Taves, *The Household of Faith* (South Bend: University of Notre Dame Press, 1986).

70. Ann Taves, *The Household of Faith,* 35.

71. "Roosevelt on the Bible—A Letter to the Epworth League," *Christ's Poor* 1:11 (June 1902) 33–35. This letter was orginally given at

the thirteenth anniversary exercises of the Epworth League of Straw-
bridge Methodist Church and was reprinted in the Baltimore *Herald*
which Mother Alphonsa cited, when she inserted the passage into her
own little publication.

72. Clement Thuente, O.P., spoke at the 1904 National Congress.
See Joseph P. Chinicci, *Living Stones,* 152. Chinicci points out the
close link between eucharistic devotion in the American church and
the understanding of priesthood that followed from this emphasis. At
the same time, the individualism that private devotion to the eucharist
fostered was to intensify the laity's sense of their own union with
Christ. Women were to be the principal gainers from this aspect of
eucharistic spirituality, despite its powerful ecclesiological and clerical
contours.

73. See the October 9, 1892, letter to Martha ("Mattie") Stearns.
Life in the American parish during these same years is described admirably in *The American Catholic Parish: A History from 1850 to the
Present,* I, ed. Jay P. Dolan (New York, Mahwah, N.J.: Paulist Press,
1987). See especially Joseph J. Casino, "Expansion, 1880–1930"
where Casino describes eucharistic devotion in the typical Catholic
parish, as well as other prayers and practices. including the Pious
Union of Our Virgin Mother of Good Counsel to which Rose refers in
her diary.

74. George Parsons Lathrop and Rose Hawthorne Lathrop, *A Story
of Courage. Annals of the Georgetown Convent of the Visitation of the
Blessed Virgin Mary* (Cambridge: Riverside Press, 1895), 3.

75. Ibid. 23.

76. Lillie Hamilton French, "Hawthorne's Daughter," *Ladies
Home Journal* 10 (February 1893):9.

77. Lillie Hamilton French to Rose Hawthorne Lathrop, November
8, [1892], Rosary Hill Home.

78. *The World's Columbian Catholic Congresses and Educational
Exhibit* (Chicago: J.S. Hyland, 1893), 83.

79. Most Catholic sentiment was against such an "unjust, unreasonable, unspiritual abnormality." See John Boyle O'Reilly's words in
James J. Kenneally. "American Catholicism and Women," in *Women
in American Religion,* ed., Janet Wilson James (Univ. of Pennsylvania
Press, 1980). See Katherine Conway's title essay in *The Christian Gentlewoman and the Social Apostolate.* Urging the fitness of women for
education and public service, the sometimes feisty Miss Conway was,
nevertheless, opposed to women's suffrage. As a diocesan journalist,
she represented episcopal views, but in this matter these views corresponded to her own: "The woman-suffragist, we must admit in the face

of notable examples, is often a most admirable woman, whom we are compelled to like personally, however little our sympathy with her cause. . . . Social regeneration must come from within—not from without. Regenerated society will draw its pure life from the guarded well-springs of those homes whence women trained and developed on normal lines diffuse high motives, refined tastes and virtuous examples through the channels of ordinary domestic and social opportunity— where the old-fashioned Christian gentlewoman exercises the social apostolate" (12–13, 20).

80. Of the American hierarchy, only Bishops John Ireland, Bernard McQuaid, and John Spalding supported woman suffrage.

81. See James J. Kenneally, "Eve, Mary, and the Historians, American Catholicism and Women," *Women in American Religion,* 191– 206, at 194.

82. James J. Kenneally, "Catholicism and Woman Suffrage," *Catholicism in America,* ed. Philip Gleason (New York: Harper and Row, 1970), 81–91.

83. Janet Wilson James, "Women in American Religious History," *Women in American Religion,* ed. Janet Wilson James (University of Pennsylvania, 1980), 15.

84. Alice T. Toomy, "There is a Public Sphere for Catholic Women," *The Catholic World,* 57 (August, 1893): 674–677, at 675.

85. William T. Elsing, "Life in New York Tenement Houses, As Seen by a City Missionary," *Scribner's Monthly* 11 (June 1892): 697– 721, at 721.

86. Father Drumgoole had died in 1888. He had not become a priest until he was 53 years old, but he had been overwhelmed by the poverty of the newsboys in New York City and dedicated his priestly life especially to the care of these and other neglected children, starting a mission in downtown Manhattan, which was later moved to Staten Island. Rose had clearly been impressed by his story.

87. These letters and accompanying photographs are all in the Berg Collection of the New York Public Library. A few have deleted sections that the recipient apparently did not want to make public.

88. Rose Hawthorne Lathrop to cousin Richard [Manning], February 7, 1896. Essex Institute.

89. Rose Hawthorne Lathrop to "Mattie," [Martha L. Stearns], September 14, 1896. Berg.

90. Msgr. I. Lavelle to Rose Hawthorne Lathrop. October 31, 1896, Rosary Hill Home.

91. Father Fidelis (James Kent Stone) was the son of John Seely Stone, rector of St. Paul's Episcopal Church in Brookline, Massachu-

setts and dean of the Episcopal Theological School in Cambridge, Massachusetts. His mother, Mary Kent, was the daughter of jurist James Kent, Chancellor of New York and author of the standard *Commentaries on American Law.* James' wife, the former Cornelia Fay, had died after six years of marriage, leaving three daughters. At the time he was President of Hobart College. He converted to Catholicism, resigned his position and entered the Paulists, on the condition that if he could provide for the care of his children, he would transfer to the Passionists. A wealthy California couple agreed to adopt his daughters on the extraordinarily painful condition that he never seek contact with them again. He agreed and shortly thereafter became a Passionist, assuming his new religious name. For the next 44 years he held numerous administrative offices, including that of Provincial. He wrote a conversion account entitled *The Invitation Heeded* (1870), and a sequel, *An Awakening and What Followed* (1920). He died in 1921.

92. Rose Hawthorne Lathrop to "Mattie" [Martha L. Stearns], November 25, 1896. Berg.

93. Rose Hawthorne Lathrop to "Mattie" [Martha L. Stearns] April, 1898. Berg.

94. Cited in Sister M. Joseph, 54 (See note 50).

95. Sister Rose Huber, *Memoirs,* Rosary Hill Home.

96. According to the records of the New York Archdiocese, the foundress was Annie Blount Storrs.

97. In 1910 the work of the Women of Calvary was offered to the Servants of Relief. While Mother Alphonsa was questioning whether or not she had the resources to do so, the ministry was assumed by the Blauvelt Dominicans. The Servants of Relief were then free to concentrate their efforts on building a larger house on Jackson Street.

98. J. Warren Greene was a New York lawyer, whose wife had died of cancer. Not only did he make financial contributions to the charity, but offered free legal services. Mrs. F. A. Moulton was a constant contributor. John D. Crimmins was the major contractor for over 400 buildings. He constructed most of the elevated railway mileage in New York, as well as the subways for underground electric wiring. With 12,000 people in his employ, he was a powerful citizen, a staunch supporter of Archbishop Corrigan, a member of the Board of Trustees of St. Patrick's Cathedral, and a faithful supporter of Catholic charitable works. In addition to assisting Mother Alphonsa, he helped to found Corpus Christi Monastery of Dominican Sisters at Hunt's Point, New York. He eventually became Mother Alphonsa's treasurer, although initially, he would have no part in that risky undertaking.

99. Clement Thuente had first been assigned to the parish of St.

Catherine of Siena in a thickly populated Italian section in the central part of New York. Here he was instrumental in forming what has been called the model Catholic settlement, called St. Rose's, which offered classes in Christian doctrine for public school children, as well as for adults. The administrator of this project was Marian Gurney who, as Mother Marianne of Jesus eventually founded, in 1908, the Sisters of Our Lady of Christian Doctrine.

100. Cited in S. Joseph, 84 (See note 50).

101. Robert Emmett Curran, *Michael Augustine Corrigan and the Shaping of Conservative Catholicism in America, 1878–1902* (New York: Arno Press, 1978), vi.

102. Ibid. John D. Crimmins (See note 98) recorded in his privately printed diary on Christmas, 1902: "Every year we might record the separation of a dear friend near to us as one of the family. The one in particular whose sweet memory will be always dear to me was the saintly Archbishop Michael Augustine Corrigan. For many years and with much anxiety he followed all the conditions in which I was surrounded and his tender advice and interest I am deprived of and which I feel so often the necessity for. He must have the reward of a good and faithful servant. I never met one so sincere and spiritual as His Grace."

103. By coincidence—perhaps—it was Julian Hawthorne who wrote the official description of the elaborate funeral services of Archbishop Corrigan. John Talbot Smith cites his essay in his own history of the New York Archdiocese, observing somewhat sanguinely that his essay "easily takes rank with the permanent things in literature." See John Talbot Smith, *History of the Catholic Church in New York* (New York and Boston: Hall and Locke, 1908), II 562–569. Talbot indicates his source as *Memorial of Archbishop Corrigan,* Cathedral Press, 1902.

104. *Christ's Poor* 1:11 (June 1902) 18.

105. Discussion at the Third Plenary Council of Baltimore indicated that the practice of begging among American sisterhoods had become intolerable, and the bishops discouraged as much of it as possible. Many congregations became desperate in their efforts to continue their work among the poor, some opening up shops and laundries, many adding private music and sewing lessons to their teaching duties in order to support themselves. See Mary Ewens, O.P., *The Role of the Nun in Nineteenth Century America* (New York: Arno Press, 1978).

106. *Report: Dominican Cancer Homes for the Destitute,* (New York: January, 1908 to October, 1912), 28.

107. Eventually male orderlies were employed for assistance with men patients. M. Adelaide Nutting has noted that in some Catholic

hospitals, the sisters assigned the menial tasks to hired personnel and did not themselves engage in such patient care as would be "demeaning" or threatening to their concept of chastity. See M. Adelaide Nutting and Lavinia L. Dock, *A History of Nursing,* 4 vols. (New York: Putnam, 1935), 1:503. A balanced account of the problems European-based religious congregations often faced in the work of nursing, as well as of the achievements of nursing congregations in America, is given in Mary Ewens, O.P., *The Role of the Nun in Nineteenth Century America.* (See note 105.)

108. Cited in Maynard, 331.

109. "Letter from Mrs. Rose Hawthorne Lathrop," (June 9th), The *Hawthorne Centenary Celebration at the Wayside* (Boston and New York: Houghton, Mifflin 1905), 14–15. Julian, however, was not present. He sent a paper entitled "Hawthorne's Last Years," which was read by Margaret Lothrop.

110. Ibid., 146–47.

111. Mother Alphonsa to Sister Rose Huber, August 1, 1908, Rosary Hill Home, Hawthorne, New York. In 1900 Father Thuente was assigned to Holy Rosary Priory in Minneapolis, Minnesota, but returned in 1903 to become Prior of St. Vincent Ferrer's. In 1906 he was reassigned to Holy Rosary Priory. During the years 1913–1916 Father Thuente was the head of the Northwestern Mission band, preaching, and giving retreats and missions at a considerable distance from New York. His direction had to be by letter, since he got to Hawthorne only occasionally for a retreat or visit. In his absence diocesan authorities did not appoint an official successor to the office of Ecclesiastical Superior, although various Dominicans, such as Father Eugene Daly functioned somewhat in that capacity. Father Daly was appropriately cautious in his advice to Mother Alphonsa, but she often felt frustrated because he did not consider them a religous community in any canonical sense at all and could not be so considered until she and Sister Rose were permitted to make final profession. In 1908 Father James McNicholas arrived to function as adviser and spiritual director. In 1914 Sister Rose Huber complained to Cardinal Farley that the community had been "spiritually abandoned" and asked that Bishop Thomas F. Cusack be appointed Ecclesiastical Protector. He agreed willingly and the appointment became effective immediately.

112. See note 98.

113. John Talbot Smith, 354.

114. In 1900 the bull *Conditae a Cristo* recognized congregations of sisters with simple vows as authentic "religious." In the following year other problems were clarified, particularly the relationship between

religious superiors, their local bishop, and Rome. Problems continued, neverthless, as the history of religious congregations testifies.

115. See note 111.

116. In that article he speaks of Mother Alphonsa's many "crushing disappointments" and her devotion to her own community of sisters, citing from one of her letters: "Around these wonders [the novices] circle our little crowd of old professed—all of us just about as naughty as we can be. Yet what sublime goodness these older Sisters have displayed in so many ways."

117. See Reginald Coffey, *The American Dominicans: A History of St. Joseph's Province* (New York: St. Martin de Porres Guild, 1969), 624–36.

118. Mother Mary Rogers to Mother Alphonsa, [1912] Rosary Hill Home.

119. The other side of this debate is inaccessible. It exemplifies, however, the kind of collisions many religious foundresses were experiencing with their male mentors or with those who thought themselves their mentors. See in this context, Margaret Susan Thompson, "Discovering Foremothers: Sisters, Society, and the American Catholic Experience, *U.S. Catholic Historian* 5 (Summer, Fall, 1986): 273–290, at 288: "Consider, for example, that dozens of American congregations successfully sought pontifical status during the decades just before and after 1900. The reasons to do so were many. Not the least was the desire to lessen the authority that idiosyncratic and autocratic bishops were otherwise able to wield over them. For this status to be achieved, however, a religious community had to satisfy several requirements, including the securing of endorsements from every bishop in whose diocese their members were located—from the very men, in other words, in whose control the sisters were trying to free themselves." The writer comments that Mother Cabrini, "whose connections in Rome were unparalleled, was well known for the skill with which she advised other Superiors General to proceed." Mother Alphonsa's conflicts, however, were generally not with bishops, but with others who worked with her or who, like Father McNicholas, had a certain degree of unquantifiable influence.

120. Mother Alphonsa to Sister Rose, Rosary Hill Home.

121. Ann Taves, 73 (See note 69).

122. See especially Joseph P. Chinicci, O.F.M., "Spiritual Capitalism and the Culture of American Catholicism," *U.S. Catholic Historian* 5:2 (1986): 131–161. What is especially remarkable is Mother Alphonsa's absolute resistance to other forms of American spiritual capitalism: the fund-raising techniques urged upon her by charlatans

and clerics alike. She was never to succumb to the lure of bazaars and charitable fund-raising motivated by self-interest. Nor is there any mention in any of her diaries of the lure of indulgences. All of her petitions were for wisdom and counsel in her own life, sanctification for others, and the material means to relieve suffering in those to whom she ministered.

123. See John Farina on this point. In his Introduction to *Isaac T. Hecker, The Diary* he notes that the devotional life of the church in the first half of the century was designed to foster docility to Roman authority (See note 40).

124. Julian Hawthorne, "A Daughter of Hawthorne," 373 (See note 20).

125. Ibid., 376.

126. Carolyn de Swarte Gifford, "Women in Social Reform Movements," *Women and Religion in America: The Nineteenth Century,* eds. Rosemary Radford Ruether and Rosemary Skinner Keller. (San Francisco: Harper and Row, 1981), 297.

127. M.T. Elder, "Put Money in Thy Purse," *The Catholic World* 50 (February, 1890):618–28. Elder was a prolific journalist for organized social action within the church. See also Aaron I. Abell, *American Catholicism and Social Action: A Search for Social Justice 1865–1950* (Doubleday: Garden City, 1960); Winthrop S. Hudson, *Religion in America* (New York: Charles Scribner's Sons, 1965), 305 ff.

128. Cited in C.M. Thuente, Mother Alphonsa, O.S.D., *Torch* (1926):23, 27.

129. See Carroll Smith-Rosenberg, "The Female World of Love and Ritual: Relations between Women in Nineteenth-Century America," *Signs: Journal of Women in Culture and Society,* 1:1(Autumn, 1975):1–29. "These female friendships served a number of emotional functions. Within this secure and empathetic world women could share sorrows, anxieties, and joys, confident that other women had experienced similar emotions. One mid-nineteenth century rural matron in a letter to her daughter discussed this particular aspect of women's friendships: 'To enter into all her little needs and in whose bosom she could with freedom pour forth her joys and sorrows—such a friend would very much relieve the tedium of many a wearisome hour . . .' "(p. 12).

LETTERS

To Nathaniel Hawthorne, 1856 [RHH]

This is the first letter Rose Hawthorne is known to have written. It is in large cursive script. She was five years old.

> dear papa,
> darling, sweet,
> dear, I have written it.
> > *Rose*
>
> 1856

To Nathaniel Hawthorne [Berg]

An early concern is sounded here: one must be of some use. This letter was written shortly before the return to Concord.

> *Bath, 13 Charles St.*
> *May 20, 1860*

My dearest papa,

This morning I awoke and sow the bright son beating on the houses oposite and thanked God it had come at last, these rainy days without any thonder or lightening—unless Una has a letter are very dull in deed. But now papa cannot you come and stay with me to-day it's my birthday you know, and I shoun'nt have half such a nice time if you don't. I shall be sure to have a doncky ride to-day as it is Saterday. Dear papa, mamma wants me to write you a song if I can but you know it says *if pots and pans were ifs and ands ther'd be less work for idle*

hands, but my idle hands are'nt of any use so you must exuse (I beg
your pardon I have not spellt it right) me till another time.

>   My best wishes
>   to you
>   Good by

>   your daughter Rose
>   nine years old to day

To Mrs. Fields [Boston Public Library]
        Nathaniel Hawthorne and Sophia were close personal friends of
his publisher James T. Fields and his wife Annie (Adams). Aunt Lizzie
Hawthorne is Nathaniel's sister Elizabeth. Rose was often encouraged
to write to the Fields to acknowledge gifts or hospitality. After Hawthorne's death, Sophia became disaffected with the publisher, and the
friendship dissolved. Rose, as this letter suggests, disliked being alone.

>   *The Wayside 1861*
>   *Concord, Mass.*

My dear Mrs. Fields
        Mamma and I are going away soon, and mamma is so very busy,
that she does not know what to do. She has been making me some
dresses and has to make two or three more now. I have been longing for
paper dolls, and now I have two and one set of furniture, and I hope
that I shall have a larger family soon.
        I have a perfectly black kitten, and she is very cunning and loving,
and I love her very much indeed! I am very sorry that I shall not see you
when I go through Boston, I am going to the mountains first, and then
to Salem. My Aunt Lizzy Hawthorne is here, and she is going to stay
here to take care of Una while mamma and I go to the mountains, and
then we shall come home, and go back with her to Salem. I think that it
is very hot to-day, though I believe that it rained in the night. We have
so many flies, that I wonder we were not eaten up before this time, but
we soon shall. We are having a few apples now, though you may have
had them before this time. I have a very pretty doll, though I never play
with it, though I try to. I have a great many things to play with, but it
seems so desolate to play alone that I never play with my play things
now. Mamma says that I want a thing, and get it and I throw it away
with all my other things, and don't play with it, and I say because I have

no one to play with me, but I suppose it is no use; I never have any one to play with me I might as well play by myself if I could.

> Good bye dear Mrs. Fields.
> Rose Hawthorne

[Note in Sophia Hawthorne's writing]
Sunday.
My dear Mrs. Fields. This is quite a melancholy cry for companionship. But Bud has *one* playmate when she can come to see her, though it is too sure that she is quite lonely. I intend to play with her myself this winter. I have never thanked you for your nice long note. But now I am a needle and not a correspondent. But I love you and think of you all the same. Ever yours,

> S. Hawthorne

To Patty [Berg]
"Patty" is Martha L. Stearns, the Mattie of many subsequent letters. This childhood friend corresponded with Rose Hawthorne for almost forty years and is the recipient of many of Rose's most personally revealing letters. The "Aunt Lizzie" of this letter is Elizabeth Palmer Peabody, Sophia's sister. Alice Wheeler remained a close friend for a long time, later living near the Convent of the Sisters of Charity in Wellesley Hills where Rose went years later to make a retreat. Rose's personal orthography is maintained in this transcription.

> *Concord 1862*
> *Massachusetts*

My dear Patty,
Do excuse my not writing to you before; but it has been quite impossible for me to do so. Alice Wheeler has been to draw with me this morning, as she always does. *The prisoners are coming home and I am going to see them.*

The prisoners have come home, and such a time was made about them! I must describe it as well as I can. First Alice and I were at the depot at 12 o'clock. Soon the soldiers came with a large company of other soldiers, and with some little boy soldiers too. Then they were taken all round town to be looked at which I should not think would please them very much. They were all grown terribly fat in every way. There is a Sidney Rice who came home. When he went away his face was very thin and he had a red moustach and red whiskers and beard.

Now his hair is shaved close and his moustach is black his little tiny beard is black and his whiskers are shaved off and he is fat with splendid blue eyes, and he looks very handsome. The Boston band came up and played "sweet home, there is no place like home" very softly and then for the first time the soldiers began to wipe thier eyes. There is one that came home that looks the heartiest of them all, and *he* has a bullet in his shoulder. They are to have a fiest at the town hall. I am afraid this is not very interesting to you. I rode home with Alice and as we were coming home I sprained my ancle.

I have not the honor to know your address so I must write to Aunt Lizzie. I hope it won't be long before we see each other again. My new garden is florishing very well, I think, considering how scanty it is. I do go to school now a little; but for only two weeks more for then the vacation comes of eight weeks. Alice and I are drawing [illegible—possibly for Alice's aunt] Now breakfest and this noon I had no dinner, so I have a right to be hungry for my supper. Give my love to all my friends in Dorchester and excuse my bad writing.

Yours truly,
Rose

To Sophia Hawthorne [Berg]
The following letter exemplifies what Theodore Maynard, in summarizing this period in Rose's life, has described as "the unutterable woes of adolescence." Rose's roommate is Bessie Whitwell.

Darling Mama,
I have ever so much business to talk about. First, my new short dress don't fit me in the first particular. What could have been the matter with the pattern? And Una too, for it is above my knees, And too short waisted, and too small round the waist, and everything is wrong. It is guilt to the last degree. because all the hem won't make it long enough. I hope Una hasn't cut out any more of my dresses. I have nothing to wear, and am in an awful pickle. I don't know whether I shall send it right home or not. I cannot do anything next week, for my purple dress is tearing in every direction. That also was uncomfortably short, and altogether as far as my clothes question goes, I am rather poorly off. I have no waist to reveal, and must try hard to put belts on those loose animals. I need to have that balmoral skirt fixed, and one or two white short skirts. I need stockings and aprons, and my hoop skirts are unhappy. I think the only way for me to do is to tell Fullerton that I

must go home a few days to have dresses fitted. I don't see what else to do. Please send word imediately whether I may, and a note to Fullerton saying you wish me to. I never should have come away without a full outfit. Last night Bessie and I fell out, And about the fire too. She said she wished to go to bed but would not go till we had put out the fire, All the evening the fire had been very low, and her aunt and I were very nearly frozen, and decided to have a good roast before we went to sleep. So I bundled in a big stick of wood into the stove, at which Bessie set up a wine that I was real mean. She continued to wine in such a weak disgusting manner that I decided her selfishness should not have the upperhand of me. She pretended that she was an injured angel, whereas it was exceedingly selfish to wish us to freeze for a peak of her own. I told her if she would knock me over or scold instead of moping and calling me mean and saying that she was not angry at all, I should have a good deal more respect for her, but the rediculous goose's enthusiastic affection for me dissappeared as soon as I would not freeze Lucy and myself for her sake, and she probably knows what a shallow puddle of dish water she is. I thought we should have a healthy fight over the fire that would warm us up beautifully, not that she would be so doubly mean as to sit there and call names angelically and I was very much surprised this morning that she spoke in the same injured wine. Fullerton says I must get a note from you saying that I may stay at home from Church if I wish to, that I shall show to him because he cannot let me off without having a written permission from you. You see the preaching is so vile here, that I cannot go possibly—but if there comes a good preacher I will go. I shall go into the Shakespeare class, as I believe you said I might, And learn Arithmetic and Geography. The other night Mr. Lewis said tickets were to be got for R——[illegible] but they were for Wednesday. I don't think I wish to go even if you would let me; but I don't know as I ever get off as I said I wanted to go there. I was quite excited as there had been a great deal of fine singing and playing this evening, and did not know what it was about. I shall probably have to come home to get my dressed fitted, and so I guess he won't make me [buy] a ticket. I feel horribly out of order as I have nothing to wear, and Bessie is so disgusting and don't believe I shall go to Miss Ripley next Wednesday. At any rate I must come home to get clothes. I have ever so many things that I want, but there is no use trying to name them. I don't beleive you will be able to keep me here long for if I say I must have ever so many things that I can't have. You can't do anything without money and I . . . [illegible] very good, feeling that I am rising up everything. Besides when one comes away from home, one has to get things that otherwise would seem . . . [illegible, possibly commonplace.] [I] feel extremely disgusted, and probably you will see me before this letter. I guess I will finish up now.

Truly your loving daughter,

Rose Hawthorne
Nov 4, 1866
Lexington, Mass.
Sunday

To Mattie from Rose, 1869 [incomplete] [Berg]
The clearest picture of the Dresden years are in these letters to Mattie, many of which are fragments only. They do contain, however, vivid descriptions of favorite art masterpieces (Raphael's Madonna) and Rose's impressions of German culture.

February 13, '69 Dresden
You dear, dear Mattie!
What a delight it is to me to get this letter from you, you can't imagine, and you can't imagine how I have longed for it. Seems to me it takes your letters unnecessary ages to come, and yet the direction is quite right. I have perfect loads to tell you, about every conceivable thing, it is so long since I wrote to you last. But, darling, I was so sorrowful to hear that your sister's husband had died—it seems too short a time ago that we saw her blushing at the mention of his name at the Fulsomes' that summer day, to have her new married life cut off so now. It is very sad, dear, I sympathize with you with all my heart. Such exerience either makes one tremble as if walking by the edge of a precipice, or feel safer and more confiding in God. On Ash Wednesday Mama and I went to hear "Stabat Mater" at the Opera or Hoftheater. I had hesitated about going, for at the Terrace Concert we had not liked the style of Rossini's music. So little I knew! for the beauty of the "Stabat Mater" as performed by this orchestra is quite beyond any description of mine. But I must mention one or two parts that particularly enraptured me. Before the voices begin the orchestral introduction is, as you might think, full of low moaning and then throbbing music, till it ends in a wailing, low and passionate like a storm of sighs and tears. Then the chorus sings "Stabat Mater dolorosa. Juxta crucem lacrimosa" and when they come to the words "Dum pendebat" each deep tone was followed by a pause of horror, but the word "Filius" was a shriek of anguish, torture, agony. One sees the mother, hears the cry she utters through the wild grief of the women and the groans of the

men. It is some time before the music subsides, and then the tenor voice sings. Now the tenor was Herr Schild with a voice like unto a seraph, not so powerful as of wonderful refinement and quality. Some notes were so rare and remarkable I saw some people start forward almost from their seats with intensity of interest. Many a time I caught myself open-mouthed with absorption, having for once entirely forgotten there was such a wight in the flesh as your's truly. Herr Schild's voice can't last long, it is too perfect, and yet not very strong. For this reason he hates to sing in the Opera, besides, I daresay he don't relish hugging the tremendously fat old Prima Donna as I suppose it is necessary he should in tender parts of the acting. She goes by the name of "that awfully great" etc. So Herr Schild departs soon for Friberg, accompanied with a unanimous groan from Dresden, for he is the best singer for miles round, I have heard. There was one very stirring part of the performance. There is a monkish chant of a chorus of male voices, which the bass voice led like a high priest, and sometimes the female voices joined in the chorus. At the end the Quartet sang "Quando corpus morietur. Facsit animae donetur. Paradisi gloria" the last two words being sung with such delicacy and joyousness the house seemed full of angels, or that we had been elevated with the music into a new sphere of hope and comprehension of immortality. They then played Beethoven's Symphony eroica in E flat. How I pity you poor creatures in America who never have such a grand Orchestra as there is here! I am so sure the best German musicians stay at home instead of gadding off to America. And certainly I never heard music till I went Ash Wednesday, still I have no doubt they have more wonderful performances still.

To Una [Berg]
The following letter was written on shipboard during Rose and George's return to the United States during the winter of 1871–72. They had been married less than four months.

January 8th 1872
"Oceanic"

Dearest Una,
I am afraid that before now you have begun to wonder what can have become of us. And when we reach New York we expect to be received like creatures long ago commended to the floods and forgotten! for we have not hailed a high vessel since we last saw land, and

have had squalls, head winds and two storms in continuous succession. Only of late a few days were calm so that it was possible to go on deck, and after a squall of last night we have a fine though rough day. My dear girl I have just witnessed the saving of drown men from a wreck, which drifted in sight. It has been very exciting, for their brig was expected to sink every moment. The poor fellows came at first close alongside of us—that is, as near as was at all safe for them, but we could not hear what they called out. At last, one of the sailors flung up his arms and flung them down again with a most expressive motion; the vessel was sinking, the dear American flag at the top of the mast was upside down—signal of distress-and one of the sails was torn to shatters. Her sides were split all along, the water had filled her; and as she tossed came rushing out and over her. She was scarcely above water. The excitement was most intense among us, and the sailors and Captain were received with open arms. We had been in such similar peril ourselves, that we could thoroughly sympathize with these unfortunates. However, they were not so *much* to be pitied, after their escape, and under the charge of our great, bluff Purser, who took charge of them as regarded pantry matters. They had been twenty nine days on a week's trip from New York to Portland, and for four days they had been unable to go below deck, and in biting wind and storm and snow, had remained exposed *without food.* Imagine the horror of it! And we can only be glad now that we have delayed six days. The Captain of the Oceanic says he has never in nine years' experience seen such weather as we have had, and we all believe that any vessel less splendidly built would have gone down long ago. The Screw was seriously damaged in the *first storm,* Christmas night, but otherwise the vessel was unbroken. The motion has often been frightful, and we feared to be out about the [illegible] altogether. I suffered a great deal for the suspense you would feel, but now we shall soon be in New York, and you will see by the papers that we are safe. I cannot bear to think of what we have been through, and what we have escaped. George saw a small bit of a wreck yesterday floating past. The first four days and nights as you may suppose, I lay in misery in my berth, unconscious to everything but disagreeable influences, and when my condition at last allowed me to rouse myself and feebly grin at George from my wretched place of residence, I had *no idea* how many days we had been afloat. Now I am regaining strength and flesh. And since long ago when the Captain ordered the food to be distributed with less freedom, and our meals, tho' admirably sufficient, are not always entirely palatable, to say that I eat as much as I can get—which I do—is not so extraordinary an assertion as you might think. George is well too, except when it is roughest, when he becomes pensive in the extreme. To feel the quivering of the ship, the waves rolling and thumping at her sides, lifting her and often rushing *beneath* her over and out again was enough to make me cling to George and scream idiotically as was my custom. I assure you we ladies have been well frightened, and many of the gentlemen too. I never shall forget New Year night at twelve o'clock! We had been very gay at dinner and had been spectators of some fireworks on deck, and most of us I daresay disposed to sleep soundly, although a cannonading of waves soon began after George and I had retired to our stateroom. I fell asleep, but presently was awakened by a great lurch which almost rolled me out of my berth. But I had so often experienced the same inconvenience, that I held myself as an old hand at the crisis, and prepared for sleep again when a confusing peal of bells near and distant and the clattering of some instrument like a policeman's whistle struck horror to my soul. Louder and louder waxed the din and I got possession of my faculties sufficiently to call out to George, who slept calmly on. I then rushed to him and set up a howl. But this time every door seemed opened and male and female voices clamored to know how soon the vessel would sunder and go down. George woke and bidding me be of good cheer! proceeded to array himself, bidding me follow his example. Oh dear! I obeyed the dictates of necessity and sat quietly applying stockings to my legs. Suddenly George dropped his arms in sleepy disgust and exclaimed "New Years!"—I leaned my head on my berth—and became the personification of gratitude. Not long were the cackling passengers in finding out the same fact, and discovering that the pans and soup ladles were chief malefactors in the riot. Cries of "Now that *is shocking*" were emitted in accents of the bitterest contempt from those *costumed* wights who had emerged from their lairs without much preparation—pale lions. Those persons who were more elaborate in their toilets came late upon the scene, and appeared far more angry at the real state of things, a seranade by the stewards, than relieved that the vessel was not really in her last moments. A German lady, of the teacher grade, who had favored us with her presence on board, and who always affords great amusement, quite convulsed the by-standers by her contributions to the disturbance. She arrived late in the entry by our cabin, where everything occurred, vociferating— "Stewardess! fwhat was the matter?" and when informed—"O to— mein Gott! but dat was wrong; O to mein Gott, fwhat shall I do." Etc, in a stentorian voice. She was taken in charge, and she afterwards explained that she had put on two dresses and three or four other wrappings in order to drown warmly.

I have been reading "Jane Eyre" to George and we have laughed and I have scolded at almost every paragraph, so unnatural, vulgar and absurd is most of the book. We cannot finish "it"; our patience is exhausted. I have sewed a great deal, and I sat up on deck of late, and got angry with the looks and ways of some of the passengers, as it is my wont to bother my temper with these failings of persons over whom I have no control, and in whom I have no reason to be interested. I am well, I seldom have a disagreeable sensation now; still, I don't know what the future will bring forth, I supppose I shall know soon. I am cultivating a great desire to see America, and trying to love it as a place of long residence, for I think we shall stay there two or three times as long as I thought when I said goodby to Liverpool. I am determined to find it beautiful and interesting, and study hard in it all sorts of lore. And when I reflect upon my husband's ever present love, and before the example of wise living that I shall have in him, I am inclined to think any home with him as heaven. And after all America is a dear grand country. I believe we shall both visit Newport after seeing Dr. and Mrs. Lathrop because [mss mutilated here] . . . anxious to settle down into some cubby hole. I shall post this on arriving in New York, and quite soon send another letter to my dear sister of our land experiences. Meantime, with a great heartful of love—goodbye in the epistolary sense, with affectionate remembrances to Aunt Lizzie and Frank, and love to you from your own sister.

                                                             Rose Lathrop

I never got a letter from my dear girl in Liverpool! probably owing to the . . . [mss torn]

To Lily [Essex]
    The otherwise unidentified addressee may be Lily Fairchild, mentioned in one of Una's letters as a friend of the family. She is possibly related to Senator John Fairchild of Maine, who had supported Nathaniel Hawthorne's appointment to the Salem Customhouse. In addition to its historical interest this letter reveals more of Rose Hawthorne Lathrop's inner struggle than any extant correspondance of this period

of her life. She is already worried about the bonds of marriage and childbearing, deeply concerned about her own intellectual life, and struggling to reconcile herself to exclusively domestic responsibilities.

Thomas Henry Huxley (1825–95) was one of the first to be convinced of Charles Darwin's theory of organic evolution. His writings include *Evidences as to Man's Place in Nature* (1863) and *A Manual of the Anatomy of Invertebrated Animals.* When Rose was a student in London, she had attended some of Huxley's lectures.

John Fiske (1842–1901). American philosopher and historian who helped spread the theory of evolution developed by Charles Darwin and Herbert Spencer. He was the author of *Excursions of an Evolutionist; The Destiny of Man; The Beginnings of New England; The American Revolution;* and *A History of the United States for Schools.*

Herbert Spencer (1820–1903). British philosopher and author of *Programme of a System of Synthetic Philosophy.*

Charles Robert Darwin (1809–82). British naturalist whose theory of evolution through natural selection caused a revolution in biological science. He is the author of *On the Origin of Species by Means of Natural Selection, or the Preservation of Favoured Races in the Struggle for Life* (1859).

Othniel Charles Marsh (1831–1899). American paleontologist. Professor of vertebrate paleontology at Yale College who conducted research on fossil vertebrates of the western states.

George Eliot (Mary Ann Evans) 1819–80. English novelist. Her writings include *Middlemarch, A Study of Provincial Life; Adam Bede; Silas Marner;* and *The Mill on the Floss.*

August 27th [1876]
Petersham, Mass.

My dear Lily,

At last the Huxleys have been here, staying only from Monday noon until Wednesday noon; but giving all of us full hours of enjoyment and enlightenment. I meant to write you instantly about them; but had become so fatigued by constant attention to what was said, that I have been obliged to wait a few days before going over it. I hope I have got a few things to tell you out of the mass, which you will really like to hear. They are both unusually genial and socially intelligent persons, Mrs. Huxley being as impressive as her husband. He is keen-featured and keen-tongued, expressing himself with graceful volubility, and seeing the opportunity for a sinewy joke with unfailing alertness; nor

does he waste the opportunity by any chance. He is full of warm-
heartedness, speaking of his seven children with fervid tenderness, and
softening and gleaming at sight of any of the children here. There is not
the least pomposity about him, even when speaking about subjects on
which he is so great an authority. In fact he is one of those men so truly
great that they can afford to forget themselves, and never find that this
abandon has led to a blunder. We saw the Huxleys in the best possible
light, for they are very fond of Mr. Fiske, and they came into the midst
of a happy summer crowd, all full of welcome and admiration. Therefore they bloomed out to the breadth of their circumference, and may
seem colder and less interesting in certain other surroundings, for this
is the way with everyone. They expressed so many extreme terms of
gratification to Mr. and Mrs. Fiske on taking leave,—seemed to have
linked hearts with them so, too, that we all know they must have been
in a rare glow. Mrs. Huxley has a happy, perhaps once pretty, face, and
gentle, refined manner, and withal a brightness and piquancy, and
far-flighted wit, which reminds one of a french woman, plus tangible
qualities, which one hardly gives a frenchwoman credit for, I imagine,
—or at any rate the bright English woman is a finer combination in my
opinion. She has brought up the seven children entirely by her own
wisdom. When these began to come in rapid succession, she said in
despair to Mr. Huxley—that her life, her individuality, her power, were
all to be given up to this one end of childbearing,—that she should have
to give up all hopes of study and progress with him, and become an
impersonal force, as it were. How many women must have felt this
dagger at their hearts! I among the rest. But just think how encouraging
to hear your husband say, as she did—"Stop there! you have said it—
'*only* childbearing.' It is the greatest work, beside which all other, man's
included, is secondary. Nothing I can ever do will approach your power
in magnitude." And Mrs. Huxley has found that in some way her
development has gone on without the personal and deliberate study
she had hoped to carry out. Her intercourse with her children, and
self-discipline in studying out the best course for *their* developement,
had reacted upon him as an educator, and his cognizance of her husband's work and object in life has given her a critical faculty which is of
the greatest benefit to him, and which seemed to define her place in his
intellectual world as divinely ordered and absolutely necessary. Mr.
Huxley never writes anything that he does not read to her before print-
ing, and depends immeasurably upon her advice concerning it. In several instances where he hesitated about taking it, and finally did not, he

has incurred failure. Mrs. Fiske tells me that she holds the same position with her husband, and I am proud to say that George always defers to me also, and I have been able to give him assistance by criticism and suggestions to an extent which enables me to comprehend all this, and feel perfect satisfaction in so dear and great a function as this is possible to become. If a woman is impelled by a sturdy, invincible power to create intellectually, she will find time to do great things, without interfering with her peculiar order of work. And how much less of trash would be offered to the world if such a limit were put upon her literary and artistic endeavours! A genius cannot be denied utterance, and a woman who properly orders her time, reads as every being ought to do, and developes also through intercourse with the persons of intellect and endowment who almost always are accessible to her, will progress to that extent that if she can write or paint with more than the average result, she will do so, without lifelong practise. If she is a Michel Angelo or Shakespeare, or even less! She will soon know her destiny, and without one misstep will place herself upon a summit which is to isolate her and enthrone her, and where she will work unhindered. If women are cultivated with more care and conscience—if their time is not wasted as it almost always is by pure nonsense half their days, the woman will become so much nobler and more inspired, that instances of great genius will not be so rare, so qualified—And perhaps the effect upon their sons would be immense, too. For every great man has had a rare mother. I cannot help writing you my thoughts, partly because I want your sympathy, and partly because if you do not agree with me, I should be so glad to hear your views on the subject.—Now I am going to tell you the Huxleys' opinions about certain English people. In the first place Spencer, whom you may have heard about, but I never did; I mean as an individual. Here is an indication. He and Huxley were invited by Lady Derby to meet the Czar. Of course court-dress was required, and Huxley had his made, accepting this necessity,—as he would that of wearing a white neckcloth to a dinner, however absurd the custom might be in itself. But this was against Spencer's principles, and he went to consult Huxley as to what he should do. "For heaven's sake," said Huxley, "don't refuse to go. Stay away, if you must, but don't write your views to Lady Derby. Why should you bother her with your determination not to put on a court-dress, or your contempt for Monarchy. She has enough to do without giving her attention to such matters of other peoples private opinions." But Spencer decided to write the bald fact that he did not approve of the court-dress, and

therefore could not be present. Of course Lady Derby courteously returned that she should be glad to see Mr. Spencer in any dress whatsoever; which he had not anticipated—, and suddenly remembered as
well that if he went in an ordinary frockcoat he would be the observed
of all observers. His attitude was therefore ludicrous; and they say he is
always getting into such scrapes. Mr. Huxley said in comment, "life is
too short and serious for us constantly to be stopping to pick up the
pebbles beneath our feet, and scratching ourselves with them. It takes
as little time to put on a court-dress as a frock coat, and we do not jar
upon customs which will not be otherwise by our open contempt, and
are perhaps a very good means of keeping society in order and of easy
management, petty as they may be." It seemed to me quite a novel trait
in one who looks less flinchingly than almost anyone into the grim
depths of the world's Hows and Wherefores, that he should recognize
patiently the relation of what is so momentary to what Herbert Spencer
respects solely. At the same time Spencer is more particular than most
men about the quality and order of his dinner, and has been known to
have a serious struggle with his cook upon the point of whether or no
quails should be served as an entree, which the cook objected to. He
dines with the Huxleys every New Year's day this twenty years, which
betokens intimacy and good fellowship. He at one time thought seriously of marrying; but has given it up. I believe it was not long ago,
however, that he decided it would be a good thing to fall in love out of
hand, and fastened himself for three days upon a young lady with such
absurd intensity that the whole campaign was begun and ended in this
length of time, and the young lady's old nurse perceived the Spencerian
intention directly and was very angry. The hero was not atall reduced
by his failure, but decided that spontaneous falling-in-love was a mistake after all. Darwin in complete outfit is, they said, an extraordinary
sight. He wears a cloak reaching below the knee, a broad-brimmed hat
(I think) and carries a tall staff. He has a long white beard, which
enhances the effect. He has a reputation for being very peculiar in his
habits and for having a liking for nonconformity of all sorts. A lady
who very much admired him was surprised one day to see him as she
passed in her carriage, squatting in the road at a few rods distance from
a farmer who was similarly occupied. The fact was Darwin had discovered a train of ants of unusual length, and finding the ant-hills between
which they were working, was stationed with his temporary assistant
for observation of the ant-motion. He and Mrs. Darwin were first
cousins, and the children are extremely nervous. One night when one

of his children gave him a great deal of trouble, Darwin is known to have quieted him by showing him pictures of monkeys. One of his daughters being admired by a lady at a party, the latter remarked, "Charming! but what a pity that her father is not quite in his right mind!"—The Huxleys told us a good deal about George Elliot and her husband, which coming from personal acquaintances (I believe however that Mrs. Huxley herself has not *visited* Mrs. Lewis) will perhaps be news to you. Mr. Huxley first knew George Elliot when she was assistant editor of the Westminster Review (?), and when she wrote an article for it upon scientific questions, which Mr. Huxley said was so superficial that he wrote a critical article in answer to it, which was actually printed in the Review and which made George Elliot very angry. I wonder if her scientific knowledge, which has been said to be so great, is now solid; but I did not remember to ask Mr. Huxley. Mrs. John Brooks and I had only a day or two before been talking of her, and Mrs. Brooks thought that her course in regard to Mr. Lewis had been based upon the noblest motives and sincerest convictions, as the moral tenor of her books would indicate. That she was always pointing out the case of a woman who places herself in a questionable light to the world, when she thinks it is to the advantage of one she loves, as Maggie's sacrifice in "Mill On the Floss"—I was inclined to think her unjustified, although mistaken not foully but unfortunately. Mr. Huxley however had no idea that she was under an impression that to live with Lewis without the marriage bond was a high duty and a noble sacrifice; and described Lewis in justification of this opinion. He said Lewis was a fascinating man, endowed with wit and graciousness to a remarkable degree, so that one is instantly enthralled by him. Although Huxley said that to him the charm wore off with alarming suddenness, and he found Lewis really to be of ephemeral substance. Lewis is a thorough Bohemian, having no high ideas of morality, but coarse in the extreme. His wife and the man who seduced her (Theodore Hunt, I think) lived together under Lewis's roof for about a year, Lewis accepting the situation so long, that when he wished for a divorce in order to marry George Elliot, the law was incompetent to give him one! His wife was then dismissed, and George Elliot took up her abode. Since the first wife's death they have been married, not on account of property belonging to Lewis, for he has none. While George Elliot was obscure no one would visit her; but since the accession of fame she has had attention enough! But she never goes to other peoples houses, saying they may come to her if they please, and implying that she does not forget previous treatment. Mr. Huxley said he was not himself squeamish about having intercourse with persons who had taken laws into their own hands simply because they had done so; but that as he considered monogamy one of the, in fact, the very most valuable institution of civilization and as he must consider the effect of irregularity upon his children, he had not allowed an acquaintance to spring between the Lewises and his family, though he knew them himself. He said he did not see the justice of making exceptions of people of genius or position, from a general condemnation. He thought George Elliot had been overcome as George Sand was overcome, the latter being to his mind a far greater woman, by the lower forces of nature—one might say, by the deseases of nature—I suppose. He says George Elliot was shockingly ugly in her earlier days; but that now age has softened the effect, in some way. The first Mrs. Lewis was one of the prettiest women Mr. Huxley ever saw. Very bright too in conversation, and, if she had married a man of any principle would have led an excellent life. But this young Hunt was living in the house, and as Mr. Lewis professedly believed in the law of free love, it is not surprising that a woman of not great moral force should be persuaded to abandon him. He was probably a disgusting little fellow in many ways, and I certainly should no longer lay the charge of a preference for wickedness rather than goodness, at Mrs. Lewis's door. When Mrs. Lewis No. 1 came to want, Lewis supplied her with sufficient means of support until her death. Mr. Huxley has a belief that there is neither a benevolent nor a malevolent creator, but that life is cruelly hard, and that nature is too beautiful at her best for us to ignore the good in life; or as he said, "look out at that sky, and then say the motive power is malevolent, if you can!" He says that from the evidence of Marsh's collection at New Haven, which he has examined,—*evolution is proved.* Marsh, you probably already know, has been collecting specimens out West (is it?) in that region called the "bad country?" where he was obliged to hold onto his scalp with one hand and dig up specimens with the other, so to speak. And Mr. Huxley says it is all a wonderful discovery, and that when the collection is put in order, all doubt as to evolution of species will be removed. Of course this will effect religion very seriously. But in the bringing up of children Mr. Huxley thinks the chief thing to be avoided is giving them a feeling of superiority of conviction over their companions; and that as far as possible they should be held to the prevalent belief, judicious freedom being given them to draw their own conclusions from the establishment of facts. His children go to the church of a liberal minded preacher, and when even he preached of the devil as a person, Mrs. Huxley scolds to her husband about it, but leaves the children to reject or tolerate—according to their developement, and they already show much good sense. Of course knowing the discoveries of science, they don't understand how anyone can be so foolish as to suppose the world was made in six days. I was sewing during the psychological discussion, and when Mr. Huxley said there was no such thing as chance—that every act was ordained (by an act-evolution, I suppose) any length of time ago—and I expressed my horror of such a law, he said "the stitch you are taking now will effect an infinite number of successive acts, and was itself inevitable." I cannot understand just what he means, although he talked some time about it; but hope his essays, or treatises, will elucidate. In Fiske's Unseen World, he speaks of the effect of a thought upon the particles of the brain, which in moving effect the atmospheric particles, and so on, and I suppose the facts—if they are facts, are related or the same. We read several of Huxley's, "Lay Sermons, etc" before he came, and admired and enjoyed them extremely.

August 30th—Alas, dear Lily, I look over my too long letter, and behold it filled with sentences that seem to be standing on their heads, and will give you much trouble to understand, and when you have found out what I am saying you will be very much disappointed. But if I am sending you one word which will amuse you, and if I give you one correct idea about Huxley, I shall expect you to forgive my prosiness. If George were not in Boston for a few days, I should get him to give his opinion about sending this to you. —Your kind note came yesterday, thanks be to you. I *have* secured a very admirable nurse, Mrs. Bruce, who nursed Mrs. Whittemon, an acquaintance of mine who very much delights in her, and one or two other ladies I know. Dr. Walcott has corroberated Mrs.W's opinion, so I am quite at rest. You are sisterly indeed, and give me very great happiness. I am quite well, but have lost a little of my energy, perhaps because this is the seventh month, which is trying, I believe. I think the 10th of November is very near the time when I shall be confined, and I have asked Mrs. B. to come on the 6th. I had a letter from Una a day or two ago, very sweet but she is not very well, she says, and she and Minne were at the sea-shore for strength. I hope soon to see you, dear Lily. With heartiest love to you and yours, and congratulations upon the lightness of the hay-fever.

Yrs, Rose Lathrop

To George Lathrop [1880] [Essex]

This is one of the very few extant letters from Rose to her husband. Lily may be the Lily Fairchild to whom Rose's letter from Petersham was addressed.

Tuesday Evening

My darling George—

We went to Keene to-day and had a *splendid* time. In order that all of us should go, I had to hire Mr. Lardley's horse, and so there were three teams. You must try to imagine what fun it was, and how we carried a lunch that we ate in the big hotel bedroom, which I hired for Francie's nap, who was tucked away in a little inner room that came with the big one—He had a fine sleep while we lunched, which was very jolly, as we had bought a few canned things and some lemons and berries. We all felt built up. The children throve more and more every mile and hour. Francie had glorious fun, and was bewitching, with his roundalays all the way home. But I have felt broken hearted at hearing how near you came to being turned over at the foot of the hill! I was very anxious from the moment I saw you mount behind that wretched beast. My darling, you must be more careful, or when I see signs of danger listen to me—for you might have been seriously injured or killed. Mrs. Craigin said the gray horse behaved shockingly on its way from the Morses yesterday at some time, for no reasonable cause. I wish you were a little slyer about taking care of yourself. I am wretched to have you out of my sight, and fear the stage turned over on your way to Greenfield! You know you came very near having an accident when you left me in the car at Cambridge, for it was moving quite rapidly when you got off. Isn't this a silly lecture? but I am too scared and lonely to help a bit of it, and besides its all true. We are very, very well. Dear love, goodnight. Lily's note I have not read atall, but opened as for me.

Your own,
Rose

To Rebecca Manning [Essex]

The Essex Institute assigns this letter to 1894. Julian moved with his family to Jamaica in December, 1893. Rebecca Manning is the daughter of Nathaniel Hawthorne's uncle Robert and one of Cousin Richard's two sisters. "Aunt Louisa" is Nathaniel Hawthorne's sister Maria Louisa who had lived in Boston and drowned when the steamboat *Henry Clay* caught fire and capsized in the Hudson River. Minutes before the fire started she had been seen in her stateroom reading *Pilgrim's Progress.* The memory of her tragic death troubled the Hawthornes for years. Rose had met a Miss Wilder who studied under "Aunt Louisa" at a "night school" in Boston. Rose had not known of her aunt's work.

June 24th
New London
Conn.

Dear Cousin Rebecca:

We made a little trip to Boston, from the 14th to the 19th; but were not able to go to Salem, as our time was over-filled as it was, and it proved impossible for George to be absent from home and work any longer. I look forward with eagerness to seeing you before very long. It is very interesting to hear that you taught with Aunt Louisa in the night school. I will call on Mrs. Wilder, before I close this letter, and find out what her maiden name was. Since my little article in The *Ladies' Home Journal* about papa, which they urged me to write, I have received a number of invitations to "read"; it seems to be the latest fad of people to get persons at all before the public by their writing, to come and be seen and heard! At first I objected, and disliked the idea very much; but friends and the need of money prevailed to make me do this strange thing. It is not as unpleasant as it would seem. I read anything of mine I choose, essays or poems, and next autumn have half a dozen places already half arranged for. Julian likes very much to have me enter upon this mild form of contact with the world; and of course George has been pleased with it, or I should not have concluded to do it.

The meeting friends in Boston and Cambridge at receptions is perfectly refreshing and delightful, it is so long since we have been able to go thither, either together or on separate trips. I am so grieved to hear that your means are dwindling, and I do so hope some investment will fortunately turn the tide! We expected quite a large sum *all at once,* but we find we can only have it in instalments, so that our money difficulties are not exactly straightened out, as we need in *some way* to get a good sum very soon, though those *instalments* will come in beautifully by and bye, all the same. We think we could make so much more if we could stop short articles and stories, to make solid books, either fiction or others; but we are a little set back of late as our lawyer was a trifle too sanguine as to the arrangements he could make for us.

When I see you, I can easily tell you how it seems the best thing for the Hawthornes to go to a place like Jamaica, all interests considered.

But in some respects it is a very hard thing, and certainly so for me. I hope sometime we can go and visit them there, if only for a week's stay. I cannot give up the idea of seeing you and Maria in my home, and if our affairs brighten soon enough, it must be this summer. I am not quite such a shell-bound oyster as I was once, and I should, I think, be able to make you talk to me; and it was always so good to see you; it brings back the past so beautifully to be with long known friends and relatives. Lovingly yours, with a goodbye for a little while only, I hope,—

Rose H. Lathrop

I have waited all this time to see *Miss* Wilder (I find she is). Her father was a Congregationalist Minister at the church in *Howard* St. Salem. Again with love. Yours,

Rose
July 24

To Julian and Mary Albertine Amelung [Berg]
    This letter is dated 1889 in the Berg collection, but since it refers to the conversion of George and Rose, and is a probable response to Julian's 1891 letter to Rose, it must have been written at least three years later. [The watermark on the stationery is 1889.] Rose suggests that Hildegarde had been chosen as a Confirmation name. Julian and "Minne" Hawthorne's daughter Hildegarde had been born just before Rose and George's marriage.

March 29th
New London

My darling brother and Sister:
    You know, you must know very well, how much gladness your letter brought me, and to George, too. I do not think anything could express my joy in your blessing of our new life in this way, but some jubilant anthem sung by fresh young voices, lovelier. When I wished to choose a patron saint for myself, whom I might particularly love and appeal to, it made me very happy to find that there once lived Saint Hildegarde, Abbess in a convent near Bingen in the 12th century, who is worthy of all remembrances. One of the things she is known to have written is this—so true of all the Catholic preachers we have heard: that "those who would do the work of God must remember that they are as trumpets, uttering the secret things of God, not as of themselves, but as

another breathes into them." It is delightful to me to think of this beloved name in connection with the devout and generous soul whom I have determined to love and honor. Dearest Minne, may heaven bless you more and more everyday for your precious kindness and warmth of heart. I wish I were with you on this promising spring day. With love from both to you all,

Your happy sister
Rose

To Mattie from Rose, 1892 [Berg]

These are the reflections of a new convert to a Catholic environment. The reference to George's venture is probably to his disappointment that Thomas A. Edison lost interest in collaborating with him in writing a futuristic novel.

October 9th, 1892
43 Federal St. New London, Conn.

Darling Sister Mattie:

Your letter was a great event to me, a great blessing, dear, for I hardly hoped you would find the strength to give to writing when you needed all the strength you could muster to bring you back to healthy life again. Your "will write soon" seemed too good to be true. And then *once again* (precious phrase) your hand writing came to me in a whole letter! I was so thankful, but at the time you wrote I was very much hurried in getting ready for the Catholic Summer School which came to New London in its first session. Mr. Lathrop was on several committees, and I had a world of hard work to do, besides trying to attend to his literary engagements not connected with the School. He had a lecture to write for it, also. We had to help him all we could, Miss White the stenographer and I, and then all of August was one wild scene of people from all points and four or five lectures a day and calls and receptions and so on. I call it a wild scene, for in some respects it was, being hurried and crowded; but I could not find words to tell you how deeply edifying it was to hear the lectures, to see the priests of holy and generous lives, and to note the sincerity and sweetness of most of these Catholics; many young women teachers, of all people the most earnest to me, except those devoted more completely and definitely to God, as the nuns, Sisters and Priests. We may say that we can serve Him as thoroughly and nobly in the midst of life's ordinary perplexities and sorrows and efforts as if we were clothed in flowing dark robes or devoted to lives of abstemiousness and loneliness among the sick in body and mind but to know these priests and nuns at all intimately is to know that their daily energy, their daily renunciation of natural impulses for comfort and ease and freedom from moral severity possess a power and virtue beyond our lay energy, our lay asceticism. I feel that I have passed close to spirits that purify and give strength as though their very robes too partook of their virtue; such a feeling as I have had in the presence of the elect of the society we all have known. [Mss obliterated here for two lines.] But how few comparatively of such there are in the world: yet among these religious of whom I speak the most (apparently) ordinary nature is lifted up to dignity, and healthy power over the spirits not so blessed, to such an extent of numbers that the preponderance is on the side of that power we feel so seldom in a different system. The absolute self-immolation and constant prayer—how seldom it is found where people are not trained to it by a beautiful law that cannot be set aside, and at last is a blessed yoke.

It is a long, long time since you wrote, dear heart, and I am hoping that your summer has been passed largely out of doors, and that you are now much stronger. Oh, do let me know about you, and forgive my silence, for it has been caused by the most hurried summer I ever passed, and the many cares crowded into the month since the Summer School took its departure. You know I have to spend some time always saving pennies by sewing and housework. I trust we can make some cheaper arrangement next year, so that we can have freedom from so much anxiety and petty labor. When we came into this house, which is rather expensive, we expected to have more money, but one of George's ventures turned out badly, and we have been hampered ever since. Don't imagine, dear, that he speculated in Wall Street! His ventures are all with the pen, and in this case another man did not keep his word. George is pretty well, and is doing some very noble writing. He has lately finished a poem on Columbus which I think wonderfully lofty and poetic, which he is to read at a great celebration in New York. I write a few stories and verses for money solely, having no time to make more heroic attempts in literature, and am getting old enough of course to begin to lose that fine agony for artistic effort which has made many an hour exquisite pain for me, and yet a sweet pain after all, as pain goes! Oh, what delight I feel in the great writers and painters and musicians, and why should they not be quite enough to satisfy my art—instinct! I fear selfish vanity is at the bottom of my desire to paint and write. Write to me dear, and Mattie, pray for me that I may be kind and useful to others.

Ever your loving sister,
Rose

To Henry Oscar Houghton from Rose H. Lathrop [n.d] [Houghton]

The following letter was written shortly before Rose and her husband separated definitively. The operatic version of *The Scarlet Letter* opened on the evening of March 6, 1896, at the Academy of Music in New York. Rose with a friend saw the performance from the balcony. A New York *Times* review (March 7, 1896,4,col 6) lists performers in a January production as Mme. Nordica, Signor Campanari, W.H. Rieger and Conrad Behrens. Walter Damrosch (1862–1950) directed both performances. The *Times* article says in part of the March 6 performance, "The new opera was received with warm encouragement if not with unbridled enthusiasm and the general verdict seemed to be that it was an uncommonly good piece of work for a young and inexperienced writer" [Damrosch]. The reviewer praised George Lathrop for structure and faulted him as a librettist. The problem of the opera was the matter itself. As theater, the story is over before it starts, and the mood can only be treated successfully in narrative prose.

Overdale
New London, Connecticut
December 17th

My dear Mr. Houghton:

The Brooklyn Institute asked Mr. Lathrop to give two lectures upon Thoreau, which have just been very successfully accomplished; and it seemed to me that these lectures might be given to advantage in Cambridge or Boston, especially in view of your new edition of this wonderfully artistic and noble writer. My husband's study of him is very sympathetic and thorough, and would, no doubt, bring forward points that might be overlooked by many readers. Would you care to suggest any way in which an audience might be secured for the lectures?

We are asking a number of our friends to be present at a Concert in New York, in which Mr. Walter Damrosch will render, with the assistance of Mrs. Emma Eames and Companari and others, and with a chorus of five hundred voices, the 1st Act and a Forest scene from his Opera of "The Scarlet Letter," for which Mr. Lathrop has written the words. We are naturally eager to have you hear it, and hope you will give us the satisfaction of doing so. It is expected that the Opera will be given entire in the spring, with Alvary as Dimmesdale. The concert occurs both on the *afternoon* of January 4th, and the evening of January 5th. We shall be present at both performances, with friends, and we will send you tickets for whichever date is more convenient to you, if you can grant our request. I should like to speak of the interest and beauty of this Opera, and my enjoyment of the frequent occasions when I have had Mr. Damrosch play and sing the music in private, and also when I have been present at rehearsals, but I must not encroach further on your time.

> With our very earnest regards,
> Yours most truly,
> Rose H. Lathrop

To Mattie, 1898 (Martha Stearns) [Berg]
    Rose's thoughts on the death of her husband correspond very much to her diary reflections. Minne is Julian's first wife Mary Albertine Amelung. Jack, Hildegarde, and Beatrix are three of their children. Frank is George's artist brother (see Introduction). Mary Mahoney was a mutual friend who was one of Rose's first volunteer helpers. Augusta St. Gaudens was the wife of the American sculptor, Augustus St. Gaudens.

> *May 29th*
> *668 Water St.*
> *New York*

Dearest darling Mattie:
    What can you have thought of me in this long silence? I have been shocked at the fact that I have not written to my friends, and especially to you, my sister, for a month, and in spite of receiving such loving letters. I have twice been really ill, scarcely able to be up, yet obliged to work, and twice confined to my bed for two days. I am not strong now, but cheerful, and am doing a good deal each day, tho I work much more slowly, so that a day from seven a.m. till eleven p.m. does not see so much accomplished by half as once it did, in my little hospital. I was crushed by George's death, not having ever dreamed that I could bear his death at all, if it came before he had accepted my work as a wise

measure, and helped in it, and raised our lives to a high, united service of God. My heart was filled with love and misery. He looked very beautifully as he lay dead, and very noble. How well I knew that I loved him, and that the shadows were not to live, but the beauty and joy of the past. But I could not bear to live, and work with George dead, and no goodbye. But I heard lovely things of what he had said and talked about me lately; and the morning after his death he seemed to come to me and say, in his most enchanting mood of boyish tenderness, that of course he loved me, and of course we never could have any real misunderstanding of each other. But I have had many struggles to bear the tragedy of the whole situation, and to cling only to God's blessings all along the rough way. The funeral was sublimely beautiful in the great Paulist Church, with the men's and boys voices chanting, and the organ giving forth Chopin's funeral march, and the coffin laden only with fragrant violets. Mrs. Lathrop and Frank were very lovely to me; and so were all. Minne Hawthorne, Jack, the eldest, Hildegarde and Beatrix came. They have been so good to me since; and my helpers have been heavenly kind. I have had several deaths and new patients here, since then, and so much to attend to that I hardly could do it; but I am gaining health every day now.

Your Auntie, and my Auntie's letter was most perfect and so needed. All she said was wise and kind and blessed. Give her my tenderest love and thanks, please, dearest Sister.

I have cut off my hair close now, and wear a hood and put on the full working costume on the 19th of May, and am very happy in having at last quite given up all thought of "the world," as they call the least interest in personal appearance, and personal effect. The costume I first planned was thought too religious in aspect by his Grace Archbishop Corrigan, and so I look now something like a Quakeress. My three helpers are eager for their garbs, I am happy to say. Some rich men are thinking of giving us a big house, in this region, and we are praying very hard that they will do so soon. I am so happy in Alice Huber, my Kentuckian assistant—she is like a sister to me, and as straight-forward and good and noble as you can guess. How you would love her! Thank you for your dear, dear love, my Mattie, and do not punish me for my silence, the result of a sort of paralysis of the faculties. Dear Mary Mahoney was here, and too lovely to let go! But I am unable to lay hold upon her at present, and must pray for her help by and bye.

With love to you all and such blessings on you my own darling!—I ought to write to Augusta St. Gaudens, who writes a second time from

Paris that she is *agonized* at my silence; [the last two lines of this letter have been effaced, probably by the recipient].

Your own
Rose Hildegarde

To Houghton, Mifflin and Co. 1898 [Houghton]
Mrs. Herman Melville prevailed in this dispute.

May 30th
668 Water St.
New York

Messrs Houghton, Mifflin and Co.,

Dear Sirs—
I enclose two letters from Mrs. Melville, which may lead you to have the words she objects to in her husband's letters in "Memories of Hawthorne," omitted. I have argued with her by letter as well as I knew how, but this does not seem to have made her any happier than she was before. If I can or should do anything about having the words erased, will you let me know? Perhaps the opinion of someone else would, if favorable to my idea of leaving a man of genius safely in care of his own expression have effect in inducing Mrs. Melville to let the printed record stand as it is.

Yours very truly,
Rose Hawthorne Lathrop

To Alice Huber, 1898 [RHH]
Here begins the twenty-eight year correspondence with Alice Huber, the first to commit her life with Rose Hawthorne Lathrop to the care of the cancerous poor. Rose, like her mother, whose epistolary style must have been her model, was effusive in her expressions of love, but the gift of Alice Huber's loyalty to her was never to be underestimated. That love was her strength in her darkest moments and it enabled her to sustain her own commitment to and love for the poor. Very rarely in church history do we see such an extraordinary demonstration of the love of two religious women for each other.

Jan. 31st
668 Water Street
New York

My darling:

It is so sweet to be writing to you, but it adds to the sweetness a thousand flavors to believe that I shall seldom need to write to you! There is a pair of silk mittens here, which I think may be yours, and they give me an excuse for writing, that you may remind me of them tomorrow you come, as your head is clear, and mine is a medley of remembered and forgotten obligations.

I pray for you, my dear, with all my heart. You are my first-born in this enterprise of burning love for our Lord, the warmth of which can be proved only in burning love of outward acts for His words, crushed and set aside by the courts of the world. You have brought me so much peace, for your first kiss was like the slow, still enwrapping of a thick snow-storm, or a flame quiet with holiness. How can I give you half the help you are giving me? Perhaps you really like gratitude, and in that way I could repay you.

Forgive the smudges on the other page—the black cat is to blame, who sits on my lap always, as I write, and rubs her ears into my most tender thoughts as if she had some right to share in my real life. I could not give any reason why she should not, for a good animal seems much more respectable than a bad Christian, whom neverthelesss, we ought certainly to treat well, if we love St. Francis of Sales.

Have *courage!* my darling Alice. Let each day be as if it were the probable extent only, as the saints say, of your contest with the arctic cold of isolation with Jesus. God bless you, soldier! Your own

Rose Hildegarde

P.S. I write carelessly, it would seem. The *arctic cold,* when the victory is won, is heavenly summer for eternity; and every hour the ecstasy of Our Lord's mercy can bring this summer for as long as we win by a stroke a moment's advantage over self.

To Alice Huber, 1898 [RHH]

As Alice Huber was arranging her affairs in order to join Rose Lathrop, she continued to receive encouraging letters. The following was written a month before she moved to Water Street

Feb. 26th
Water St.

Dearest Child & Sister

I have no time, and can find no more notepaper easily, and yet I must tell you that I love you and pray for you, and wonder that I am permitted to be the sister of such a very generous woman as you show yourself to be to me, and of course to our Lord. I marvel that you can look forward eagerly to coming to me to share my labors and misfortunes which are all dear to me now; but I know that God must bring you to me and so even our small work and poor home seems to you the best for you in all God's creation. It will be our aim to forget ourselves and our finite life of work in our Lord & the spiritual quality of our work, which we are taught is heavenly in so far as it is honestly done. So that you and I may find that our life is radiantly beautiful, in not being ours, but the life of Him we desire to be at whatever cost of our will, and ease. We must try to be brave in order to be made brave, for our ambition is to die daily for Christ, and it is so hard to have the wakeful energy to know how to die.

I am writing a sermon when I ought to be attending to my duties. Will you tell Sr. Mary of Jesus that I was ashamed to have *seemed* to think my choice of work better than a nun's life. I only meant I was cut out for a servant; and so must not ask to be an angel.

Your own Rose

I am very well today. I received.

To Alice Huber, 1898 [RHH]

Rose's insight into the theology of vocation is unusually mature. God uses human love to draw Alice to a work she might otherwise resist, and Rose prepares her for possible disappointment in that love. But the work is the work of God and Alice's own virtue will keep her faithful to it.

March 18th
668 Water Street

My darling Alice:

Your delicious letter made me extremely happy, for many reasons. You love me, oh, so much—and if our Lord loves me (something of miracle I am only now beginning to think of definitely, so wonderful is it to my poor mind) then indeed you may possibly love me, for some reason. Then, you do so love our dearest Lord, that I fear nothing for you in anything you may attempt. Then, you promise me that our little rule can and will be kept, however like an untrained colt or dolt your mother is. That you so love me and desire to be with me, is nothing in the world, but our dearest Lord's gentle way of inviting you to a severe work, though I ought not to let you into the secret. Perhaps a sad strain in your life will be finding that I am really trash—but I think your love for your work will make you indifferent to that or anything else, soon; and no pain will come to you but the real sorrow of not suffering enough for your Beloved. Then, I rejoice that the prospect before you brings you peace, and am as certain as I am of the sun's warmth, that this proves you are to help build up a charity dear to God. In naughty recreation instead of my waiting work, I am writing, with all my love,

Your Rose

To Alice Huber, 1898 [RHH]

Written two days before Alice moved to Water Street, the following letter reveals much of Rose's new found happiness. Alice arrived in time to support Rose in the sorrow she was to experience a few weeks later: the death of George Lathrop. The third woman referred to in this letter could be Mrs. Corcoran, a volunteer who died of tuberculosis the following year. Father Edmund Hill, C.P., was an English convert who was a close friend of the Huber family. At the time Alice joined Rose Lathrop, Father Hill was giving a retreat at St. Gabriel's parish in New York.

March 22nd
668 Water St.
New York

My darling Alice:

I am thinking of you constantly, and though I am deeply moved by your courage, I can have very little sorrow or pity for such a servant of Christ. I tremble in the hope that we may keep those tiny rules of which you speak so respectfully, with great fidelity, thus training ourselves—we three women here —to be useful servants, always at our posts, & alive to every call for aid both temporal & spiritual—so that you, my sweetest dear, may have more fit companions than would otherwise be the case. Never did a bluebird or butterfly watch the skies for spring & the bushes for leaves more eagerly than I look for Thursday's season of my true friend's opening life near me, for such an end as you have in coming. Never was a year so beautiful to me as this one.

May I forget myself forever in our Lord and you, and be an instrument of usefulness for dear souls, as simple and serviceable as rake or hoe, or jug of water for reviving roots! I thought of you so often on Friday, when I am sure you were satisfied in friendship by dear Father Edmund, who must have given you the greatest consolation & vigor of sympathy. Dearest daughter, do not fail to remember that you will not love me in any way so truly as by teaching me exactly my faults of behavior towards our Captain, Christ, & that every reproof you give me will be a profound blessing, for which I shall never be ungrateful. I shall not be able to tell you when you come how your steps over the doorsill are blessed, and sound musically to me; but as the earth seems soiled and dark, yet holds all sorts of miracle in color and delicate texture of flowers, so in this hum-drum and noisy hole I can realize that beauty is coming forth, not to be spoken of except in prayers to our Beloved and His saints.

My lovely child, come to join your mother—

Rose Hildegarde

To Sister Rose Huber and Cecelia Higley [RHH]
The following letter was composed in 1900 when the Sisters were advised by Father Clement Thuente to make retreats that year at the Dominican Motherhouse in Caldwell, New Jersey. The letter is interesting for its observations on local preaching as well as for a clear indication of how Sister Alphonsa was reflecting on the practicalities of religious life. Her sense of her own religious identity is very sure. The Mother Superior mentioned in the letter was Mother M. Mechtilde Ostendarp who was appointed superior of the Caldwell congregation in 1894. Mother Mechtilde eventually became the first Prioress of the Akron, Ohio foundation. She returned to Caldwell in 1929 when Akron became independent. She died in 1944.

Academy of
Mt. St. Dominic
Caldwell, N.J.

My dearest Sisters, and the Sister-to-be.—
While the nuns are skimming about the grounds among wide vegetable beds and under trees and into the handsome farm-buildings, I will write home some of the many things I am longing to tell you. I got ready a postal-card soon after arriving, which a Sister said she would give the man to post, but she forgot it, and so I will replace the few words with what I fear will be a small volume.

First of all, this place is most beautiful, and grand in proportions of buildings and estate, and the air is deliciously refreshing. The nuns and many children all look in beaming health and good spirits. But so far as I can see, the Sisters have as hard a tussle to accomplish their crowds of duties, as you do in our busy Home;—many steps hurried past my door long after I was in bed, the Sisters carrying baskets of clothes etc., and the children are full of activity and are noisy, all of this being wisely permitted for their benefit, so that my heart ached at the revelations that even these dear Sisters know in their superb convent the confusing sounds and constant appeals that make us dizzy, and that these tasks and turmoils hurry the poor angels along from one week's end to another. Sunday, too, is a very busy day, as those precious relatives haunt this work as they do ours,—the only difference is that here the scrimmage is rather pretty and goodnatured, while with us it is cruel and gruesome. Now, we should be glad that we are taking up a thing avoided by all but our Lord, instead of sorry that we have not children to mind. It was heavenly to hear the Sisters singing at Vespers, so stately and noble a strain, in honor of our Beloved. Do you think I am part of that adoring band? Oh, no; they scarcely know that I am anything of a Dominican, even; and although they are exquisitely kind, and more like sisters by blood than any but Sisters of the Spirit can be; still it will take a course at some new University to explain to them how one can be dressed in this funny garb and yet be a daughter of St. Dominic; and how one can be blessed by God in a work and not be blessed first by the Holy Father. If this were otherwise, we should never learn what our Lord's friendship really is, how His consolation is sufficient to make the heart glad, and how He makes life abound with interests that are so much more absorbing than any other companionship could be, for a visit to Him is more resplendent with intercourse than any other visit in or out of the Community.

It is nice to find that the Altar has a covering edged with the same style of crocheted edging that we used on our first altar-table. Another item to assure you of, is that the coffee may be made of carrots, such as I wished to try, but is so weak that I cannot guess its ingredients. The flaked rice is flavored with a dash of vanilla and a little sugar, and is delicious. But I must encourage you by relating that we live like princesses at table as compared to these Sisters, which shows that your health is somewhat safeguarded, after all. As for me, there is all of everything I want, for I begged for bread and milk as the staple of my food. I do not know what comfits they may offer you, but be assured that economy is studied here. The potatoes were nice and mealy, and flavored with a remembrance of ham, in some way, and were greedily consumed by the prize eater. The lettuce had no oil with the vinegar, and was very nice; but the oil is so nutritious that we poor nurses ought to retain it. Acres of land are beautifully cultivated with vegetables, and so they are fresh and fine for the table.

I was up early this morning, looking out upon the enchanting row of trees along the hillsides, the birds singing and cool breezes humming. I long to have you drinking in the nectar of this air. I received with the Sisters before Mass, of course, and it was sweet to be accorded this privilege. Many thoughts come to my mind, as to what we need most for our constitutions and for our environment, and I pray that I may have light as to what is best for us. I have seriously considered the wisdom of simplifying our complex days by having the Relief Room work (eventually) relegated to a house by itself, supplied by the half year at a time from the hospital house, as this would distribute the turmoil more bearably, and give more room for a Chapel or a least a community-room. At the same time, I am, so far, more convinced than ever that the weight given to the *enjoyment* of religious observance in a charitable undertaking is not so much to the credit of these Sisters as our cramped conditions would be to us, if we were as good as these Sisters are. I am sure our idea is the best, that we shall have the patients out of sight if we please ourselves more than we do, and share less with them than we do. They are now given the best of all we have—rooms, chapel, food, time. God grant that we may make this generous principle our own by doing all that the sacrifice can cover with real love and grace.

There were three Masses today, one celebrated by the brother of the Mother Prioress, one by the oldest little priest I ever expect to see, a thousand times older and more tremulous than old Mr. McCarthy and one in the village chapel, to which some of the Sisters went, celebrated by the parish priest, who gave a very long sermon, covering penny offerings and all that vast complaint priests with waggish and stinging tongues so often enter into; and also giving a withering attack upon objects of devotion that are "sold in every Jewish shop, to get money under the pretence that Catholics can save their souls without self-denial, if they only buy these gewgaws!" Imagine this dear old priest in our sitting-room! He was a witty Irishman, with a brogue that grew with his rage, and he said some terrible things of America and medals. And as for the pennies, he said they were so dirty that it would take a pair of tongs to pick them up. First he gave a slap, and then he stroked his congregation, and told them that if they were to be found among fools they could remember that their priest had warned them where the fools were. I could have listened to him for a week, but still I *expected* a spiritual uplifting, as Rev. Mother had said that this Father Byrne was one of the most eloquent preachers of the diocese. Rev. Mother is very intelligent indeed, young and energetic and sweet. The Sisters all show (so far as I have spoken with four or five) great refinement of feeling and courtesy from their entire oblation to God; so that they evidently remember Him in each act. Shall we not be as gentle and active and careful to be finished in all we do? One thing, however, surprises me, and that is that in the entries and about their work I have not noticed any effort to be low of voice in speaking, or deliberate of movement, so that we are not so odd as I feared in this respect. It is better to be very quiet, however, as these Sisters lose in dignity in contrast to others I have known, when not in the Chapel or receiving company, in which case they are perfect. Pardon this long letter, as I may not be able to write for a week. Let me hear from you, I beg, as soon as you can send me a letter. My prayers for you constantly ascend to God, my dear ones, and for our sick. Please pray for Miss Mary Burke's sister who is not a good Catholic, and for her epileptic sister.

I could write much more if I were to say all I have wished to, but have not the audacity to go on. All I insist on till I return is that you get rosy and fat—I can have no other surprise from you, my brave friends. Love to Mrs. Leonard and Mrs. Owens, who were dozing when I left.

Your little Mother.

To Sister Rose [RHH] 1901

Father James Augustine Daly became the confessor and director of the Sisters after Father Thuente was transferred in 1900 to Holy Rosary Parish in Minneapolis, Minnesota. Miss McCauley received the habit of the congregation in 1902, assuming the name Sister Mary Hyacintha.

+J
July 7th
Rosary Hill Home
Neperan P.O.

My darling, darling, darling Sr. M. Rose,

Your little Mother has a moment in which to tell you that she loves you and thanks you. Your letters, and the correspondence sent, have been such a comfort each time—and you know a little coward like me needs comfort from you at every turn. We are really getting on very well, seeing that we are a pack of fools, with little memory or virtuous determination. Our black sheep changes shade a trifle every few hours—now dark as thunderclouds, and then pearly gray for a moment. I am awaiting Father Daly's answer as to what I have to do about the thunderous sheep. I do not think $25.00 would by any means supply clothing and larger meals for this poor dear, and fear I must buy the clothes and the wig! I hope our blessed Mother will teach me what to do, that I may please our Lord in the matter. Miss McCauley wished you to learn that the cat—we do not know how to distinguish it from the one which did not—caught a big rat on the very morning you advised a death sentence for cats. I must say, they are hideously dirty; but then many people about here are hideously unreliable and deceptive, and take our money too fast. Are the cats as bad as these latter creatures? Perhaps we had better leave all delinquents alone, lest we have a scene of carnage in destroying so many creatures as would deserve death at our hands. The broom stick would not be hard enough to discourage them.

You must not grieve at the hardships we meet, unexpectedly as well as expected. "Death to the world" means more of death than you quite realized; it means that nothing will be our joy but God; that if one loves us, we must be separated from that one, and if one dislikes or maltreats us, that one shall be our companion. It means hunger and weariness and martyrdom if it means deep love for Christ. It means that wherever our heart is deep and tender the sword of penance is to enter; that we may in so far resemble Christ as to suffer with Him and for Him. I should weep more for you darling if I did not know that the more bitterly you suffer now, with a devoted heart for God; the more you will congratulate your soul in eternity. But it is hard to have you suffer so much fatigue and anguish. Christ be with you!

I will write to-morrow, hoping for you on Tuesday.

I think I shall have to go to town on Thursday, about the legacy and I shall need to have you stay here while I am gone.

Cannot you plan to do so?

> Your own loving Mother and
> hanger-on which means servant—
> M.M. Alphonsa, O.P.

The doctor came, and was lovely and delighted with it all. He will come *once a fortnight.*

John Burke is here, very helpful. The Spanish Father is learning English with great energy—a very nice Father.

My love to my dear children.

To the Sisters at St. Rose's Home, [1901] [RHH]

This letter was probably written a few months after the move to Rosary Hill in what was then called Neperan, now Hawthorne, New York.

+J

August 11th
Rosary Hill Home
Neperan

My dear Daughters:

We have come within the most sacred light of the Feast of the Assumption, wherein we all see our shortcomings more distinctly than ever, and rejoice proportionately in the beauty of our Blessed Mother, who does not neglect us, though we are such poor, shabby beggars at her feet. She leads us to see in each other all the little virtues which make us dear to her, if we are sincere in our love of our Lord and of herself. No matter how ragged and unlovely a rosebush may be, it still has some bud upon it that has a lovely tint or a breath of fragrance, for which we like it, because the rose is so beautiful that a single petal is charming. So, if we strive to love heavenly spirits, we become part of the family of the Saints, and a tiny fragrance at least tells to whom we belong. We must not be sad over our faults, or those of our companions, but take up our time completely in thanksgiving of all sorts that we are in a state of grace, and will strive daily to become more diligent in obtaining victories. I have been so silent that you could not know how much I have thanked you for your prayers, and felt their aid, and how happy I have been to think that I have been at all connected with the calling together of such loving servants of God, who have borne the heat and distress of a city summer with the best cheer any good soldiers could show. May God bless you with numberless years of happiness for every moment of your pain and faintness in the past months, and for your patient fidelity to your resolutions and vows. We here pray for you every day, with true fervor, and on the blessed Feast of the Assumption we shall not forget you.

I was reflecting yesterday that every great event in the history of the Redemption was surrounded by suffering as a bird by its nest. Our Mother could not receive the blessed happiness of possessing our Lord in His Infancy, until she had been driven to the utmost anxiety and humiliation, in being repulsed in Bethlehem, and forced to house herself in a manger. Our Lord could only win the hearts of all sincere people who saw him by suffering infinite toils of fasting and prayer and hard journeys, having no home to rest in, and only bleeding feet to carry from one crowd of sick poor to another. The sublime wonders of the Resurrection could only come after such disaster and misery and scornful indecency of treatment, as the world never knew before or since. So much value in suffering and crushing contempt must encourage us to hope for the very best God can give, in the midst of our very worst moments of fatigue and seeming fruitlessness of effort. When the yoke God gives us presses most keenly and heavily, we may know that we are working most effectively to drag this burden that God has set for us to bring to Him, at the end of our life. All work done for Him is paid in His love-nothing less, and it could not be more. We feel that you need nothing from us but congratulations for your past firmness, and prayers that the future may be still more faithful, and even heroic. Pray for us, that we may crucify ourselves.

Your loving servant of our Lady,
M.M. Alphonsa, O.S.D.

To Sister Rose Huber [1901] [RHH]

This letter suggests that there may have been a disagreement between Mother Alphonsa and Sister Rose, but it could not have been too serious. In any case, Sister Rose Huber sometimes needed encouragement as her memoirs suggest that she often took a darker view of events than did M. Alphonsa.

+J

August 29th
Rosary Hill Home
Neperan P.O. N.Y.

My darling Sister—

This letter contains a love for you that is growing more true than when you felt I loved you first, and which partakes more than ever of the light and security of God's love. But you see day by day how imperfect all that I do and feel still is, and you will have much occasion to instil generosity into your true and beautiful love for me. If I seem harsh, and am harsh, at times, it is the imperfect effort of a poor wretch to bring to your soul and mine a greater share of God's truth, which will bless us, no matter how roughly we strive for it; for certainly our God must be willing to let us arrive at the truth according to our poor will and understanding, since He gives us "free will," and knows that when we act of our own impulse we must be somewhat faulty, and if not full of charity, the fault is proportionately great.

May St. Rose of Lima, our great and beloved American, help you and me to a complete union of intention and action, that our work may flourish, but still more, that our souls may come to Paradise one of these days, hand in hand, and simple and gentle as two little doves that move shoulder to shoulder over the sward.

My darling, we all love you as few women are loved, and long to see you, and miss you very much. May the gem of the year that is enclosed by two Feasts of St. Rose, be to you brilliant with supernatural flame and angelic purity from venial sin.

May God bless you, in the Trinity, in the Sacred Heart, and in our Mother's care.

Your own, M.M. Alphonsa.

Love to my dear children, sick and well.

To Sister Rose Huber [1901] [RHH]

Mother Alphonsa usually managed to pay her bills, but she did not always know how she would do so. "His Grace" is Archbishop Corrigan.

+J

September 12th
Rosary Hill Home
Neperan, P.O. NY

My darling warrior and sweet child—

Your lovely letter came in good time today, for although all goes well in most ways, and I feel nicely, our poverty is really enough to shake the nerves, since we have nothing in the bank, it seems. You will have poverty for daily sustenance for several weeks, unless our dear Lord wishes us to receive an immediate gift to help us out of our plight.

When you go to the bank today, you will learn that I overdrew $42.00, and the check was protested. Horrible, but true. I had a check for 75.00 to make the disaster good, but I wanted that for Cox and Taylor, not to mention our plumber, etc. I really cannot understand how the bank ran dry so soon, and hope there was a mistake, as once before. I am going to send several appeals out at once. It is true that these are very dry and almost useless when we have a fat little sum in the bank, to which I of course always plead guilty; but it is a striking—bottom—shock that feels dreadfully, when we cry out that we are sinking—for we always really mean it. God help us, is all I can say—nor do I even expect to say anything else, until I am a downright coward, and cease to venture growth. Your love, solicitude, tender good advice are a mercy from God at this juncture of many worries, and so I will not worry a bit, but live peacefully at our Lord's feet. I could get Mis Cox's 70.00 and a hundred or so from Mrs. Woodhouse, but I would rather battle it out, for both measures would be against the principles I have laid down for the work—to ask money of our women helpers, or of individuals. Yet I will if it seems best later. There is no startling news from here. His Grace has not written and so I suppose he will ignore Your loving

> M.M. Alphonsa, blessed
> be your generous love

To Cousin Rebecca, 1922 [Essex]

Hildegarde Hawthorne, one of Julian's daughters, remained close to Mother Alphonsa all her life. Mother Alphonsa used to publish her poetry occasionally in *Christ's Poor,* as a way of encouraging her initial writing efforts. Among her other publications, Hildegarde once wrote an article about "Aunt Rose" for the *The Catholic Digest.* Mother Alphonsa's letter to her cousin Rebecca (Richard's sister) suggests an effort to bridge a relationship that must have faltered over the years. It provides a brief commentary on her own life, and her awareness that illness was beginning to threaten it more and more.

> *Rosary Hill Home*
> *Hawthorne, Westchester County, N.Y.*
> *The Servants of Relief for Incurable Cancer*

+

J.M.D.   *September 4th 1922*

My dear Cousin Rebecca:

Our Hildegarde was here the other day, and we spoke of you, and she said she had lately received a letter from you, in which you remem-berd me. I was so happy to hear it, for I have often thought of you, and can see you, after all these years, as if I had but just parted from you, recalling the times when you came to visit Una, with your beautifully quiet manner, and ever kind spirit lighting up your face. Here I am, at 71 years of age, quite an invalid after years of hard work in this under-taking for the sick, and several severe acute illnesses beginning seven years ago, (Erysipelas caught from a patient, Grippe, pneumonia, "Flu") nearly at the end of my life; and being unable to spend crowded hours from 4:30 a.m. to (sometimes) 2 a.m., have time to reflect as I could hardly do for twenty years; and I wonder very often how I could have been so foolish as to let slip from me the chances I had to know you all very well in *many* meetings, which I am sure you would have granted me. In my earlier life I was a thing of reticence and silence, and after my marriage, laden with many sorrows, so that I had small energy. Now I can ponder on what I missed in not seeing more of you and yours, and appearing to be so without appreciation and feeling. Hildegarde, now married to the dearest John that ever lived, has kept me informed about you through a long space of time—Lest I die before a loving word goes to you from me, I write to you today, and beg for a letter from you.

Lovingly yours,
Mother M. Alphonsa Lathrop, O.S.D.

(Rose Hawthorne Lathrop)

To Sister Rose Huber [RHH]

In 1926 The New York Rotary Club selected Mother Alphonsa Lathrop to receive a medal for "outstanding service to humanity." She initially requested that the medal be given to the congregation "which," she explained, "had been doing the Work for so long."[1] When the Club pointed out that it could only be given to an individual, Mother Alphonsa consented to accept it. The little ceremony occurred April 18, 1926, just three months before Mother Alphonsa died. She was clearly touched by the event. Father John J. McEvoy was the chaplain of the home at the time. Clifford Smyth was the husband of Beatrix Hawthorne. The only extant photograph of Mother Alphonsa in the religious habit was taken on this occasion.

J.M.J.D.   *April 18th 1926*

My beloved Sister Mary Rose—

I am not yet sure whether I am standing on my head or my heels! Such an afternoon. First a Reporter and 2 photographers! Publicity was to be paramount, and the Reporter was a Hearst man, and one of the brightest, most like a trained *American* gentleman of the three. So now everyone will know about the Servants of Relief. Clifford was present when these came in. We all talked for 15 minutes, and then an auto or two came up, and finally another with the President of the Rotarians, 20 in all, and then the fun began. Fr. McEvoy behaved like a prince. We all went to the Com. room, which had been duly arranged, Sister at the end near the altar, and I in the middle of the room, the President

---

[1] See Sister M. Joseph, O.P. *Out of Many Hearts,* 204. The medal read, "To Mother Alphonsa Lathrop, O.S.D., in recognition of her mercy and valor and the free gift of a life of service to hopeless and destitute sufferers."

opposite me, and Fr. and Clifford near, and then the address began. Well I never heard or read more genuine eloquence, and all on the highest plane. I cannot report any of it here, but may be able to give you an idea when we meet. Besides, it was all taken down. When the President was ready to pin on the medal, I stood up, and received it, and said a few words, but soon came near sobbing, such great things had been said,—and I said—"Clifford, speak for me!" But he motioned to Fr. McE. who jumped up and made a fine short downright little speech, ending with thanks and recommending all to Almighty God. It was all distinguished and noble talk, manners and spirit from beginning to end among them all. Only two Catholics were there, and one was born near the little red house in Lenox where I was born. So many nice things happened. The medal is fine, and a new design made by the President. More next time!—

Sister says you have had a little cold, and I felt sure you had no such weather. She says it is over, but you know I cannot trust your statements. All the Sisters seemed aglow, and they may be sure that this marks a great access of success to us, being widespread recognition. Clifford was charming. Your own loving

M. Alphonsa, O.S.D.

I had probate paper of a legacy from Alice M. Lee; no particulars.

To Sister Rose [RHH]

The following was among eight letters written the night before Mother Alphonsa died in her sleep of the heart ailment that had troubled her for years. It is included here not only because it *is* her last letter, but because it is so indicative of Mother Alphonsa's attention to every gritty detail of the work to which she had committed herself thirty years earlier. To the very last day, she was thinking not only about patient care and religious life but about money, sewers, utilities, repairs, workmen—the daily claims on the life of anyone in administration. Her love for Sister Rose never diminished and her opinions remained vigorous. Quite appropriately she concludes this letter with a happy reference to the harvest.

Brother Julian, member of the neighboring religious congregation of Christian Brothers.

Augustus St. Gaudens, American sculptor. Rose had met him in New York at the home of Richard Watson Gilders in the early days of her marriage.

J.M.+ D.   *July 8th 1926 Evening*
Beloved Sister M. Rose—

I want to write again today, as you might not get a letter till Monday night if mailed tomorrow p.m. I took a nice dose of Mr. Rich's inocuous tonic before dinner, and I am sure it did me good. I had 2 hours' sleep from 2 to 4 this p.m. and yet am awfully sleepy—I had a very broken sleep all night, but was at Mass. Then I took a walk with Sister, to see the building-work, and also speak to Mr. Hang about some things. Meantime, let me tell you I got a check for 500.00 from the executors of Catharine Wynn's legacy. It has been in our list of coming legacies for long. I can send you some of it if you prove to be short, but my coal will be 1,600.00 when all in, so I am careful. The notice has come, but not the bill so I do not know just how much yet. I was so glad to have the check back from Brother Julian, to send you, and hurried it off, lest you needed it as soon as possible. I have written some important letters to day in my personal appeal effort. Mr. Hang was mending chimneys, and found the one over the Chapel front door so ready to fall, that no one liked to touch it, but finally two carpenters went up and put boards round it, and then built a scaffold. Mr. Hang is going to attend to our well and power plant after Tom goes, until the new man thoroughly understands it. He expects Mr. Walsh to employ him in setting the hollow tiles. Sr. M. Siena telephoned to the nice Agency that sent the nurse, and the man is going to select a thoroughly good man, at 75.00 a month. He will come up and be here before Tom goes. So there will be time for a change if either side wants it. The place seems half alive without you, and I miss your loving ways very much, and am looking forward to your next visit, very soon. I have to get old Mrs. Cox up tomorrow, to witness my signature to the Will receipt. I shall probably take a little dose of the sleeping potion (but very little). My old friend, Mrs. Augustus St. Gaudens has died; but as she became madly jealous of me because her husband gave me that great photograph of *Caritas,* autographed, she ended up not very faithful to me, and I cannot care for her very much. *His* mother was a devout Catholic, but Augusta would have put a match to a Saint! She had great abilities, all the same. But *he.* The "hole" did look very huge and charming today. A lot of wooden tracery was on the Area Side—I do not know what for; and a man was hacking a trench for the sewer. May God and His Blessed Mother bless us all! The hay is in splendidly, and load after load of it. Your own loving

Mother M. Alphonsa. O.S.D.

DIARY

The 1896–98 diary begins auspiciously in formal prose, but Rose clearly did not have time for long narrative discourse after her work began. Alice Huber eventually took over the task of maintaining the records. Persons mentioned here who are not identified in the Introduction include Father William O'Brien Pardow, Provincial of the Society of Jesus, whom Rose had known in her New London days, and who was pastor of St. Ignatius Church in New York at the time she was beginning her work. He became her spiritual director after Father Charles Parks. She mentions also Father Edmund Hill, C.P., a convert from Anglicanism who had been a close friend of the Huber family and spiritual director to Alice. "Mamie" is Mamie Corton, a fourteen-year-old girl suffering from meningitis, who aroused Rose's concern. She needed work to help support her family, and Rose hired her temporarily, offering her and her family food and other necessities. Mrs. Corcoran's name is sometimes spelled "Corchran." Rose uses the ampersand, which is transcribed here and in all of the letters as "and."

On the cover of the document are the words:
   Items in my experience of association with the poor, as a
   Servant of Relief

                                        Rose Hildegarde
                                        September, 1896

September 29th. 1 Scammel St., New York:
   I took a street-car anxiously one day, a Sunday, in order to hunt for the region in the city which should strike me as best fitted for my attempt at nursing among the poor. I prayed to Our Lord to give me intelligence to know when I had come to the place He willed me to

settle in, if He so willed. The East Side proved much the most crowded and desperate.

As soon as I could take another afternoon from my Hospital work, I wandered about the East Side, looking for the very street and the sort of house where I should conclude to make inquiries. It was a lonely and frightened season in my determination; but I always thrust the care upon Our Lord, assuring Him that I knew my incapacity. I was alarmed by the faces I saw, both of men and women, and feared that I should be robbed and even murdered, if I lived alone among such characters. As I found my announcement of desiring to bring cancer patients into the apartments about which I negotiated, made everyone draw back in dismay, I concluded to appeal to a real-estate agent.

The real-estate agent was deeply interested at once, as he had lost his father by cancer six weeks before. He elaborately described his father's illness, and his own nursing of him, and assured me that he would do all in his power to find me a small house, or an apartment.

As he sent me no further word, in a day or two I called upon him again, and got the address of a house in Scammel St., corner of Henry St. Every window pane was broken, the house seemed abandoned, and a defunct liquor-store formed the base of the broken-down abode; but it was just what I should have liked to take, if I had had the money to repair it a little, and if the whole block had not just been bought by the city for a school building. Feeling very brave, and crossing myself, I opened the door in the wooden fence of the yard, and, after greeting a cat with a green and a blue eye, set out to look through the house; making up my mind to it by realizing that if I turned away in dread, my cowardice would upset all my future efforts, where similar alarms would most likely be numerous.

Instead of concealed thieves and cut-throats, I found a goodnatured Irish family stowed silently away upstairs. A fierce dog in the basement would, however, have closed my earthly career, they said, if I had stumbled upon him first. The family revealed the short lease of existence of the building, and so I had to put aside all desire for it. I began to be heavy of heart at the difficulties in hiring a place in which to begin my work; and I allowed myself to wonder whether God intended at last to show me that my work was not in this field.

But I had learned not to dread the most unpromising appearances in a house or the aspect of tenants, and penetrated the worst corners with a feeling of security; always finding people polite and helpful. My manner was all trust and good cheer—the only preparation needed for success among the poor.

It became so discouraging to look for rooms that I decided to appeal to the priest of the Church nearest to the quarter I had selected for my search; and I found a young priest at St. Mary's one morning. He set out to annihilate me, by manner and speech, probably thinking me a perfect fool. He said, there was very little cancer hereabouts; that the Catholics were all moving uptown, and the Jews moving into this neighborhood; and he gazed his contempt over my shoulder.

I answered that cancer was very prevalent, though not often known even by those afflicted with it; that it made no difference whether my patients were Catholics or Jews; and that I hoped, if I came into the parish, he would give me advice.

He seemed interested and aroused, and suggested my trying to hire a loft for my purpose. I had already thought of this plan, as giving me plenty of room for half a dozen beds, with free circulation of air, and I was delighted at his ratifying my idea by suggesting it himself. I spent several hours along the waterfront, looking for a building where lofts were to let, and where a row of liquor saloons would not obtrude themselves alongside of every possible foundry or lumber-yard.

A loft free from rum was finally to be discovered, and very kind persons listened to my scheme with respect; and I went back to my little lodging room excited and glad with the belief that my first step had been irrevocably taken.

It was now necessary for me to drop preparations, and go to Boston for a week to visit a dear friend who was extremely ill, and with a feeling of faintness, as if tearing myself up by the roots, I went away from my scene of action.

During the days of interim I realized that a loft was utterly out of the question, and that I must take a few rooms, and go out to my patients, excepting such as were well enough to visit me daily for treatment. This conclusion had been forcing itself upon me for sometime, although it sickened me with regret not to plan for bed-patients, under my constant care, in a place of my own. As the Nurses' Settlement in Henry St. I had been encouraged to think a *visiting* scheme an excellent preparation for my work.

Upon my return to New York, I went to Mass at St. Mary's on Grand Street, and set out afterwards to look for rooms, begging Our Lord to lead me directly to those I needed. I had been told that there was a nice apartment in Scammel St. and I reluctantly concluded to hunt that up first; yet was convinced it would be too expensive, and moreover not the kind of quarters I wished to occupy, as I wanted to be *of* the poor as well as among them. A prominent little sign of "Floor to Let" at No. 1 Scammel St., caught my eyes; and penetrating darkness and dirt and shattered stairs, I looked at the empty rooms, all unlocked and forlorn, two little cells being almost entirely shut off from air and light by a house-wall close to the windows,—and I immediately decided to take this apartment. In every respect it answered to my idea: it was as inconvenient, as devoid of necessary arrangements as any poor person could have endured; and, on the other hand, there was an absence of liquor saloons.

Ever since selecting these dreary little rooms their advantages have been revealing themselves, with the crowning charm of delicious uncertainty; for the city may pull the house down at any moment—the agent alone being sanguine on that point—it forming part of the block which cowers under the hammer and pick-axe of the city.

A housekeeper of brightest countenance and pleasantest manners narrowly scrutinized me as I made enquiries, but was very hospitable nevertheless, and made me feel that the rooms were already mine, and the neighborhood by no means as *dangerous* as I had fancied. I begin to doubt whether there is any neighborhood in the city that would be dangerous, if properly encountered—that is, with cheerful sincerity and thoughts of God. Near the house trip along unceasing cars all day and night, and a pleasant little square gives breathing space; and between the houses, across the way, the moon makes glorious scenes of cloud and light, while the salt breezes drift over pretty freshly from the harbor. The black holes which I had looked upon as hideous bedrooms are gladdened in the mornings by a miraculous sunbeam, shooting in at a little square window high up in one chamber-wall, and rays that insist upon coursing across the little sitting-room through the doorway of the second sleeping-apartment.

The frightful dirt everywhere was scrubbed and painted into flight, and light colors have sent thrills of ecstasy through every bosom that has felt relief from the sorrowful tints existing before in this tenement. Smells have vanished also, and the very crannies which were most repulsive have, by special attention, become almost fascinating.

The Jewess on the ground-floor, who was called "that thing" by the other tenants, shines with happy smiles now, and everybody is growing to like her, because I liked her, and said respectfully that she had a soul, and Our Lord loved her, and she was very kind indeed to me.

The lady over me who was said to be unbearable, because she fought so unmercifully with her husband, has been so good to me that I have wept a little over her thoughtfulness, her tea, and her gentle accents.

I have set out to love everyone, and to try to make them love each other; and I do very little, and am as stupid as I can be about it; but even this imperfect effort is so beneficent in being according to God's plan, and in so far as it goes, free from selfishness and sloth, that each person coming into contact with it is refreshed—while I myself tremble to see the power, even in me, of a little of the right spirit. It is as if God brushed me aside each moment, saying, "I am here!"

My first thought in putting myself upon the same plane with these people was, that I was making a concession—one needed, but, still, somewhat abnormal and self-abasing. My second thought was, that there are no planes in persons, but only in circumstances, and that the circumstances which career above the poor, the ignorant, the darkly corrupt, are a disgrace. When we rise, let us do so gently, with backward looks now and then to the countless poor, whom we must return to, and uplift when our development is sufficient for the mission. God surely loves them better than He loves us, unless we love them.

It was like a draught of wine to my spirit to find that, in this deplorable region, the College Settlement had planted its flag, and the Settlement of Nurses, and Miss McDowell's Kindergarten, and Mrs. Van Renssalaer's beautiful parlor for a girls' club; so that I was stepping among a stalwart company in coming hither.

I went to the Board of Health to ask if I should be permitted to nurse patients without the constant supervision of a doctor, and learned that there was no hindrance. The functionary whom I saw was arrested by the word "cancer," and told me that his wife had died of the disease. It is impressive to find how often people have this seldom-mentioned disease at the very core of their history; and a silence occurs before they reveal particulars to me which I have come to understand is the prelude to revelations. The interest these people take in my undertaking satisfies even me. First comes the tremulous question: "Have you found that cancer can ever be *cured*?" Then they cannot talk enough of the great sorrow, or dread of a recurrence in the case of a child who seems to be cured, and so on.

The interest, the incentives which invigorates every day of a nurse who works with love, is to perceive the hungry longing of patients, and those who love them, for sympathy and relief. The flattery of being needed so much is sweet as any there is; (I think sweeter, because so absolutely genuine); and the interest of doing work so largely left undone is one easily understood by an earnest housekeeper of business-man, who are accustomed to begin where the most congested spot is discovered to exist. The repulsion once overcome, one wonders that there was any hesitation in deciding to eradicate so dreadful a state of affairs. So in deciding to listen to the moaning appeal of a sufferer, or to attend to the loathsome state she is in, we suddenly find ourselves afire with enthusiasm, because without us *this* sufferer would have been without love—without *relief*: horrible thought! Let those who desire to keep the fire of charity from their hearts, never come near the agony of the poor.

September 17th, 1897. 668 Water St.

No chance for making these notes has been found between these dates [Sept. 1896–Sept. 1897–Ed.] nursing from five to 11 at night, or doing all it involved to set out as a nurse, soon prevented my sitting up till 2 a.m. to write a description of the East Side.

Rose H. Lathrop.

"I am the Lord Thy God and thou shalt have no other God but Me. Read the Scriptures."
Year from beginning my effort.

Wednesday, Sept. 15th

Offered Mass for *wisdom,* at St. Rose of Lima's, as I went there first after coming to the East Side. At noon, *Angelus* and *Litany of St. Joseph,* and *Chapters IV and V of I Corinthians.*

Thursday, 16th

Offered Mass for *means* to meet daily expenses of charity. Prayed especially to the Sacred Heart. Received $100. Too busy, and ill with a cold, for much prayers. *Angelus.*

Friday, 17th

Ill with severe chest cold. Read St. Teresa's *Interior Castle, II and III Mansions.* Mrs. Corchran went to St. Rose's for *Benediction* and prayed for us.

Saturday, 18th

Too sick to go to Mass. *Angelus,* and prayers. *Angelus,* and *Litany of Loretto.* Began *Novena* to Our Lady of Good Counsel for wisdom. Sisters of Charity from St. Mary's called.

September 19th, Sunday

Unable to go to Mass because of a cold. *Angelus* rung for the first time at 12 noon by Mamie. St. Paul to the Philippians, I, II, and III Chapters. *Novena* to O.L. of G.C. *Litany* of Seven Dolours of the B. Virgin. *Novena* to O.L.G.C.

Monday, 20th Sept.

Angelus. Litany of the *Holy Angel Guardian. Wisdom,* III Chapter.

Tuesday, 21st

Mamie was away, and I forgot to ring the *Angelus,* being ill and very busy. Alas, what a scatterbrain I am! But morning, and night we said it, as always. Read "Never Forgotten," describing Good Shepherd Order. Novena to O.L.G.C.

Wednesday, 22nd

Honored St. Joseph. *Angelus.* Read in "The Following of Christ." Forgot Novena to O.L. of Good Counsel, being excessively busy and very ill. Alas, again!

Thursday, 23rd

Angelus. Read in "A Year with the Saints." Began Novena once more, to O.L. of Good Counsel. Rosary with Mrs. Donovan. Mother Superior and Sister of the Assumption called, and expressed great approbation of our little beginning. Litanies of Sacred Hearts of Jesus and Mary.

Friday, 24th

Angelus. Novena to O.L.G.C.

Saturday, 25th

Angelus. Rosary with Mrs. Watson. Litany of Loretto with Mrs. Donovan. Prayers to St. Anthony. Father Doyle told me of the difference between material and formal sin, saying young priests often made the mistake of judging the former harshly, whereas it was *conscious* and *intentional* sin that was to be condemned to the full. Also, let people be accused out of their own mouths, according to their professed intentions. If they try to be devout, it is much, even if they do not act upon their tenets, from stupidity, ignorance, or weakness, rather than daring effrontery. My belief had been this, but some in authority had argued more fiercely against the sinner of the East Side. *Rosary* at Church offered for Miss Fischer, who came in at 7 p.m. to ask to be received by our charity. She had been offered to us by the Sisters of the Assumption. Novena to Our Lady of G.C.

Sunday, 26th
Offered Mass, the first for me in ten days, for my husband. *Angelus. Novena* to O.L. of G.C. Read in "Following" and "A Year with the Saints."

Monday
Angelus. Novena. Responsory to St. Anthony.

Tuesday, 28th Sept.
Angelus. Novena to O.L. of G.C. Litany of the Holy Cross. Responsory to St. Anthony.

Wednesday
Mass at 8. Offered for means for my work, especially linen for our nurse's dresses and a first class Remmington type-writer for my work. I besought the Sacred Heart of Our Lord. *Novena* to O.L. of G.C. *Angelus.* Read in "Following." Also Our Lord's sermon about becoming as little children. Began Novena to St. Joseph for charitable help for our work.

Thursday
Angelus. *Novena* to O.L. of G.C. *Novena* to St. Joseph. *Rosary* said for Father Pardow's greater perfection by Mrs. Donovan and me.

Litanies of Sacred Hearts of Jesus and Mary. *Little Rosary* of the Sacred Heart.

Friday, October 1st

Mass at 9 for the First Friday's Thanksgiving and for the beginning of a *Novena* of First Fridays for the entire conversion of my husband to God. Also for wisdom. Also, close of *Novena* to O.L. of G.C. *Angelus.* *Litanies* of S. Hearts of Jesus and Mary, and other prayers to the Sacred Heart. *Rosary,* offered for Father Pardow's work in religion. *Seven Words* upon the Cross. *Novena* to St. Joseph, for hospital.

First Friday, November 5th

Mass, offered with Holy Communion for my husband's complete conversion to God, and for wisdom for myself. Began trying to have special examen of conscience for five minutes every morning, and five minutes of reading in the 4th Book of Thomas à Kempis.

. . . .

Presentation of the Blessed Virgin　November 21

Offered *Holy Communion* for complete *consecration* to God of myself and my husband, and for the choice of a spiritual Director for myself. Have been somewhat successful in daily reading of "The Following of Christ." Not so successful in thinking about my conscience clearly, though the special examen for temper is distributed all along!

November 28th, Advent

Began 4,000 Hail Mary's in aid of the Holy Communion at Xmas of persons who are negligent of their duties.

November 30th

Holy Communion received and two masses in aid of my wisdom, and my husband's entire conversion to God, in honor of Mary Immaculate, to whom St. Rose's Church are making a novena. Reading III Book of the "Following" this month. Mamie, without being asked, arranged a little altar in the bedroom I now occupy. A great consolation and help.

Dec. 3rd, 1st Friday

Communion offered for my husband's entire conversion to God, and for the intentions of my *Novena* to the Immaculate Conception.

Dec. 7th

Ended Novena to Mary Immaculate for wisdom to know God's will, and for my husband's complete conversion.

Dec. 10th

It is likely that Father Parks will be my Director. At his suggestion got Faber's "Growth in Holiness" and "Spiritual Conferences." And also "The Light of the Conscience." Great relief and light from this spiritual reading, tho I have so little time until night. Have asked the Blessed Virgin for a director, since Father Parks says (with so many others) that I should have one who is constant. Father Pardow really has been, though I have not let him feel the weight of my selfish needs. Four Communions, besides Sunday.

Dec. 16th

Holy Communion, offered for our money.

Today had the satisfactory help of a talk with Father Parks (who, it proves, was a pupil and constant companion of Fr. Pardow) who is willing to be my director. He gave me the Memorial of a Christian Life by Louis de Grenada simple little rule inaugurating my obedience. Visit to the Bl. Sacrament. Rosary for spiritual growth. Letter in answer to two from Fr. Fidelis.

Dec. 17th

Holy Communion at 7, offered for spiritual growth. Fasted till 12 a.m. Visited St. Laurence's, and was present at 9 a.m. the Canon. Arranged with Father McKinnon to come at once to Mr. Southall (very ill) with the Blessed Sacrament, and was present. Visited St. Rose of Lima's with Gertrude Tuttle, at 2 p.m. and asked Our Lord to win her to this work, which she leans towards.

Dec. 17th, Friday, Ember Day

Began Novena to the Miraculous Infant of Prague, for means to carry on my work.

Dec. 25th

Great emotion to think of the poor heart I had prepared so badly to receive the Divine Infant. Offered Holy Communion for the future of Alfred Chappell, Jr. and gave to orphans for him.

Dec. 26th

Began Novena to the *Miraculous Infant of Prague* for the hospital to come, D.V., and the means to be given for our work from the general public. Mrs. Corchran had given me a beautiful little image of the Infant.

A call from a Trappist, Father Murphy of Canada, was a blessed event. He came from Tessie Gethim, and brought a Cross of St. Anthony from her. He is collecting gold for a chalice to be used in his Monastery, and I gave my last bit of jewelry, the pin Mr. Winans gave me, worn for twenty years almost constantly. He was very encouraging to us as to our work, and blessed us, and told us to pray for helpers among women, subjects, to St. Anthony. I began prayers to this end at once.

Dec. 30th

Began Novena to the Divine Infant, with Mrs. Watson and Mrs. Salmon, for patience under irritation. Also *Litany of Loretto* for Mrs. Watson's happy death, and growth in virtue until her death.

Jan. 4th, Tuesday

Alice Huber decided to give her life to the work. Finished Novena to the Miraculous Infant of Prague, in aid of my obtaining a hospital for 300 patients, and means to carry on my daily work at present. $50.00 came since I began the *Novena.*

Praying to St. Anthony for "subjects."

Jan. 6th

Finished *Novena* made with Mrs. Watson and Mrs. Salmon to the Sacred Infancy, that I might have patience with all the sick I tend, (they having their own intentions) and to *St. Anne* that they two might get better. Also the *Litany of the Blessed Virgin,* that Mrs. Watson might be more reasonable and resigned.

Jan. 7th, First Friday

Offered Holy Communion for my husband's holy life, and for patience for myself and my sick, and for the growth of love of the Sacred Heart.

Jan. 8th

Offered *Holy Communion* for *Direction.* Sent acknowledgment to the Messenger of the Sacred Heart for temporal aid received in answer to prayers.

Jan. 12th

Began Triduum for adoration of the *Holy Name of Jesus,* and in aid of my helpers and myself who are ready to devote our lives to the hospital. *Mass* in the morning, and evening devotions at the Church, with Benediction of the M.B. Sacrament.

Jan. 16th

Miss Bogue came "to help me" from Boston, and convinced me that she must stay. She had a vision, about 2 weeks ago, of our Blessed Lord, surrounded by a bright light, when she was in Church. I had the same vision after Holy Communion at, so far as I can remember, just the same time. The vision came to me all at once, with a heavenly sense of joy and peace. I could not tell why Our Lord had so responded to my cry of adoration and longing. God grant Miss Bogue and I may work together for good. On the 11th, beloved Alice Huber assured me, again, that she would soon be with us, only a previous promise preventing her from staying "then and there." Ellen Ryan promises to come on the 1st of Feb. for life: So has St. Anthony in 8 weeks, answered my appeal for "subjects." Glory be to God.

Jan. 17th

Visited St. Anne's Shrine in E. 76th St., while out on a visit to the sick. Great happiness from praying at the shrines in the Church, and kissing the place where the relic rests.

Today we received $53.00 in answer to our prayers for help. Father Parks has given us a little rule for our present life, which we keep. Mrs. Corchran seems likely to stay always.

Jan. 20th

Am allowed five Holy Communions every week. We keep up our little rule for prayers and reading quite well, in spite of crowding and interruptions. Mrs. Corchran is always strong to obey any religious admonitions, God bless her! Am able to go now and then to Church in the evening, which is a great comfort. Mr. Southall told me yesterday that he could *cure* Miss Hanan's tongue in 6 weeks! We thank God so deeply that all of us are as if celebrating a feast. Miss Hanan was given up as hopeless at the Cancer Hospital.

Second interview with Director was very helpful and encouraging. He seems to have real respect for our aims. Miss Bogue appears to be most desirable, does quantities of work, *most* thoroughly, and seems to mean to stay always. *Yesterday* Margaret Corchran assured me she should *stay.*

Jan. 24th

Miss Bogue's inspiration to come to us has thus early seemed to her an unbearable Cross, as she cannot endure the smells and sights, and turns out to be rather flighty in spite of her efficiency in cleaning a room. She has been up to Miss Swift and Miss McGinley, and shown her queer streaks, and I must give her up at once.

Have undertaken to mortify myself in little things hourly, before grasping at any higher method.

We are praying to the Miraculous Infant of Prague for help to carry on our work and build a great hospital.

We are praying to St. Anthony for women to help us. The Sisters of St. Joseph at 81st St. have promised to pray for us.

Jan. 30th

Am gaining much peace and some simplicity through the wise direction I receive, and reading Faber's "Growth In Holiness," and sincere prayers. It is decided that I *must* speak before the Mother's Congress.

Feb. 4th, 1898
First Friday. Holy Communion for my husband.

Feb. 6th
Began offering my communion for overcoming impatience and anger. I desire with all my heart to have no feeling of resentment or unloving displeasure towards *anyone,* like St. Francis de Sales.

Feb. 23rd, Ash Wednesday
Began a *Novena* to Our Lord in honor of *His Passion,* and for *aid from the public* for our work.

Feb. 24th
Was told by Fr. Parks to take the altar table and hanging lamp devoted to the Sacred Heart out of our workroom or dispensary. It was very hard to do it, and I thought the room would be unbearable to me.

March 4th, First Friday
Novena (6th month) for my husband's conversion to God. Also end of *Novena* to Our Lord in His holy Passion for aid from the public. Have during this novena obtained exactly the sum I asked for—$200.00.

Thurs., March 10th
Began a *Novena* to St. Joseph, for a large hospital *very soon,* as well as help for daily needs at once. After several days, decided to promise a donation of 5.00 every month to St. Joseph's Hospital for Incurable Consumptive, if my prayer is answered.

16th
Have promised 6 Stations of the Cross in reparation for leaving one, in a Novena to the Passion of our Lord, not fully completed. I

obtained my request. I promised to love our dearest Lord to the exclusion of all else. Also to work *much harder.* I have begun to realize that Our Lord loves me, even me, and everyone, though he so suffers from contact with us when we are sinful in our lives or from our past.

March 19th, St. Joseph's Day

Finished Novena to St. Joseph for a great hospital *soon,* and for my husband's holy consecration, and my own holiness of life.

March 22nd

Began a *Triduum* to Our *Blessed Mother,* in honor of the Feast of the *Annunciation,* in aid of the perfect service of the four Servants of Relief. Alice Huber comes on the eve of the Annunciation.

....

On the first night at 12 when I got up to say a prayer to St. V. de Paul, I felt great happiness; and on the second night, not waking till 4 a.m. and getting up, I joyfully prayed, and saw Our Lord as if upon the Crucifix, not upright, but before being removed from the Cross after it was lowered.

....

Our Lord seemed to say to me, on a visit to the Blessed Sacrament after confession—"I love you, and you love me—then what is the trouble?" Great peace overflowed me. I begin to love Him only, as I have prayed to do for three years. My shocking unworthiness strikes me almost more in the point of my having so little life left to offer, so little sacrifice to make in offering it. Yet Jesus loves me, and everything is simplified and exalted.

March 25th

Finished the *Triduum to Our Lady* for the Servants of Relief, going to St. Gabriel's with Alice to five o'clock Mass, where we heard a short sermon to the men's mission by Father Robert. Then we received Our Dearest Lord, and afterwards were present at Father Edmund's Mass at the Blessed Virgin's Altar. He was like an angel, so simple, so absorbed, so peace-giving. He offered the Mass for Alice and me.

April 1st, 1st Friday

Offered the Mass and my Holy Communion for my husband. Alice "received" with me. She says she shall give me one holy Communion every week. This last week, Father Edward, the very dear friend of Father Fidelis, called on Alice and me—a Passionist from Baltimore, Superior there, with Father Joseph, who is one of the four priests who come next to the Provincial of the Passionists. A beautiful visit. They have great faith in our work. A letter, most kind, came from Father Pardow.

April 3rd, Palm Sunday

We all went to first Mass, Mamie being left on guard. Alice offered her Communion for me. I offered mine first for the softening of hearts towards our work day by day to enable us to live, but above all, to bring about the principle object of our work, to spread charitable feeling. I remembered my husband, and then prayed for the "perfect service" of the Servants of Relief. I found, by the paper, that Father Pardow is to preach the Easter Sermon at the Cathedral. I have no hope of being able to hear him; but shall try to send Alice and Mrs. Corcoran, Father Hyacinth, Passionist, and Alice says, thought by his Order and all nuns to be a great saint, called for a long visit. He brought us a relic of St. Paul of the Cross. He gave a great deal of good advice; he seemed to me a truly inspired man. Much that he said was contrary to our wishes, and some advice from others. He says that he shall call again, and as he is often in town, we expect often to see him, Alice being a treasure in the estimation of Passionists,—how otherwise? I was much exhausted after his call, being tired already almost beyond endurance. The chance to hear the truth, to gain light for my aims and conduct—the blessings, and all that goes to move my soul and heart, are hard though sweet to hear. I feel more than ever my unfitness, my longing for a great life of simple perfection in Our dearest Lord's service. I cannot bear to have the Fathers or Nuns go away—their atmospheres seem life, their absence illness. Then I miss more, when they go, others who are always absent. God be praised forever for His mercies to me, and to us all!

April 8th, Good Friday

Father J. J. Fullam lately came to propose Miss Roddy as a member of our group. He gave her a splendid endorsement, and said she had 12 years experience as a *lay* Sister of Charity, but had a great desire to find some sort of thing which my undertaking seemed to correspond to. Alice Huber was frozen stiff at the idea of even a lay Sister who wanted to leave her Convent. Miss R. is evidently remarkable in many ways; but our director said he knew of her quite thoroughly, and refused his sanction. She could have diverted a good deal of money into our coffers, as all the circumstances were such. But come she could not. Father Parks will write out for us a little rule, to be pondered over by us. Holy Week Service, and visits to the Blessed Sacrament are most beautiful.

I have been begging through the papers, and much help comes most cordially—$350.00 already, and two offers of larger houses. We feel that our earnest prayers for a large home, given to St. Joseph, have been heard. But one house (at a nominal cost of $175.00 a year) is at Ocean Grove; the other is suggested by Theo. B. Starr, by the fact that he asks what a large brick house such as we want would cost per year. Which is enough for us Servants of Relief to raise our hopes to the zenith!

April 15th

Yesterday I went to see Father Pardow, who had expressed a wish to see me, and had an interesting call. He showed me the new Church of St. Ignatius, which he, as Provincial, had caused to be finished in a noble style of architecture. Everything he does and says is satisfactory —none like him.

Afterwards, I had a talk with our director, who gave me our rules for the community in its present infant state; very simple. He is truly in earnest, and we feel that all he plans is come with prayer and therefore is blessed. He thinks he has a fine house picked out for us, that we may buy.

Money still drifts in from my appeals, and we have had over 500.00.

April 21st

My beloved husband died on April 19th, about half an hour before I reached him. I had made seven offerings of Holy Communion on the 1st Fridays, beginning in October last, for the entire conversion of my husband to God and to holiness. As I stood beside his body, soon after death, the beauty and nobility and the exquisite gentleness of his life, and the eloquence which breathed from the unbreathing being of one who has died in the Lord, spoke plainly to me of his virtues, and the welcome our Lord had given him into His rest. My own soul was trembling in the dark uncertainty of all unworthiness. Yesterday, early, his soul came, I am sure, to console me, in his loveliest way of forgiveness.

On the 19th, we began *Novenas* to St. Joseph, St. Paul of the Cross, and St. Anthony, to obtain the house we have chosen for our work, in Cherry St.

On the 14th, Alice Huber and I began a *Novena* to St. Fidelis in aid of Father Fidelis, whose feast day is on the 24th.

April 25th

Began *Novena* to the Miraculous Infant of Prague, for the obtaining of the house we want on Cherry St. Finished Novena to St. Fidelis yesterday. I am trying not to sink down and do nothing.

April 28th

Am striving to keep above the waves. A talk with Our Director day before yesterday helped me to gain a little courage for our work. Thousands of prayers are ascending for my husband's translation to heaven. Alice is most brave and helpful, as all are who care for me or the work.

May 1st, 1st Sunday

Holy Communion *for Forty Hours,* for *direction* in my work and the building up of my community. Also for the repose of my husband's soul, and for the intentions of our Archbishop, whose silver jubilee comes soon, and the people are all praying for him. Began Novena to Our Lady for *our faithful service* of Our Lord. Have last evening, for the first time since George's death, felt courage, and am very cheerful, *in Christ.*

May 5th

We began a Novena to the Blessed Virgin on the 1st of May, to become faithful in all our work as Servants of Relief. Mrs. Watson died on the night of the 3rd.

May 8th
Was obliged by illness to interrupt *Novena* to the Blessed Virgin, but began it again next day, the 6th, Friday. Could not go out, having cold in lungs, and rainy weather, on 1st Friday, so had to break Novena for my beloved husband. Could not receive Holy Communion today for our *Novena* to the Miraculous Infant of Prague. Hope to begin another soon. Am still confined to the house.

May 11th   Tuesday
Lighted candle beside our image of St. Anthony, for my husband, and for the addition to our nurses which I crave. Began on the 10th, a *Novena* to the Miraculous Infant of Prague for our home in Cherry St. Today a hopeful letter comes from J. Warren Greene about it. Glory be to God. My heart had almost failed in long waiting, but I knew God's will was our only desire, and so was a little at peace in the prospect of rebuff and perhaps failure. Now I hope indeed that God blessed our outlook in this direction. *May 14th began Novena* to St. Jude for patience.

15th
Father O'Mahony of Lawrence, Mass. the first priest who prayed during Mass for my work's development, and prayed for a long time, came to see us, and cheer us on.

18th
Began Novena to St. Joseph for consecration. Began *Novena* for Mrs. Jennings' eyes, according to the advice of Father Joseph (Passionist) to St. Paul of the Cross, with relic and prayer. Letter from Fr. Fidelis.

May 25th
Yesterday received Holy Communion for the first intention of Novena to St. Jude. Began another Novena to him for patience.
Letter from Fr. Edmund day before yesterday. Yesterday, Alice Huber and I went to the Cathedral, to show the Archbishop the dress we now wear, and obtain his permission to go singly to cases, and to be out till 9 p.m. in twos. Could only see Fr. McMahon, but he was very kind and favorable, and advised me to write to His Grace, which I did

that evening. The dress is so like a nun's simplest costume that we are taken for Sisters. Many persons, and boys, take off their hats to us. Alice feels as if she had always worn it, and so do I. I put mine on the day before the 19th, to obtain Fr. Parks' approval, and began to wear it regularly on the monthly date of my husband's death. My hair was cropped as close as possible. Alice and I stayed a long time in the Cathedral, and made an offering to St. Anthony. Lovely letter today from Fr. Pardow.

June 3rd

First Friday. Offered my Holy Communion for the respose of my husband's *soul,* as the beginning of a *Novena* to First Fridays for him. Also in honor of St. Jude at the end of a Novena to him for *patience* for myself. Also for the help of our work and that the Sacred Heart will grant us daily aid from the public. For Mrs. Moulton's temporal help and conversion.

Began Novena on the *1st of June* to the *Sacred Heart* for temporal aid, to the *Blessed Virgin* as Our Lady of Perpetual Help for temporal aid, a *Triduum* to *St. Joseph* for Mrs. Moulton's temporal affairs, and to the *Miraculous Infant of Prague* for our home-to-be and *temporal aid.*

June 11th

Have received more than $160.00 for current expenses since our Novenas for temporal aid were begun, and being within a hundred dollars of collapse as far as the next two months go. We are very grateful. We are all making a Novena for temporal aid to the Sacred Heart to end on the 17th, the Feast. Also for *nurses,* to St. Anthony, to end on his Feast, the 13th. We have offered a Mass in his honor. The gentlemen interested in getting our house, Mr. Starr, Mr. Crimmins, and first in our gratitude, J. Warren Greene Esq. and also some others, are having quite good success; and they send me themselves fifty and twenty-five dollars for daily work. God be praised for blessing our efforts.

June 18th

Our Novenas have ended with the happy result that we have received through my appeal, and the appeals of Mr. Greene, Mr. Starr, and Mr. Crimmins about $250.00 for our current expenses! This, when we were nearly reduced to bankruptcy, having but $100.00 in the bank to last two months. Glory be to God for His mercy to those who pray to Him! The Sacred Heart of Jesus, St. Joseph, and Our Lady of Perpetual Help, be praised!

We began, today, Saturday, a Novena to the Sacred Heart of Mary for true charity of heart. The readings we find in the book made up from the writings of Blessed Margaret Mary, are very beautiful, especially that of consecration of all one's heart, forever.

August 5th

1st Friday. Last month, and today, continued the *Novena* for the repose of my husband's soul. Miss Foley (a patient) has been faithfully offering prayers daily to the Miraculous Infant of Prague for our increase of funds, *that we may never* be obliged to turn away a person in desperate need. Mr. Greene endorsed the idea of helping such people, and we have had considerable money to meet these cases, ever since the prayers began.

Mrs. Corchran seems to be dying, of quick consumption, much to our sorrow. She put on our working dress and hood the day she was taken very ill. Miss Spety, my dear friend the trained nurse, came and offered some weeks of nursing free [to] us, just as were at a loss what to do for someone to nurse, scientifically, Mrs. Corcoran. Praise be to God.

Feb. 3rd, 1899

First Friday, finished the Novena of 1st Fridays for the repose of my husband's soul. I prayed that he might be received into heaven on Xmas Day; and I then felt that he was in bliss. God bless his beloved soul.

Feb. 2nd

Began *Novena* to St. Anne for the recovery of my mother-in-law from her blindness.

Went to visit St. Anne's Shrine with Mrs. Lathrop.

March 3rd

Began second Novena to St. Anne, for Mrs. Lathrop's cure, in conjunction with her.

First Friday

Began Novena of 1st Fridays, to the Sacred Heart, for the success of our charity, and the holiness of the S. of R.

April 10th

Have been able, through donations made in answer to weekly appeals in the newspapers, to half pay for a house, 426 Cherry St., to which we move on May 1st. St. Joseph and the Sacred Heart were long besought for this house. A Novena of Masses in thanksgiving to St. Joseph are being said by Fr. Edward, C.P. of St. Joseph's Retreat, Baltimore, Md. A Mass is to be said monthly in honor of the Sacred Heart, *always,* beginning with this month, in thanksgiving. Our Home is to be called S. Rose's Free Home, in honor of St. Rose of Lima. We prayed to the Holy Ghost for three days, and then drew the name from a box, in which others had been placed.

Received on the 1st Friday for the success of the work, etc.

ESSAYS

FROM 'THE WAYSIDE'
CHAPTER 14, *MEMORIES OF HAWTHORNE*
(BOSTON AND NEW YORK: HOUGHTON, MIFFLIN, 1897); RPT. 1922.

Editor's Note: When Rose Hawthorne Lathrop was in the first months of her work on New York's Lower East Side, and beginning to spend long hours attending the sick, she composed and edited late at night her *Memories of Hawthorne.* An earlier version of four of the chapters had already appeared in the *Atlantic Monthly* (February, March, April, May, 1896). Much of the book, including the final pages of this chapter consists of letters of Sophia woven together with her daughter's commentary. Chapter 14 gives us a sense of the ambience Rose experienced as a little girl and her adult conviction that smiles and conversation could both be "illusive joys" if the philosopher's optimism was unfounded or high ideals never acted upon. Only Thoreau survives her benevolent critique in these remembrances. The spelling in her childhood letters cited in the text was improved considerably. The original texts, as the present edition indicates, were far more inventive, sometimes reflecting her Boston accent. ("Mama has influenzer," she once wrote.) The final incident in this selection tells us forcibly of Hawthorne's famous distaste for most women writers. Rose, fortunately, eventually abandoned her efforts to sustain a career in fiction writing, but not until she had spent several years ignoring the paternal command.

*

In order to give an idea of how it happened that our family could return from Europe to Concord with a few great expectations, I will rehearse somewhat of the charm which had been found in the illustrious village when my father and mother first knew it. There a group of people conversed together who have left an echo that is still heard.

160

There also is still heard "the shot fired round the world," which of course returned to Concord on completing its circuit. But even the endless concourse of visitors, making the claims of any region wearisomely familiar, cannot diminish the simple solemnity of the town's historical as well as literary importance; and indeed it has so many medals for various merit that it is no wonder its residents have a way of speaking about it which some of us would call Bostonian. Emerson, Thoreau, Channing, and Alcott dispersed a fragrance that attracted at once, and all they said was resonant with charity and courage.

The first flash of individuality from Emerson could hardly fail to suggest that he resembled the American eagle; and he presided over Concord in a way not unlike our glorious symbol, the Friend of Light. It must have been exhilarating to look forward to many years in Emerson's hamlet. My earliest remembered glimpse of him was when he appeared—tall, side-slanting, peering with almost undue questioning into my face, but with a smile so constant as to seem like an added feature, dressed in a solemn, slender, dark overcoat, and a dark, shadowing hat—upon the Concord highroad; the same yellow thoroughfare which reaches out to Lexington its papyrus-strip of history. At the onset of Emerson—for psychic men do attack one with their superiority—awe took possession of me; and, as we passed (a great force and a small girl) I wondered if I should survive. I not only did so, but felt better than before. It then became one of my happiest experiences to pass Emerson upon the street. A distinct exaltation followed my glance into his splendid face. Yet I caviled at his self-consciousness, his perpetual smile. I complained that he ought to wait for something to smile at. I could not be sure that he was privately enjoying some joke from Greek fun-makers, remembered under a Concord elm. After a time, I realized that he always had something to smile *for,* if not to smile *at;* and that a cheerful countenance is heroic. By and by I learned that he always could find something to smile at, also; for he tells us, "The best of all jokes is the sympathetic contemplation of things by the understanding, from the philosopher's point of view." But, in my unenlightened state, when I saw him begin to answer some question, however trivial, with this smile, slowly, very slowly growing, until it lit up his whole countenance with a refulgent beam before he answered (the whole performance dominated by a deliberation as great and brilliant as the dawn), I argued that this good cheer was out of proportion; that Emerson should keep back a smile so striking and circumstantial for rare occasions, such as enormous surprise; or, he should make it the precursor to a tremendous roar of laughter. I have yet to learn that any one heard him laugh aloud,—which pastime he has called, with certainly a familiar precision that indicates personal experience, a "pleasant spasm," a "muscular irritation."

In maturer years I believed that his smile brought refreshment, encouragement, and waves of virtue to those who saw it. To be sure, it was a sort of questioning; sometimes even quizzical; sometimes only a safeguard; but it was eminently kind, and no one else could do it. His manner was patronizing, in spite of its suavity; but it grew finer every spring, until it had become as exquisitely courteous as Sir Philip Sidney's must have been. The arch of his dark eyebrows sometimes seemed almost angry, being quickly lifted, and then bent in a scowl of earnestness; but as age advanced this sternness of brow grew to be, unchangeably, a calm sweep of infinite kindness.

It was never so well understood at The Wayside that its owner had retiring habits as when Alcott was reported to be approaching along the Larch Path, which stretched in feathery bowers between our house and his. Yet I was not aware that the seer failed at any hour to gain admittance,—one cause, perhaps, of the awe in which his visits were held. I remember that my observation was attracted to him curiously from the fact that my mother's eyes changed to a darker gray at his advents, as they did only when she was silently sacrificing herself. I clearly understood that Mr. Alcott was admirable; but he sometimes brought manuscript poetry with him, the dear child of his own Muse, and a guest more unwelcome than the *enfant terrible* of the drawing-room. There was one particularly long poem which he had read aloud to my mother and father; a seemingly harmless thing, from which they never recovered. Out of the mentions made of this effusion I gathered that it was like a moonlit expanse, quiet, somnolent, cool, and flat as a month of prairies. Rapture, conviction, tenderness, often glowed upon Alcott's features and trembled in his voice. I believe he was never once startled from the dream of illusive joy which pictured to him all high aims as possible of realization through talk. Often he was so happy that he could have danced like a child; and he laughed merrily like one; and the quick, upward lift of his head, which his great height induced him to hold, as a rule, slightly bent forward,—this rapid, playful *lift,* and the glance, bright and eager though not deep, which sparkled upon you, were sweet and good to see. Yet I have noticed his condition as pale and dolorous enough, before the event of his noble daughter's splendid success. But such was not his character; circumstances had enslaved him, and he appeared thin and forlorn by incongruous accident, like a lamb in chains. He might have been taken for a centenarian when I beheld him one day slowly and pathetically constructing a pretty rustic fence before his gabled brown house, as if at the unreasonable command of some latter-day Pharaoh. Ten years afterward he was, on the contrary, a Titan: gay, silvery-locked, elegant, ready to begin his life over again.

Alcott represented to me a fairy element in the up-country region in which I so often saw him. I heard that he walked the woods for the purpose of finding odd coils of tree-roots and branches, which would on the instant suggest to him an ingenious use in his art of rustic building. It was rumored that nobody's outlying curios in this line were safe under his eye, and that if you possessed an eccentric tree for a time, it was fated to close its existence in the keeping of Alcott. I imagined his slightly stooping, yet tall and well-grown figure, clothed in black, and with a picturesque straw hat, twining itself in and out of forest aisles, or craftily returning home with gargoyle-like stems over his shoulders. The magic of his pursuit was emphasized by the notorious fact that his handiwork fell together in the middle, faded like shadows from bronze to hoary pallor; its longevity was a protracted death. In short, his arbors broke under the weight of a purpose, as poems become doggerel in the service of a theorist. Truly, Alcott was completely at the beck of illusion; and he was always safer alone with it than near the hard uses of adverse reality. I well remember my astonishment when I was told that he had set forth to go into the jaws of the Rebellion after Louisa, his daughter, who had succumbed to typhus fever while nursing the soldiers. His object was to bring her home; but it was difficult to believe that he would be successful in entering the field of misery and uproar. I never expected to see him again. Almost the only point at which he normally met this world was in his worship of apple-trees. Here, in his orchard, he was an all-admirable human being and lovely to observe. As he looked upon the undulating arms or piled the excellent apples, red and russet, which seemed to shine at his glance, his figure became supple, his countenance beamed with a ruby and gold akin to the fruit. In his orchard by the highroad, with its trees rising to a great height from a basin-shaped side lawn (which may originally have been marshy ground), he seemed to me a perfect soul. We all enjoyed greatly seeing him there, as we wended to and from our little town. No doubt the garden of children at the beginning of his career inspired him likewise; and in it he must have shown the same tender solicitude and benevolence, and beamed upon his young scholars with a love which exquisitely tempered his fantastical suppositions.

He often spoke humbly, but he never let people think he was humble. His foibles appeared to me ridiculous, and provoked me exceedingly,—the brave cat of the proverb must be my excuse,—but I awakened to the eternal verity that some such husks are rather natural to persons of purely distinctive minds, perhaps shielding them. And I think one comes to value a bent blessed with earnest unconsciousness; a not too clever Argus vision; a childlike gullibility and spontaneity. This untarnished gullibility and gentle confidence, for all his self-laudations, Alcott had, and when he did not emerge either from his apple orchard or his inspirations he was essentially wholesome, full of an ardent simplicity, and a happy faith in the capacities given him by his Creator. So that his outline is one of much dignity, in spite of the somewhat capricious coloring of his character; the latter being not unlike the efforts of a nursery artist upon a print of "The Father of His Country," for whom, as he stands proudly upon the page, a green coat and purple pantaloons were not intended, and are only minor incidents of destiny.

Mr. Ellery Channing was, I am sure, the townsman who was most gladly welcome. My parents felt great admiration and friendliness for him, and it would be a sacrifice on my own part not to mention this companion of theirs, although I must beg his pardon for doing so. There is no doubt that Concord would have hung with several added pounds of weight upon our imaginations if it had not been for him. Over his tender-heartedness, as I saw him in the old days, played delicious eccentricities, phosphorescent, fitful, touch-me-not antics of feeling. I was glad to meet the long glance of his gray, dazzling eyes, lowered gracefully at last. The gaze seemed to pass through me to the wall, and beyond even that barrier to the sky at the horizon line. It did not disturb me; it had been too kindly to criticise, or so I thought. No doubt Mr. Channing had made his little regretful, uncomplimentary notes in passing, but it was characteristic of his exquisite comradeship towards all that we did not fear his eyes. I say comradeship, although the power which I believed touched him with its wand so mischievously had induced him to drop (as a boy loses successively all his marbles) all his devoted friends, without a word of explanation, because without a shadow of reason; the only thing to be said about it being that the loss was entirely voluntary on the part of this charming boy. He would cease to bow, as he passed. Then he found the marbles again, pocketed them as if nothing had happened, smiled, called, and hob-nobbed. A man's high-water mark is his calibre; and at high-water mark Mr. Channing's sea was to us buoyant, rich-tinted, sunlit; a great force, darkening and dazzling with beautiful emotions. He was in those days devoted to the outer air, and to the wonders of the nature we do not often understand, even when we trap it and classify it. He always invited his favorites to walk with him, and I once had the honor of climbing a very high hill by his side, in time to look at a Concord sunset, which I myself realized was the finest in the world.

Another peculiar spirit now and then haunted us, usually sad as a pine-tree—Thoreau. His enormous eyes, tame with religious intellect and wild with the loose rein, making a steady flash in this strange unison of forces, frightened me dreadfully at first. The unanswerable argument which he unwittingly made to soften my heart towards him was to fall desperately ill. During his long illness my mother lent him our sweet old music-box, to which she had danced as it warbled at the Old Manse, in the first year of her marriage, and which now softly dreamed forth its tunes in a time-mellowed tone. When he died, it seemed as if an anemone, more lovely than any other, had been carried from the borders of a wood into its silent depths, and dropped, in solitude and shadow, among the recluse ferns and mosses which are so seldom disturbed by passing feet. Son of freedom and opportunity that he was, he touched the heart by going to nature's peacefulness like the saints, and girding upon his American sovereignty the hair-shirt of service to self-denial. He was happy in his intense discipline of the flesh, as all men are when they have once tasted power—if it is the power which awakens perception of the highest concerns. His countenance had an April pensiveness about it; you would never have guessed that he could write of owls so jocosely. His manner was such as to suggest that he could mope and weep *with* them. I never crossed an airy hill or broad field in Concord, without thinking of him who had been the companion of space as well as of delicacy; the lover of the wood-thrush, as well as of the Indian. Walden woods rustled the name of Thoreau whenever we walked in them.

When we drove from the station to The Wayside, in arriving from Europe, on a hot summer day, I distinctly remember the ugliness of the un-English landscape and the forlornness of the little cottage which was to be our home. Melancholy and stupid days immediately followed (at least they were so in my estimation). I marveled at the amount of sand in the flower-borders and at the horrifying delinquencies of our single servant.

For some years I was eager to use all the eloquence I could muster in my epistles to girl friends, in England or anywhere, as to the paucity of life in Concord. Perhaps the following extracts from two letters, one written at Bath, England, and the other at Concord, and never sent, but kept by my mother from the flames with many more of my expressions in correspondence, may convey the feelings of the whole family:—

> *31 Charles Street, Bath, England*
> Dear Hannah [Redcar Hannah],—When I go home I think that I shall never have such a nice time as when I go home; for I shall have such a big garden, and I shall have little and big girls to come and see me. Never on earth shall I have such a nice time as when I am at home.

After the transition:—

> *Concord, Mass.*
> I am in Concord now, and long to see you again, but I suppose that it is useless to think of it. I am going out, after I have done my lessons, to have a good time.—A very good time indeed, to be sure, for there was nothing but frozen ground, and I had to be doing something to keep myself warm, and I had to come back after a little while. I do not know how to keep myself warm. Happy are you who keep warm all the time in England. The frost has made thick leaves on our windows everywhere, and you can hardly see through them.

I tried to bring the stimulus of great events into the Concord life by writing stories, of which I would report the progress to my one or two confidantes. My father overheard some vainglorious boasts from my lips, one afternoon, when the windows of the little library where he sat were open; and the small girl who listened to me, wide-eyed, and I myself, proud and glad to have reached a thrilling dénouement, were standing beside the sweet-clover bed, not dreaming of anything more severe than its white bloom. A few minutes afterwards, my father hung over me, dark as a prophetic flight of birds. "Never let me hear of your writing stories!" he exclaimed, with as near an approach to anger as I had ever seen in him! "I forbid you to write them!" But I believe this command only added a new attraction to authorship, agreeably haunting me as I beckoned imaginary scenes and souls out of chaos.

COMMENTS UPON THE EAST SIDE, MADE IN 1897,
DURING OUR WORK AS SECULARS
CHRIST'S POOR 1 (JULY 1902) 5-16

Editor's Note: Although published in 1902, this essay was originally written as a personal record of the ministry Mother Alphonsa
began before becoming a Dominican. Her description of the daily life
of the poor on the lower East Side of New York in 1897 shows what
kind of world Mrs. George Lathrop entered when she began her charitable work. What is remarkable about the text is its fusion of compassion
and dispassionate assessment. She has avoided impressionistic description and remarks which would have called attention to her own emotional response, or any private struggle she had to make to sustain her
commitment. In her diary of that year we read: "September 17th,
1897. 668 Water Street. No chance for making these notes has been
found between these days [September 1896-1897]; nursing from 5 to
11 at night or doing all it involved to set out as a nurse, soon prevented
my sitting up till 2 A.M. to write a description of the East Side."

*

When I started out to see what the East Side of New York was like,
the street which struck me as the most astonishing in its difference from
those up-town was Goerck Street. It was a warm August afternoon, and
the inhabitants of the houses along this narrow way were sitting on the
steps and standing about the sidewalks, to say nothing of those upon
the street itself.

I looked eagerly at the faces that should suggest dangerous depravity, and I thought I saw upon almost every countenance expressions of
the most satanic cruelty and selfishness. I find that the people who visit
me for investigation in this quarter of the city come in the same excited
state of alarm at the character of the East Side residents. But after a few
months of living among them one entirely abandons any idea of their
being so different from other human beings, and there scarcely remains
any surprise in one's mind concerning them, excepting this fact of their
living together in crowds, which seems dangerous to moral and physical health. I have found that it is a very common thing for a family of
eight or ten persons to have only one bed; so that possibly an elderly
woman afflicted with a disease like rheumatism or cancerous affections
is obliged to sleep upon chairs or to lie upon the floor, while the
younger members of the family are piled upon the bed, and the poor
little children are disposed of anywhere.

One of the most pathetic cases of sickness that I have attended is that of an elderly woman dying of two cancers—a person of lovely disposition, and formerly of the comfortable class of humble citizens—who slept at night upon four chairs with her knees necessarily drawn up somewhat, her improvised bed being near the kitchen stove, while her children slept in one bed. I felt a sharp blow, as it seemed, when I entered her room early one morning and found her still in this condition; and I have since known of a number of other instances of the chair-bed. It is a common mode of the poor to sleep without additional covering in the coldest weather, and the lack of room is repeated by a lack in every other department of need. The people are thankful if, in the first place, they can pay their rent; next, they desire to keep up their life insurance, which will bury them at death; after that they eagerly seek for shoes; and if any money is left for food (usually beer, coffee and tea, with pork; or, in the case of the Jews, I believe, cakes), the sum of their comfort is as complete as they can make it. The fuel is frequently not paid for, being all sorts of wooden planks, hoops and staves, that are dragged home by the children from places where buildings are being torn down.

When we see an overcrowded street, indicating the overcrowded tenements along it, we have a brief statement, so to speak, of the entirely inadequate resources of the poor in every way. Tenement reform has undertaken to bring to the knowledge of the public the horrid condition of the houses hired by the poor, but no descriptions had given me a real knowledge of how dark the passages are in the daytime, how miserably inadequate the water supply, how impossible that the masses of poor in tenements should keep themselves or their quarters clean.

You go into a kitchen, which is the principal room of a suite of apartments. The first thing to greet the eye is a huge tub, which to the rest of the room bears the proportion of a large centre-table; the stove is another large feature; the dining-table is still another, covered with a litter of unwashed dishes and crusts of bread. You proceed to enter the room, and the scream of a child calls your attention to a baby on which you have almost stepped as it sprawls upon the floor. You attempt to sit down upon a chair, and find that you run the risk of sitting down upon two larger children who are leaning over it. You look around for a place where you may put your cloak or basket, and there does not seem to be a single spot where some unclean article or small human being is not already in the way. If you come in about twelve o'clock, the already crowded apartment is thrown into some consternation by the arrival of the father of the family, who wishes for his dinner—which is never ready for him. If a baby is sick, it is bolstered up in a rocking-chair on two pillows, or else is brought out of the little bedroom—a dark closet —where it has been buried alive without a breath of air. In this bedroom there is a medley of things—clothing, baby-carriage and boxes. How this mother of a family, who smiles upon you and does her best to be gracious, can possibly keep things clean in so little room, and with so many children, is a question that you cease to ask from that time. You know she cannot possibly do it. It seems strange that so dreadful a place should be of infinite value to a family herding in it, but if the rent-money has not been saved or has not been earned, almost the only thought in the mind of each member of the family is that the landlord will turn them out upon the street. This he almost always threatens to do in the most savage manner, though there are some patient landlords who wait a month or two. I have known a family of father and mother and four children who were living in one little attic room, with a sort of closet attached, the mother earning all the revenue—because her husband was consumptive—by sewing for the sweat-shop. She finally became ill from overwork, and the severity of the landlord towards her, as she sat in her chair dying, as we supposed, was so terrible that he could not have spoken more harshly. This sort of thing is repeated all the time. It therefore did not surprise me that one snowy day a man came excitedly into my little room in Scammel street, with a pale, thin man beside him, to whom he pointed, saying that this man's wife was very ill, having a newly born baby, and being at that moment upon the sidewalk as the snow fell, with her baby in her arms, her other children beside her and no money (because of no work) to find another home. The man who spoke was the foreman of one of the street cleaning gangs. He said that his own pay would not come in for a few days, or he would give this man ten dollars to settle in other rooms. At the moment I was nearly at the bottom of my purse and had no resources, and was obliged to refuse to aid him. I, the one patient who was living with me then, and my one assistant, passed a very uncomfortable night, and have often wondered since if that mother and child survived the severity of their landlord.

I do not blame landlords for insisting upon having their rent; I am not sure, even, that I blame them for asking so high a price in the aggregate for house-room in tumble-down tenements, since they are so often cheated out of their rent; but I certainly blame somebody or something—I have not yet decided to whom the blame belongs—for the constant lack of rent-money among the poor. I think, however, that the blame attaches to the charitable, who should interest themselves in so vast and primal a need.

Since having a little more money given to me, I have been quite generous about rents, although told by my advisers not to "touch them." Of course, in caring for a patient, it was out of the question to have her placed upon the sidewalk, and this may give an idea of the way in which I have become involved in paying rents. If we help the poor at all, we must remember that they claim the necessity of having at least a few inches on a floor under a roof. It is about all they get, at best, in the human hives of which so much is said poetically in fiction and the daily press. If the poor want these hives more than anything else, why should we make our assistance touch everything else first, leaving the question of rents to the last? I have been told that the rent-money is always found. Of course, after living amongst these people for a year, I have found that this is not the case. Often the family move without paying the back rent, and by making a small deposit for the next month's housing. One of my patients, suffering from a most terrible cancer and dropsy, which gave her additional agony, was never without a perfect terror over her rent-money. I could give her fuel, a little clothing (which was generously donated by a city dry-goods firm), a bed—she and two daughters slept in one bed, and the son upon a couch in the same room—I could give her food, salves, medicines, doctor's advice; and after all was done, her face was still drawn up into an expression of misery, always because of the rent which must be paid, and the savage visit which was soon to come from an angry landlord. Now, I think that charity ought to take hold of this matter of rents.

As I go to and fro on my errands, I see the van which is such a familiar sight in front of some door, furniture being hustled into it in great haste, and a tearful woman with frightened children clinging to her, standing by as the men are bringing out her few chattels, and she looks at me with that fixed expression which implies that the person has come to desperation; and I pass with a guilty feeling that I have no right to escape a responsibility which, somehow, I feel concerning this stranger, whom I might have helped at a moment when she saw no possible help among the hard-hearted companions who refused to respond to her appealing glances.

One disadvantage of crowded tenements is that a family which is very depraved may be placed above a family which is respectable, and hideous noises of drunken people, the screams of women and violent tossings about of furniture and bodies (which have to my knowledge driven sick persons almost insane) bring down large pieces of the ceiling, and render the abode uninhabitable. These are frequent occurrences. Imagine a bent and feeble woman of nearly seventy years of age, racked with rheumatism, unnerved from ten years of lonely life in the same tenement, so ill at last with want of food and with pain that she can hardly leave her bed. Imagine her startled at night by an attack upon her door from a strong drunken woman who insists on entering. This drunken woman wishes to enter for the reason that the invalid has made complaint against her which has caused the landlord to send in a "dispossess." She explains, outside the door, that she means to kill the old lady inside, when she gets in. Upon which the old lady on the inside struggles out of bed, opens her little window, which is barely large enough to allow a person to pass through, and calls in the night to her neighbors on the other side of the backyard to come to her rescue. The drunken woman still threatens and pounds and shakes the door. No one appears to help the poor old woman who is being attacked, and in terror she struggles through her small window and falls some distance into the yard. The consequence is that she has months of illness and semi-aberration. If these tenements were not often made a place for the indiscriminate herding of any one who will pay the landlord a few dollars, such contrasts between the inmates would not exist; but the fact is I could cite many instances truly horrible to show that landlords use very little of their Christian light in these dark abodes.

On the first night when I arrived in the poor district and trem- blingly took up my new life in a little tenement of a few rooms, where I thought I had every reason to expect marauders or hopelessly drunken invaders, the voices of children along the street at nine or ten o'clock, prattling close to my low windows were the first notes of that sweet element of the amenities of the poor, which exists in many dark places of fortune.

The children of the poor are in many respects the blessings of the poor. We must keep fast hold of this truth in treating of the question; for, while the loveliest element to be found in poverty, as in wealth, is child life, of course, there is nothing so sad as a suffering child, whether from disease or starvation. Also, there is nothing so shocking as a blas- phemous child, and there is almost nothing so dirty as a neglected child on the East Side. But do not let the rich suppose that they monopolize the exquisite happiness of parentage, or that their children are so very different in their contentment of play from the little urchins who con- struct their playthings for themselves and gaily sing the same song day after day, it being the only one they happen to know.

Of course there are crowds of children, and we cannot see any good excuse for their existence. Little things of six months or a year old, even those of three years old, are tenderly loved and petted by parents who cannot support them; but when they get beyond the fascinating age of helpless infancy, they receive a wonderful amount of hard treatment, and it astonishes me to see a mother adoring her infant and very nearly swearing at her child of four years. It seems as if instinct was the only factor in the matter, and it is fortunate that God made it, because at least the babies come in for a share of gentleness.

The fresh air which the children imbibe, being turned out of doors all day to make room for their mothers' work, is not of the best, unless a good, strong wind fills their lungs. But playing out in the open air must do good, and consequently they seem merry and comfortable, even if full of naughtiness and extremely hungry.

The children of the poor also have the advantage of constant excitement. The guarded and regulated pastimes of children of higher life, however varied by individual mischief and unruliness, cannot compare with the frantic enjoyment of an East Side street. Up to a late hour in the evening, with liberty to scream and shout at the top of one's lungs, to build bonfires anywhere, to seize an abandoned wash-boiler and drag it at break-neck speed over the stones in a rabble of boys, creating a noise that strikes delightful misery to every housekeeper's heart along the route, is an outline of the fun. No apple-orchard in the country, or elaborate gymnasiums, could possibly vie in interest with the back-yard sheds, over which the boys clamber at the risk of their necks, and upon which they stand defiantly as aged and much-injured men and women argue with them, fling flower-pots at them, and swear they will have their life-blood.

The staid and elaborate pirouettes of the dancing-school are wearisome in comparison to the gay waltzes of the children around the piano-organ, which is a constant visitor. Very pretty and graceful measures are footed by the girls, from little midgets of two years, up. One of the prettiest scenes I ever saw in my life, I caught a glimpse of from my back window, finding in the yard a group of little girls who had dressed themselves in tissue papers of various colors—these colored streamers and sashes making them very beautiful at a small expense. A girl of ten, one of the brightest and oldest, was director of ceremonies, and put the children through a series of elocutionary numbers and songs, in imitation of the kindergarten to which they all went. The superior talent of the smallest child, who knew her verses perfectly and sang sweetly and moved charmingly, was not more entertaining than the melancholy stupidity of an older little maid who could not be induced to say more than two lines of her "piece," which she repeated with a most amusing inefficiency. The finished manners of these little things while performing under my gaze were most surprising. One would have supposed that they had been accustomed to quiet and orderly homes. It encouraged me to believe that the barriers between the children of the poor and a true refinement are very slight and pliant. God seems to have placed this in the poor homes—whatever else Satan places there—a quick susceptibility among the children to what is beautiful and gentle.

I very soon began to long for the relief which the greetings of these small people gave me as I started out on my somewhat painful rounds of work, or came back weary from them. Their sweet voices, sincere smiles and caressing hands I thanked heaven for as much as for the glorious skies toward which I looked for a similar consolation. I have never found, in a long year, that the children failed me; they are as dear and necessary to me now as ever, and will always be kind.

I have not touched at all upon the deep problems suggested to the wise by the fact that the children of the poor are so disproportionate in numbers to the means for bringing them up. I do not believe that there is any help for that, and so it does not interest me; but I think that it is a most hopeful fact that they give to this class its finest sentiments. As a poor woman said to me: the only consolation the poor have is to bring up their little bit of a family—meaning its dozen.

I have had occasion to notice the children of the poor, although I never expected to have anything to do with them. They insist upon having hip disease and curvature of the spine; and try as I will to get rid of such cases without doing anything for them, the mothers prevent this convenient scheme from being carried out; and they even succeed in making me plunge deeply into the dilemmas of a godmother (dragging after me the females connected in my work), because these little infants have nothing to wear and their parents nothing to eat—and, to tell the truth, because it is one of the happiest moments of my life when I know that the little child in my arms, or whom I send in the arms of one I trust, is being brought to the Lord by us.

Many children come to me with sores of graded seriousness, and please me by becoming well. Sometimes there is an exclamation in my rooms, "Where did all the babies come from!" infants and little children being collected there. I cannot step out of the door, or appear at the window, or pass along the street, without some cheerful childish voice calling out, "Hello! hello!" and pronouncing my name with affection and politeness. The rough boys who receive from most of the population nothing less expressive or severe than pails of hot water and loud harangues of reproof as they sit smoking cigarettes upon the crowded stoops, are so good as to spring up at my entrance, with soft murmurs to each other, urging haste. To be sure, there have been times when my indignation has been so aroused at improper behavior toward some one in whom I was interested, or by profanity overheard, or the smoking of cigarettes by extremely young boys, that I have sallied forth, like some dangerous harpy, and pounced upon the first offender within reach with no sparing of a rough shake or dire threat. But this very seldom happens, and the boys never seem to like me the less for it.

The saddest side of the life of the children of the poor is their unfortunate sharing of excited broils in the family; their witnessing of gross immorality, and their familiarity with wicked conversation. I have known a family well, because living in the tenement's basement, which I first became acquainted with through drunken fights that I could not but hear, while the children cried loudly in abject terror. I meddled somewhat in this state of things several times. For many months the scenes have not recurred, and dozens of happy incidents have been evolved during the summer in these formerly perturbed lives. The children seem happy; the parents seem gentle. Verily, it is not worth while to give up hope in any situation.

Another distressing element in the lives of the children is the necessity for their working. The law as to age is not regarded—at any rate, under some administrations—and parents and children have both told me that fifty cents have managed the difficulty of being under age if the right official is approached. Then the schooling is interfered with; the child is made old before his or her time; and, on the other hand, the parents as well as the children are supported, when, without this juvenile help, the family would starve. In the last year or two, when grown men and women could get no work, the children have brought in their pittance regularly. Both the children's being cognizant of immorality and every adult misdemeanor, and their proper development being retarded by being made penny-earning machines, are abominations that should be eradicated; and I consider it a disgrace that wise and good people in our government, and in the departments of thought and science, should not turn their chief attention to such poisoning and stunting of young souls and intelligences. I am sure I cannot imagine how these abuses are to be prevented, unless by the slow but sure process of widespread personal influence. The college-settlement idea and the kindergarten idea are valiantly laboring to this end; and if men and women who could be better employed than they are now, would say to themselves that they would go as missionaries not many yards away from their own homes and interests and uplift the poor and train the children by many a night-school, many a reading room, the ignorant misdemeanors of profanity and vituperation and personal violence would be driven out, because other ideas would be introduced. And if the poverty of the poor were studied by men and women with a quarter of the fervor which is given to the study of mathematics, the classics, and all other paraphernalia of high-schools and colleges—

studied on the ground, personally, thoroughly understood and met— the children of the poor would study more mathematics and classics, and would develop, mentally and physically, as every human being has a right to develop, after being, with no option of his own, brought into the well-seasoned happiness of human existence.

Slumming has been dabbled in, as children in white cambric frocks poke at frogs, along the margin of a pond, with pink parasols. English persons were the first to parody the life work of certain great men of the last fifty years, by performing in this matter of visiting the poor in a way which left nothing to the imagination of the editors of Punch. They had only to copy as they copied the fantastic art of the aesthetic school, which made good taste grotesque. In this country the best papers have endeavored to show up, as they always do any absurdities, the offensive charity of the call by the rich in broughams and the twenty-five cent donation, which have invaded the dignity of poverty in worthy families who are starving. Personal effort in regard to the poor is not meant here to include any thing of this sort, and no Catholic of cultivation in the archives of our Church would be really amused by studying these harlequin attempts to spring into the position of a dispenser of mercy.

The distance up Fifth Avenue sometimes seems as far and as frozen as the road to the now famous mines of Alaska. That is, it seems so, when I stand in my little rooms very nearly at the end of my money for the time being, and ask myself if I have the courage and the skill to enter the homes of the well-to-do and the rich and beg for the homes that are destitute. The greatest possible encouragement has been given to me by individuals sending donations—principally small, some large —and I am convinced, as I have often said in print, that charity can be dispensed adequately (Oh, wonderful word, which I dare to use!) if we only know how to explain the need for it to the avenues of means through which it shall be sent.

What am I trying to do down here among the poor? To make impossible the homeless condition of incurable cancer patients; to make impossible their semi-neglect in homes that are unfit for them; to take the lowest class we know, both in poverty and suffering, and put them in such a condition, that if our Lord knocked at the door we should not be ashamed to show what we have done. This is a great hope, and may never be fulfilled by me.

I have with me in this first year of 1896–7 two women of mature age who are wonderfully active in carrying on my housekeeping and visiting among the poor; and a young woman who helps me with short hand and typewriting; and a young girl who does an immense amount of housework, and an old, nearly blind patient who is busy all day long in the kitchen; I have a washerwoman who needs work for her large family, which she finds it very difficult to obtain; and also three women from uptown who promise to help me a great deal this winter in visiting, etc. The helpers proper give their labor without remuneration. There are five cancer patients in the house, and we expect one more very soon—all destitute and perfect instances of such need as I am striving to meet with assistance; and five families outside who are troubled with ulcers, cancers or other diseases; and several pensioners whom we could not turn away, because of their worthiness and their hunger. I have several excellent examples of imposture, I am told, who will not be turned away until detected in misdemeanors of which they are accused by their neighbors, but of which they show no signs to me. I have a reputation among some of those people, who judge one harshly and whose opinion is of less than no consequence, of rather liking to help drunkards. I never do, if I know it; though I may some day help a drunkard in some manner, as a matter of high principle. I have looked for it, but cannot find a strict ruling out of sinners from charity by the authority we ought to serve.

The afternoons are filled with relays of persons, principally women, suffering from ulcers. It is safe to believe that few women, who are constantly on their feet at work, constantly deprived of proper food, constantly worried, are not afflicted with ulcers, which are the result of non-nutrition and general debility. Men are also treated if they come to the house.

It will be seen from the above statement that the charity which I have attempted to start is no longer one to be sneered at. The likelihood is that it will grow, and our hope is that it will hit out many a good idea for the alleviation of the poor, if it only includes in the course of time, a sufficient number of bright brains among the women.

A CHEERFUL VIEW OF A HARD PROBLEM
CATHOLIC WORLD 68 (FEBRUARY, 1899): 659–69

Editor's Note: In 1899 Rose Hawthorne Lathrop published the following article in an effort to attract women to her cause. To do so, she had to minimize some of the fear most women experienced at the thought of working among the poorest people of New York City. She needed generous and courageous women, but at the same time, she did not want to suggest that hers was a life of martyrdom and unmitigated suffering. The article was illustrated with pictures of the Lower East

Side with captions such as, "City Life has a Picturesqueness All Its Own," or "A Bit of Fresh Air from the River." The most interesting picture shows the small dining room at Water Street and the three women who shared quarters there. Rose, dressed somewhat formally, is pouring coffee, Alice Huber stands unsmilingly but calm in the background, and (probably) Cecelia Higley stands confidently in the foreground, one arm akimbo.

*

I do not know that a charity is ever looked upon as a pleasant pastime. It usually is taken with a large amount of seasoning, such as fairs, sewing-bees, church suppers, and all that sort of thing; and even then the real work is done by persons at the seat of war, so to speak. When the idea is suggested, to people who do not even attend sewing-bees or affairs in aid of the poor, that one should diligently labor for the destitute in the worst condition of disease and want known, the response is usually one of genuine horror. It is said that there is no such condition of things, just as I fancy some of us would be very apt to say there were not certain conditions of sin which a long life sometimes brings to notice.

The subject about which I write, and which I would gladly make interesting to the general public, is one that can hardly be made agreeable; but nevertheless I can testify that such a life as I lead with a few companions in a poor district, among the sick, has many agreeable points. As it is my earnest desire to get women to join me who have a natural talent for nursing and a natural inclination to nurse those who need it most, I think it might be well for me to present the bright side of the care of the cancerous poor.

I suppose any one thinking of half a dozen women working on the East Side of New York, living in a tenement and working in tenements, would think first of all of the suffocation of bad air, the unpleasant aspect of things generally, to say nothing of the frightful dangers from footpads and drunken creatures. Now, the first thing that strikes me when I emerge from the house, early in the morning, is the fresh air from the East River, rushing towards me over a large park which could not be better regulated as to neatness and good taste in arrangement. Then I become conscious of some beautiful effects of sky and cloud, the charming outlines of Brooklyn across the water, with its lovely tints under the rising sun; and I see the Navy-yard shining with its white cruisers, that frequently boom out their salutes to incoming or outgoing companions. Often a sailboat, and sometimes a craft as large as a four-masted schooner, trips rapidly over the water at the foot of the square, past the other shipping, making a vigorous and delightful scene. There is absolutely no stifled air or loss of all particularly fine outlooks in going to work for the poor in Water Street. The melancholy notion that in living among the poor one is in constant danger as to life and property, has given place in our minds to considerable doubt as to whether there is any really dangerous place where people can live; and though I have spent a life often terrified in imagination at the memory of what our ancestors suffered from the Indians, and what we might suffer from them if we went far enough West, I am beginning to believe that the stories of Indian ferocity would dwindle down to inoffensive fellowship if I threw myself upon Indian mercy. I pass through the streets all about here, some of them with murderous reputations, and were I not alone I would laughingly discuss the wonderful neatness and quiet, and sufficiently patrolled condition, of these alarming streets. The house in which I live, a tumble-down tenement, has its front door always ajar, and the windows of our rooms on the first floor were not locked until a nervous patient came to us.

Of course a hospital home, such as I hope to induce the public to obtain for us, will be pleasant and neat as any structure can be when it is simple and adequate. Women know how easy it is to produce pretty effects without confusion, overcrowding or over-expense. I do not think that the free cancer hospital I have in prospect will have many unpleasant features, but I am not surprised to find that persons, calling upon me to investigate our little tenement home for incurables, step in hesitatingly, with a shocked expression already adjusted; and if they do venture upstairs—where they see not only the outside patients, who come to have ulcers dressed, but the real cancer cases, mostly in an advanced condition—feel very keenly the sudden revelation of suffering, because there is no way of shutting off this state of things, my home at present being as informal and crowded as a private house into which have been brought the wounded from a skirmish in war-time. It is wonderful, however, to find how soon the nurse loses her horror of a peculiar case, and takes intelligent interest in attending to and amusing a person so much afflicted. I hear a great deal in my visits to cases to which I am called about the outcries and general agony of persons who are ill with cancer, but proper dressings immediately produce some ease, and proper medicines quiet the nerves; so that it is a matter of comment among ourselves from day to day how little the patients seem to suffer who, we would suppose, would be in a state of active torture every hour. There is really very little torture even in this horrible disease when the treatments recommended at the New York Cancer Hospital are adopted. Perhaps several times a day there may be great suffering, but the sick have a great deal of comfort, if anyone tries to give it to them.

There is, of course, some difficulty to the nurses in exchanging a style of living which is orderly and comparatively quiet for the turmoil of a pauper district. I rank my sufferings in regard to noises with the other two trials of sleepiness not indulged in and weariness not rested. I really thought at one time that I should not be able to bear the constant uproar of the children and the midnight revels of the drunkards, but I must confess that I scarcely perceive now, after four months of what is called the noisiest street in New York, the rollicking or brawling racket always going on. It would seem that the human frame is really a slave whom it is possible to subject at every point, and that the strength of the slave is herculean when once the creature is fully conquered. It is impossible to get entirely away from the amenities of life! Into the turmoil of which I have hinted there constantly come, to people who have had connection with a more fortunate existence messages and visitors from the old social circle, and these sweeten life very much. Little mementos and ornaments creep in, to win our hearts over again to the joys of existence; and it soon becomes an affectionate warfare with the people we love who remain in the world, in order that the nurses who have given their lives up to hard work may not be kidnapped, to be kept in durance within the confines of luxury at frequent intervals during the year. But somehow the determination to carry the work of charity on with completeness and adequate help to the poor is the dearest aim for anyone who has once tasted the nectar of a self-denial which does not limit itself in idea, however weakly human nature cringes at some steps to be taken. I doubt if any district nurse or nurse in a hospital in a poor district, who has laid out for herself a plan at all in keeping with the commands of the New Testament, would feel so much at ease in her old surroundings of rest and amusement as under the yoke of charitable labor. Nevertheless, the glimpses of friends which she gets, through their generous pilgrimages over unfamiliar streets in order to see her and cheer her, are like refreshing draughts on a long journey afoot. The postman's budget of letters is beautiful with handwriting that is precious, and the words of encouragement brought by mail or spoken during a rapid call are found simply indispensable to her courage. It must also be noted that the humble appreciation and cordiality of the poor, sometimes awkward, sometimes refined and beautiful because of the naturally gentle natures of many of the poor, are a very sweet daily element in district work.

Often there is a great deal of picturesqueness about the pauper life itself, to say nothing of figures and tints among children and laborers which might be painted with a great satisfaction to the best art-critics. There are the startlingly effective groups of young folks around a huge bonfire, of which there is a brilliant series during the winter-time. One night, as I walked home in the moonlight by the water, I saw a row of four immense drays, seated, as it were, upon the cobble-stones, with their shafts drawn up towards the sky. A brilliant ruddy light touched off all the outlines, and close to one of the carts was to be seen the great bonfire some boys had built, the nucleus of the blaze being a barrel and the moving spirit a can of kerosene. It was a bitterly cold night, and the boys had all an air of conscious wisdom as they grouped themselves about this delightful centre. These bonfires may be found at all points roaring and dancing away to the satisfaction of the entire populace. No box or basket or old sofa, or any inflammable material, is quite safe in winter days, and no one seems to think of interrupting the boys in their ecstatic play with fire.

To wait for a car on some of the outlying streets of the city is to give one's self five minutes, very likely, of a brisk Italian scene, where a cheap tenement house is being run up in short order. Handsome creatures in artistic garb, prettily varied in colors of shirt and scarf, slide down and up the ladders with graceful motions of unburdened steps, or the equally graceful motions of struggling muscles weighted with a heavy load. Everywhere on the East Side one is likely to happen upon the never-wearying effects of the shipping and blue, windy water or misty shores; and here in New York the pedestrian always has a chance, at the right hour, to catch picture after picture of the western heavens down cross-streets, which are all the more soul-stirring from their contrast to the scene which has been looked at all day long, within tenement walls.

In regard to starting a new charity, there is an opinion prevalent that nothing will be met with but discouragement from those who are expected to be charitable. A very rich man has not only his city and country house, perhaps somewhat multiplied also, but he will be sure to tell you that he has two hospitals on his hands. In short, an Egyptian hieroglyphic of one of the Pharaohs is the only thing that could illustrate his hampered condition. You are told the the well-to-do have spent their pin-money on the foreign missions, and that in a year's time you will cease to exist as a new charity. The fact is, that a new charity which is as much needed as that dealing with orphans, a charity dealing with women destitute of care and unable to support themselves, yet in the grasp of a terrible disease, is responded to with the depth of cordiality which greets a call to arms if one's country is in danger, supposing the responder to be capable of nobility. The methods of securing aid and manipulating resources in charity are by no means as exquisitely finished and effective as those used in national defence, but let me prophesy that they will be one of these days.

The first thing to do in my opinion, is for those who can best afford the time to give themselves to the labor of so perfecting the science of charity that it may become adequate, instead of being as it is at present, often ridiculously defective. Who are these members of the race who have the most time to give, and who will least be missed in withdrawing themselves from "the world," so-called? They are women who have no indissoluble ties, and who have the good sense to realize that the life of an earnest woman, wherever she is, is one of suffering. They are the women who choose to do with less of the ameliorations of life to this good end of nursing destitute women, which I have stated to be, in my opinion, of equal importance with patriotism. I was informed about a French charity which takes care in a number of hospitals, both in France and England, of incurable cancer cases.

I was told that in America these incurable cases, when destitute, are terribly neglected; and, if attended to at all, are dismissed from hospitals after six months, whether death steps in as a relief or years of suffering must ensue. I felt that, as I had time to give to charity, this was the charity I would take up, in the hope of assisting to repeat here the success of the charity in France. Doctors told me there was great need of the work, as a large number of cases existed among the poor and were increasing constantly. Most of my friends begged me not to enter into such a loathesome occupation. I persisted; took a few rooms in the poorest district; immediately found myself appealed to by persons afflicted with the disease; soon had several patients living with me in my little rooms, and was joined by a few women as interested as myself in the scheme. At the end of two years and a half I find myself more strenuously encouraged by the sympathy of others than at the beginning of my work. Once in a while I fortify my finances by appeals in the daily press for money, clothing, and finances for the poor sick I care for, and immediately there is a moderate response from charitable persons, sufficient to keep me at my post.

It is the hope of the Servants of Relief, as we call ourselves, that a permanent home, accommodating at least fifteen patients, may be secured by methods for obtaining public interest; and we believe that this house will in itself strike the public, in future, as an argument that carries its point well. Our peculiar trait will be, that we dwell closely among the poor, sharing as much as possible, if the expression can be permitted, their deprivations, and also their cold and heat, their laborious effort to exist, and their old-fashioned harshness of convenience, in order that these things may be remembered and done away with. We trust that our own laborious effort will help to elucidate the difficult question of how a charity-hospital may be a kindly home.

As soon as a woman is incapacitated for self-support, she should be given a home by those who are capable of giving it to her; and that home should not be a travesty, but worthy of the sacred name.

We have no object in life but to supply this need, in one line of its outreaching growth from the central root of destitution; and as women never turn aside from misery without assisting it, and as we have hundreds of letters from men and women which express entire enthusiasm for our budding endeavor we believe that both women's work and men's money will enrich this charity for the immediate help of destitute souls.

CHRIST'S POOR

Editor's Note: Christ's Poor was officially a monthly report of the work of the Servants of Relief. It contained lists of donors, financial records, anecdotes, and occasional fillers, such as speeches by President Theodore Roosevelt, whom Mother Alphonsa admired. Occasionally the periodical (or Mother Alphonsa, who wrote it almost single-handedly), responded to criticism, either oblique or direct. In such cases, she would publish the letters, along with her response. Most of the issues have printed on the outside back cover the following citation: "As He hung upon the cross, His enemies dared Him to come down if He were the Son of God. But He descended not; leaving them to conclude that He had not the power, that He was an imposter, the basest of men. And thus He died." Sister Rose Huber's *Memoirs* indicate that someone had referred to the small community as "imposters," and that unnamed clerics had tried to influence Archbishop Corrigan against them. The repeated quotation would seem to be a response to such criticism. Another excerpt from *Christ's Poor* is important in this connection. In February, 1902, Mother Alphonsa printed a passage with commentary from the life of Henri Lacordaire, who, in the nineteenth century restored the Dominican Order in France. She comments that the original property of Rosary Hill had been owned by the very French Dominican missionaries founded by Père Lacordaire and that "the spirit of Lacordaire lingers about Rosary Hill." The excerpts from the biography she cites are almost exclusively references to the social dimension of Lacordaire's preaching. She entitles her brief article, "The Elasticity of Apostolates." By citing one of the most prestigious of Dominican authorities she was able to justify—if that were necessary—a congregation whose life and ministry was less directly educational than most of the Dominican congregations in the United States. She insisted quietly that Dominican spirituality, which she had grown to love, especially through the example of St. Rose of Lima, included a conspicuous pastoral concern for the poor and that her own congregation proclaimed that concern. Every issue included a print of Francois Millet's "The Man with the Hoe" and an excerpt from Edwin's Markham's poem of the same name.

Christ's Poor was first printed at the Novitiate of the Dominican Fathers at Somerset, Ohio. After 1904, it could no longer be sustained financially.

THE OBJECTS OF THE WORK

Editor's Note: The following essay appeared in every issue of *Christ's Poor* as a short mission statement of the charity Rose Hawthorne Lathrop envisioned. In it we see both her realism and her imagination. She believed it possible that every parish have two houses for the relief of the sick poor. Apart from implementing that astonishing plan, the congregation has remained faithful to the principles which were elaborated at the inception of the work.

*

To provide for destitute incurables of both sexes. The first forlorn condition to be met by adequate accommodation and care is that of cancer, at present left in dreadful neglect.

Other diseases in the incurable stage among destitute persons of both sexes will be attended to when the members of the Community become sufficiently numerous to extend the work, either without, or with, hired help.

Hired help will never be allowed in such force that the Sisters will lose personal control of cases, and will only be admitted when the benefit of the poor demands that the exception should be made, as in the case of male cases, who will sometimes require hired male help.

An important object of the charity is to look carefully to the interests of the poor, especially whenever the interests of science are held in autocratical estimation by persons of inferior judgment, as opposed to the enlightened and noble verdict of eminent physicians. Incurable cancer is now a matter of general and exhaustive study, and the poor supply the principal material used. This clause is of deepest concern to those who are really devoted to destitute misery. Reference cannot be made to policy or special approval of a human order, but to God's approval alone, notwithstanding the unfailing accompaniment of opposition from Pharisee and Money-changer which such a course involves.

To prove that cancer is not dangerous to nurse, with the precautions used by any neat method, or even when accidents of contact unfortunately occur. This is one of the chief uses of the charity, since the dread of cancer is so great that much inhumanity is shown in the neglect to undertake proper "dressings" of wounds, and the desire to be rid of a member of the family who is afflicted with the malady.

To show by record of experience the best methods of relieving pain, odor and excessive corruption in the disease, which are frequently increased by "dressings," etc., such as are now usually prescribed, and found in many of the cases to which the nurses are called.

To prove that the only way to meet the great sufferings of the poor sick is to enlist the interest and personal service of the women of the different parishes, who could properly and fully attend to all cases of destitute incurables of all sorts, if they would religiously devote a part of each week to them, at times never to be postponed or delegated.

To prove that the public is willing and able to provide all the money and many articles necessary for such charitable care as we undertake to give; and that in each parish two houses for cancer and its kindred diseases could and should be established, from which the cases may be sent to larger Homes in the country, when death is not imminent.

To prove that many cases of incurable cancer can be cared for at home, wherever there is a member able to nurse the sick person, or a member whose wage-earning had seemed to make an insuperable difficulty. The wage-earning can be postponed by the payment of the rent and other necessaries through the charity of the public. This precaution encourages proper kindness and devotion on the part of the family of the sick person, and obviates the bitter sorrow of the patient, who loves children and sisters, when no longer loved in return. The cancerous member of the family, man or woman, is as a rule superior in character to the rest of the members, and has incurred the disease of cancer by generous labor for those who refuse to do the nursing when tragic conditions develop. To urge Christian kindness upon dark intellects which may fall into error of this sort, is a great necessity. On the other hand, instances will be cited later of sublime devotion, difficult to imitate in any class of the human family.

To add another definite charitable activity to those already existing, which is of a nature to hasten the spread of the light of intelligence, morality and religion, and a gracious decency, in the homes of the poor of cities, from the intimate investigation and companionship afforded by tragic circumstances to the friends who bring relief.

WHAT ECONOMY IS KIND?
CHRIST'S POOR 1 (NOVEMBER 1901): 4–7

Editor's Note: Mother Alphonsa's irony and epigrammatic style is especially evident in these somewhat acerbic comments on misdirected frugality. Rarely has the identification of the poor with God's cause been so accurately expressed, or lack of generosity so targeted. "Economy is the most dangerous gift to bestow upon others, if we value our reputation with God."

*

The atmosphere of economy is very precarious to the health. It requires Scottish prudence to be prepared at all points to meet those insidious influences, from the effects of which our system may never recover. A particular shawl and wool and whiskey were invented to foil the dangers of Scotch fog, and economy demands a similar inventiveness. We must ward off chills and pessimism, when a gray, godless thief of expressionless parsimony lays its hand upon the human heart, beating for sunshine and blue sky, not for dampness and cold cessation of generosity. I will say at the outset that I believe no economy is kind in charity, except what is provided by the will of God in circumstances over which the giver has no control, because the will of God is unmistakably perceived. Obligations that must obviously be met, control obligations which we generously would like to meet. To a person of good conscience "and very good heart," duty will not dishonestly prevent our fulfilling schemes which we wish ardently to embrace for the benefit of others. The whole puzzle lies in a nicety of self-analysis, and the whole virtue in the ardor of tender compassion. Without analysis and without tenderness we race cheerfully on to death on the nag of self-righteousness, and break our spiritual necks at the goal because false righteousness balks. To be lavish towards others with our help and niggardly towards self with our ease, is a system that will not look so unchristian to the God Who died for us, as the system of being niggardly towards everyone but ourselves.

If we are endeavoring to make a good business venture of generosity, to make charity pay for itself, or even to make God's command to cherish the widow and fatherless leave us as well off as if we had ignored these poor people, we shall see at the last moment of our life, or at the first glimpse of our next home, that we have mocked Christ. Considering how much good the bestowal of money and effects can do, we should not voluntarily throw away a penny of our funds. But if by a too careful investigation we throw away charity instead of coin, we shall be asked for the multiplication of the talent without having accumulated it; we shall learn that it would have been better to err in spending money than in spending grace.

If we look at any of the charities and institutions and organizations criticized by commissioners of inspection, we shall find that various forms of meanness are the cause of abuse and suffering. We do not look for murderous brutality as a common article of circulation in such places, though always and of late revelations of this brutality have been made in the investigations of unpaid and disinterested men. But we would be foolish not to expect to find dishonorable or uncharitable parsimony in most of the places where funds are used by paid people for the people who may not complain without increased danger,—those who are dependent but held cheaply,—those especially, in other words, whom God holds tenderly and commends to noble-minded persons as likely to be in hard straits of injustice. If we read honest reports, or look into facts for ourselves, we are very much wanting in mental grasp if we do not expect offences (wholly unnecessary where supervision is earnest) in institutions for the care of the poor, whenever salaries are sought.

In the case of the navy itself, our throes of excessive adoration for sailors if they are blown up on the Maine or are killed in a brisk naval engagement, have resulted in discovering that they are fed like dogs of no particular breed or value. Cocoa made with water was good enough for them—would it have been good enough for us? Economy is the most dangerous gift to bestow upon others, if we value our reputation with God. It will be ranked in the same category as the fire-water graciously extended to the Indian by his enemies, who were Christians of the most self-righteous description.

To set an expensive precedent in the treatment of the poor is a matter of great concern, and should be done only after religious reflection, for the poor will lose their holy gratitude, through our fault, towards a kindness that is more guarded by wisdom, in case a reckless expenditure, having no justification, is made.

What shall be said, then, of the reckless elegance of buildings, and the reckless apportionment of salaries, in institutions, organizations and hospitals, and of the severe economies in these places which are enforced on behalf of the poor, for whom the places are founded? What shall we say of cold and scant meals for the very sick, while their care-takers are so well fed that their larders are a matter of delicate non-supervision? A sum of a hundred dollars is weighed with trembling precision in fingers of cautious charity, before being expended upon the poor. Upon any other department of charity it is considered most ineffective. The economies of a great institution pinch no one but those who cannot cry out. We must admit that religious reflection has not been used, but a worldly prudence that would cower before the Bible, if it ever approached closely enough thereto. Holy gratitude may well turn away from the doorstep of such charity, as the poor body enters its portal, the only resource in a hard world; and a hard resource only because gentle and noble people have not known how their charity has been transformed in hands that are not inspired by being consecrated to mercy.

It seems to me that economy should show itself above all in the manner of life of care-takers. These persons should be fed, shod and harbored more roughly than the poor of the charity; by which means the horse is gently led to his rightful end of the cart, and without any magnifying glass or tip of the cane applied to the problem before us, we can all see that the proper spirit has established the proper action. Nothing in connection with the dispensing of charity should be expensive, except the magnificent proportions of the area covered by genuine, persistent and intelligent relief. House, furniture, carriages, food should all be simple, and better than elegance in a downright shabbiness. If the poor sneer at this as human beings, always prone to be mistaken and unkind whether well or ill brought up,—God in these, His most cherished members, does not sneer; and many a true-hearted destitute creature will cheer one on by a sincere blessing from grateful eyes and sorrow-stricken hand.

SOME OF THE REASONS WHY WE WORK
CHRIST'S POOR 1:4 (NOVEMBER 1901): 18–25

Editor's Note: The first biographer of Mother Alphonsa, James J. Walsh, refers to the following essay as her *apologia pro vita sua.* (See *Mother Alphonsa: Rose Hawthorne Lathrop* [New York: MacMillan, 1930]. Mother Alphonsa knew something of the conditions of the "Cuban War" through her nephew Jack, who was seriously ill during that conflict, and for whose safe return she had prayed. A letter to Minne describes her happiness upon hearing of his arrival home. The essay is significant not only because of the topical analogy she draws between

her patients and suffering, unassisted soldiers, but because of her in-
dictment of bureaucratic inaction on their behalf. She attributes inaction to the voicelessness of the poor. Eventually the soldiers in Cuba
were attended to. If the sick poor were wounded soldiers from a popular war, they too would be cared for with the resources of a powerful
country, for responsibility is commensurate with power. If those suffering were members of distinguished families, how swiftly would bureau-
crats act. Mother Alphonsa's brutal honesty and practicality are at the
root of this appeal. So long as suffering and poverty are denied because
they are squalid and unattractive, so long as most of our energy is
consumed in debates about alleviating the causes of poverty, so long
will the poor continue to die unassisted.

*

To cull the intelligent verdict of brilliant minds against a simple
attention to the poor, whereas persons at constant close range know
that simple and direct methods are best, is very much like paying a
large bill to a doctor of eminence for the treatment of a physical difficulty, which a country-woman on a farm would relieve in a homely
and unimpressive manner. Considering the length of time that intellect
has already taken to decide how to manipulate charity, without really
progressing at all on intellectual lines, but only on those which at least
have a semblance of cardiac action, it seems pardonable to turn to
Christ, and examine His spirit and decrees. Our Lord never rejected an
expedient because it was homely, and said not one word about the evil
effect upon the poor of giving them two coats if they asked for one—
that is treating them with excessive love. We all know perfectly well
that when it comes to money, we will be mean if we are capable of
being mean; and that if we love our neighbor, the money test will alone
prove whether we are self-deceived; unless, like St. Peter, we give something immediately beneficial, which a mind not strained by culture can
instantly recognize as akin to gold. Severe theories will never satisfy a
hungry person, even if they eradicate poverty in the twenty-first century. But Christ did not ask us to eradicate poverty,—on the contrary
we are allowed to make it at home with us. The poor are a very valuable
opportunity for kindness, and help for them is never degrading unless
it is falsely given. We are many of us trying to learn how to help the
poor without false charity; and now we see for ourselves that it must be
done personally by picked people. St. Louis is especially eager to train
the charity workers, so that no ignoramuses may clog charity by blun-
dering mistakes. The sign language is wearying the more advanced
savages among us, and we are dreaming of speech. Nothing in the
world will prevent genius from creating epics of charity after a time; but

it seems long to wait; and if one is dying in destitution it is almost generous to be glad that some day Chaucer, and then Shakespeare in charity will be giving racial ecstasy to the broad earth, being the great bloom from seeds sown by Christ and His friends in the Spring of compassion.

Charities, quotes the Empress Frederick (whose noble sincerity and vigor of thought make her opinion invaluable as a type) in her saying that charity should not be regarded too much as a matter of benevolence, but that a niggardly gift or refusal is sometimes a real boon to the unfortunate who begs for relief. One knows the value of such austere impudence in religion: it can form character in masterly style. But of course a master must handle so cruel a weapon. The surgery of mediocre pruners can damage growth fatally. Moreover, it would seem that in the hands of charity such a weapon would have little chance of doing more good than a scalpel in the vocation of a nurse. Austerity is opposed to charity, which soothes. It would clear up matters agreeably if the word "charity" was used exclusively for kindness that is Christlike, and if it were remembered that the greatest of all virtues is too good to be associated even with imperial niggardliness. No doubt it is true that to keep the state from tottering worldly wisdom must prevail; the care of the poor must be practical in the accepted sense, and theorists allowed to enforce their views when their views smooth waves, and leave luxury alone in its sad contentment. Well may a sensible Empress advise that there should be "the greatest possible decrease in the numbers of the poor, by the removal of the causes of poverty existing in the poor themselves." When this nice point has been settled, poverty will be hoary with age, and crowns will have comfortably changed places down a vast line of heads. The science of imperial or civil peace is not by any means the science of the peace of God. The Empress was a woman of the utmost kindness trammelled with common sense. The Queen Elizabeth of Hungary was a woman of the utmost kindness and charity. If time made any alterations in so vital a matter as the best methods of charity, Christ would have told us so. Speaking by the Holy Spirit now, He has not said a word to contradict His first teaching, simple, direct, unavoidable, leading to personal sacrifice and immediate holy love. Can it be that we expect human friendship to be less questioning, more sure to answer appeal of the instant, than the greatest of the virtues, Christlike love? When we appeal to this, we should be certain indeed of receiving compassion in the form of a tender hearing, and a helping hand.

A cry in the distance is too often what a cry from the poor might be called, although these brethren are comparatively near us all, and often heard from. So Cuba is within five days of us, and the soldiers wrote home. But how much did we know of their terrible need of delicacies and care? The men knew all about it themselves, and the Society of the Red Cross knew. Who denied the various needs until honest testimony triumphed? Those whose signal could summon adequate help. What motives prolonged the false denial? The dignity of existing measures and the smoothness upon the surface of government. But great hearts in authority quickly called to a better sort of order the orderly criminal neglect. Red tape snapped under the sword of a general; system cringed under exceptions to a rule that was causing agony; authority itself bowed its head before men who knew the situation to be a fact which was disgraceful in a country that exists to war upon all disgraces.

A surgeon among hundreds of wounded soldiers brings a cup of water and a little care to a few of them—all he can do he does—with a groan of appeal to Heaven; and in this feeble, though devoted way a few women see and succor suffering women who are agonized and forlorn. The officers who are questioned about the battle-field which civilians do not see make answer to us: "It is too terrible to describe." Nothing but personal observation can convey the dreadful scene or the deplorable need when proper provision for the wounded has not been made. I say the same thing of conditions learned by my personal obser-vations—they are too terrible to describe, and the deplorable need of proper provision for them strikes me with dismay. Any sensible mind could have pictured to itself what must be the conditions of a war in Cuba, yet no one gave proper attention to meeting these conditions with medical tactics of any sort, except a band of persons inspired by charity, cultivated intelligence and courage, whose offers of adequate aid were at first repulsed. In similar fashion it might be quite possible for sensible minds to realize what might be the suffering of the sick poor in a city where a dozen free beds in desirable hospitals, and an almshouse hospital and limited dispensaries, are all the provision made; with the terrible clause to be added in reflections upon the sub-ject, that the non-paying poor receive treatment, in regard to care and kindness, that is akin to what some people would give an enemy who asked too much. If this were not true, half the miseries of poverty would melt away like a fog.

The time employed for fitting up Montauk for dying or exhausted soldiers who had brightened America's renown, with unstinted effort and heroic patience, was wasted by the exchange of deference between officials, by the curiosity of the public instead of its activity (except, again, on the score of a few noble men and women who had thrust themselves into the business) and by the economy of a government which really wished for proper outlay. Why? Because the wrong people were believed, the wrong people were dictators and the general public did not realize its responsibilities, which are exactly as great as its powers. Camp Wikoff was not preparing for a garden party in high life, and so it was not ready.

But officialism subsided, and politeness toward men who gave themselves for the flag is admitted to be courtesy of the best kind. Military precision in regard to the well will preserve health; military freedom toward the sick and wounded is mere Christian decency and wisdom. An army surgeon must be honored with unquestioned ascendency. If the sick poor were soldiers from a Cuban campaign, they would to-day be remembered and succored without stint of mercy; the cultivated intelligences of the city would meet together to plan immediate and lasting aid on the wisest basis, which would of course be the quickest and most generous; the Red Cross would turn its unbaffled glance upon the dilemma.

Without the Red Cross in Cuba, how soon would the public have known the needs of the sick army, or how soon would the despairing statements of surgeons have been credited? Without the members of distinguished families in the mire at camp and in the wilderness of starvation at sea—without privates of the best blood in the worst situations of the war—how soon would the sufferings of laboring men in the regiments have aroused the nation from hovel to palace?

Very many of the soldiers we were inclined to weep over were from the slums of New York. The women of the slums were waiting for their return or mourning over their death from those privations which it breaks one's heart to think of. Are we going to say definitely that we weep only for the sufferings of soldiers who enlisted from the cream of society? Do we believe that a wounded man on the battle-field or in the hospital tent, unrecognizable by his family, is a livelier sight because he went to college or had thousands to spend, perhaps unwisely? It is impossible to imagine that we should not upon the battle-field follow the example of the young men of the best families, who give their food and covering to their more humble companions at the expense of their own recovery; that we should not at least treat with as much relief the laboring man as the man who has already met with life's best advantages and can afford to suffer for a short space in this serious life of ours. Why are we so likely to look upon the question of the very poor, especially the sick poor, with contemptuous indifference? The poor are unattractive, the sick poor are nauseating. Only reflect, however, that our near relatives are often unattractive to us and that our sick friends are no more charming than any other sick persons, if they are as sick as possible. We turn from the sick poor because they displease us, not because they have sinned (the rich have done that); not because they have not treated us well (the rich do not live in true harmony); not because we believe they do not need us, but because we do not receive from them a single glow of excitement or curious pleasure. Take a pauper and place him on the steeple of a church and let the scaffolding fall, and while he falls with it the populace will tremble and weep and presently subscribe for the support of the family he leaves.

During the Cuban war, I had with me daily as seamstress the wife of a soldier who was hoping for a furlough; one of those men whom the citizens search the horizon for in order to cheer them as they march feebly from the transports. The woman came to me with her baby on her arm, and both were nearly starved. The man had left home without a word after a long struggle of no work and starvation or suicide. The unsuccessful man in the slums is remarkably like any other unsuccessful man. We fancy possibly that every one enlists purely for love of country, but many of us know what other reasons may exist. It is the same in the slums, and yet how dear the returning invalid is, either the gentleman from respectful pity or the pauper from compassionate respect! Let us face the truth as the soldiers we sent faced the hill of San Juan, and pity those who are sick unto death and abandoned because they are so, whether they interest us or not; whether they soil us as a field of blood would do and present no gleam of beauty from one year's end to another; whether or not they show us brutality and crime frequently. Need the glamour of war be so powerful with us that it can cover with enthusiasm conditions similar to that destitute sickness which is ignored and which we are usually advised that it is more ladylike to disregard?

So long as the poor are squalid and otherwise unattractive we refuse to inspect their needs, unless they live in a foreign country, Armenia or elsewhere, which makes a difference. Yet, if they were sick soldiers, we would defend them against the government itself.

What I would assert is that pity and justice might lead us to care for the incurable poor, if we allowed ourselves to admit that pity and justice have no caste or predilections, no weakness for charm, no taste for excitement. If the public knew what our experience knows of a department of suffering, a charity for that suffering would begin to develop. I assert that a great home is needed for such a charity, that of nursing incurable cancer, quite as much as if President Roosevelt had spoken for it or Lieut. William Tiffany had died in agony for the want of it.

Persons who ought to know the truth say that the incurable poor are amply cared for by hospitals already at work, and that the providing of more beds and nurses for non-paying patients and incurables would be impertinent activity. The offers of the Red Cross were refused before the facts were known, in the Cuban agony. Hospital and dispensary aid for the poor continues to be unfeeling and superficial, as is well known to people at hand, though denied by those in charge. The condition of the camps was denied by those who existed to obviate neglect in them.

There are no free beds in hospitals for incurable poor and they lie unvisited in damp basements and other improper quarters, dying from exposure, hunger and lack of medical care; or else they are shifted, roughly, perhaps, three times, at last arriving at the almshouse on the Island, usually with an experience of several hours in a stiff seat where the draught chills them. Lack of food, tents and coverings were the portion of soldiers at Montauk; or else they were "shipped" home, as the accounts put it, no matter how inadequate the home was. The sick poor work, however desperately ill, if they can find work. If they cannot find it, they are blamed as lazy paupers, and they sink down never to rise again. The statements of soldiers too sick to work or do guard duty were sneered at by some of their officers. I suppose no one doubts these often printed facts; but I certainly do not, for a relative who went up the hill, went through a subsequent illness that left no proofs wanting.

A high official in a large charity, so-called, told me that it was difficult to find a case of genuine destitution. The camp of Montauk "agreeably surprised" a high official in the government, who was noticeably lowered in official standing after his approval of the camp had been cheerfully expressed.

The sick poor need humble help, and more than two dollars a year apiece, in most instances, before they can be adequately assisted. Two dollars a year is reported as too much for each poor family calling for aid, in an American city. One would think America was a very poor Mecca. The report is like that of a charity visitor who was allowed by some rich ladies five dollars a month among fifty poor families, to supply tea and clothing when required. Her own salary was fifty dollars a month—she needed it; but the sick had at the most liberal estimate, ten cents. We are at work for those sick who get ten cents a month or nothing, unless we plead for them.

FOR THE POOR BY THE POOR
CHRIST'S POOR 1 (JANUARY 1902): 35–43

Editor's Note: A convert for less than ten years, and never educated in a convent school or within a religious order, Mother Alphonsa
demonstrates rare spiritual maturity and practical awareness of the
central problems of religious life in this unusual essay published in the
periodical directed to possible donors. We sense her own wrestling with
the problem of attracting and retaining the kind of women she wanted
for a work that few women wanted to do. She has already come to
terms with the ever-recurring problem of reconciling contemplation
and action. In an order designed "to contemplate and to give to others
the fruits of contemplation" she bears down on the ideal forcefully: "The charitable work of the Community, whatever its character,
must be dearer to it than its rule or its garb, or else the 'talents' will
remain five."

*

We may desire to secure many persons of cultivated abilities of
mind in the nursing of destitute incurables, because we learn that it is
of advantage to these charges from the hand of God that we should
have as much refinement and keen thought as a human being ought to
have: we may hope to secure a great number of such picked women
when the years unfold, although they are somewhat rare in the best
walks of life. But while we wait, as we must, we shall have ample time to
discuss the situation which is to be the object of our charity, and even
the time to accomplish admirable results with a preponderance of
poorer material. We say "poorer material" with a pang of remorse,
because a good and tender woman has nothing of poor material about
her, even if she cannot reason with clearness, and annoys sticklers.

In trying to fit a hospital and a Community together as a single
instrument for the service of our Lord's will, incompetent workers
realize the need of scientific knowledge in the management of sin and
holiness, for which a knowledge of their real properties is as important
as are very difficult niceties to a student of philosophy. Briefly, it is an
undertaking so difficult that it is likely to fail. To make bustling people
contemplate, at any time of the day, the spiritual sides of life and the
ever-present God, or to make contemplative persons do their work
with vim and finish, are problems that take the stiffness out of audacity
itself. So far has the race scrambled into the briars of mistaken activities
and interests, that simple living and working and calm thinking are lost
arts to most of us, though we daily read of how saints pursued them
with devotion.

Yet the undertaking is too sane and sweet to abandon; religious women cannot ignore the poor, and should not abandon the sick poor, especially the sickest poor. Externally simple as light,—this religious charity work,—in its means of reaching from God to the greatest distance in aid of sinners and sufferers, like electricity which seems to need no actual path to its end, the harboring and associating with abject poor, in constant service, involve for a religious person the most profound and intricate mysteries, although these two sacrifices in mercy are commanded by Christ as the "sine qua non" of spiritual strength; they involve the human heart and union with God, those extremes which we try to honor with our racial generosity and our personal austerity. If the problem is breathlessly difficult, there is but one resource. The elucidation, the real labor, must be received from and effected by God, through our appeals to Him. It would seem that the saints teach us that the thing furthest from God in His creation is His first thought; that is, abject human misery. They thought first of it. Therefore we should. The saints also seem to teach that even a good man is valueless, unless he reaches the highest grade of austerity and prayer of which his individual election renders him capable. The two efforts go hand in hand. To "do violence to ourselves" in choosing a bitter and arduous occupation of mercy, commanded by Christ, is a form of austerity which is said to take the place of much exhausting practice that would unfit us for it. To be sure, the occupation is bewildering to a common holiness, and a stumbling-block to the insincere, but can be made, it is to be hoped, a means of detachment and humility, which fit us for recollection and true prayer. Perhaps God would ask us why we came alone, if we saved our souls by vocal or mental prayer while other souls, ready to be assisted to salvation through our efforts, dropped into darkness. Possibly it is safer to trust to God's generosity towards us in this point of contemplation neglected, than to destroy our own generosity by making light of that flesh and blood which clothes our neighbor's soul. Nor is it safe to relieve others perfunctorily. St. John called us little children, not sour adults. This is indeed a lesson in charitable verdicts, based far higher than is that truth of external fact with which eternal truth has no affinity. If we have seen a little child caress its mother's cheek with a small, tender hand, we have seen how we should touch a sinner who might have faith, or a leper who might thank God. We must love them. The saints kissed the feet of the poor. They did not seem to do so, only; they did it. It is not of the saints that Cardinal Manning said, "the chief barrier to my becoming a Catholic was the example of Catholics themselves." We must come a step closer to our Light. We must be kind with loving-kindness.

We must not ape, but imitate, Christ. To earn a place near the feet of our Lord is our duty and our hope. Fraternal love and spiritual union are the factors to bring us there. To ordinary creatures this two-fold duty is a terrible problem. God alone can make a victory in such a defeat of capacities. But if we are "good soldiers," defeat is not our subject of study; success is the only thought we permit to ourselves. And having a Captain who has shown us the way, we have really nothing to do but to labor constantly, receive reverses with a smile, and know that death upon a field that is honorably lost is no failure in the divine warfare. In trying to understand the science of an active Community life, one perhaps is wisest in taking what occurs and comes to hand with as little fuss and disappointment as possible, and putting everything to the best use and advantage which we may, by the help of God, and the genius (if we are so fortunate as to be geniuses in this saintly industry) with which He has endowed us. Ask a great musician to play upon a poor piano, and whatever his secret emotions may be, he will call delightful sounds from the keyboard: his own perfection will echo there. Human beings are no doubt harder to ennoble than defective strings, but a great leader has no destructive comments to make in regard to this. The Community and its charity, its contemplative and active life, become noble in defiance of jangling tendencies and inferior developments of brain in the individual characters. The fact that mediocre people make up the multitude, and that our Lord carefully considered the emassed crowd when He abandoned select members of society without a work, points to the necessity of contriving some organization of forces that will include the multitude, by using the mediocre abilities of which it is composed. Whether the great founders planned to embrace ordinary stuff or not, they had to do it, and did it well. Triflers may rise by the patience of God to great acts. The plaint of the saints that they are the most despicable of sinners and idiots, serves to show us that sinners and bunglers can add glory to the light of God, if they love His honor. St. Francis, (but probably it was in his weaker moments), wept over the hindrance and harm caused by stupid followers, who mistook or disobeyed his aims. St. Dominic admitted to his disciples that they had broken his heart for the same reason. Words fail before the glance which fell upon Peter in the hour of his treason. It is in order to sow the seed of contrition that sublimity takes up its abode among ordinary men, or in other words, men who sleep in death. One soul is as fair and precious as another; there is no exception. Let the refined not grow faint in hope for the spiritual future of the vulgar. Christ calls them, these souls with all their roughness and clog-ging backwardness upon them, like a hampering shell. To raise souls prostrate in disease is charity in Community life as in the regions of Galilee, of which the charity of bodily ministration is an illustration and a training. It is a vast mistake to balk at mediocrity: if any are higher, they must stoop to raise it by association.

The expectation of human excellence is strewn with jagged rocks of disappointment; but the great founders made up their minds to pray right through the disasters of prevailing futility. Thus a general rides on over rough country which makes his men ineffective, sure that in the end he will have a few of the valiant, at any rate, to win the battle for him. He is sure, because he has become a general through expecting triumphs, and because example creates virtue, and a hero awakens heroism. There can be no argument that we shall not effect simple and exalted heroism to-day because no saint of flesh and blood calls us together. The world is well instructed in the 20th century, and there are holy human steps which every variety of saintliness has revealed for the benefit of the race, from the verdict of gentle women to that of austere men, as if a court were convened to prove that no one is exempt from courage. We can no longer believe that our divine Example is too great to imitate, for we are told precisely how to do it in definite records of living example, widely diffused.

Having read Catholic historical and religious records, we receive more than ever before the spirit of sacrifice, the desire to imitate and obey Christ. The simplest reiterated command is, always, to serve the poor. Christ may have placed it first in the series of His commands because we could immediately understand it, and because it abases pride at a stroke, if we serve the poor as Christ and His saints did. All else in the spiritual life develops from this act, or it never really devel-ops at all. Piety without humble works is that subtle monstrosity, self-righteousness.

We will imagine that a Community, that is, a band of women with holy interests and management in common, has been brought together to found a charitable activity, daily refreshed by religious observances, and strengthened in the midst of threatening circumstances by laws favorable to health of soul.

What is the first necessity? Silence. Silence of a sort and of a time. The word covers a series of admissions. Silence conceals mediocrity as nothing else can. The directors need to give the band of women hearty confidence, and as officers would keep cowards and awkward louts in the background of an army, so the directors do their best to make a Community represent training and capacity, or its heart fails in the advance. A decently reserved and silent person may be a wonderful one, for who can positively assert to the contrary? It being a matter of course that a large number of persons must include a preponderance of mediocrity, because it has done so from the beginning of the world, the guiding forces give this discouraging material a faculty for usefulness by checking its most obvious means of declaring its weaknesses. There are far nobler reasons for the silence of a Community than that it should be a cloak for stupidity or vulgarity; yet if there were no loftier motives, a Community could not hold together without it, for it would know itself as it is. The whole aim of a Community is to fit its members for the Beatific Vision; and although it is of the first importance that each member shall look upon herself searchingly, no one is to set out to criticize the Community except its superiors. The members are to love each other in childlike disregard of facts, simply because human facts are like leaves upon a hillside. If we, as a group of villagers, studied each leaf for its botanical points, we should do no work and see no landscape; whereas the green outline is our principal benefit as dwellers in a beautiful scene. Such beauty of general outline and color a group of persons well employed and well intentioned may always have. That our next neighbor lies, or that she lacks generosity in her work or piety in her prayers, are facts equally sad in our eyes, but equally irrelevant, although the Superior is unfortunately obliged to classify the ailments, in order that she may not give the right medicine to the wrong person; and for this purpose she is commanded to investigate the different moral diseases, minutely.

Bravely admitting that wisdom must accept the "rank and file" in a Community, although it may congratulate itself that it can exclude the insane and criminal, and giving the little concourse the radical decree that they must not be heard to the detriment of dignity, the religious rule brings to them every device that has been invented by great minds for giving infinite happiness, a happiness cosmopolitan, a happiness as deep for the uneducated and inferior who are sincerely immolated, as for St. John. Christ then deals with them. Pious practices and books lead to Him as doors lead to the sanctuary. The work of charity may expect to be well carried on by these subalterns, who, however coarse-grained, can die most honorably at their posts. Their God does not ask for brilliancy of intellect, but for fidelity of heart. He has so arranged charitable works that at their best they are simplest, and within the capacity of any honest person. He does not ask that the poor female mind, unaccustomed to study, should read the writings of St. Thomas Aquinas in the original Latin, but that it should remember the Presence of God, the Father. Being "faithful in a few things," the ordinary nun, or member of a female band of God's servants, has her abode at the feet of bliss. Let us rejoice. God will not regard us with nearly so much contempt as human beings do. Let us not leave God's work undone, in the field to which we are called, because the word "Community" has frightened us. If it requires science to form a great Community, God has proved to be so miraculous a teacher that He does not care how we stumble in examinations, if we try to answer correctly and form a merely honest company ever turning to Him.

The work of a Community is its reason for existing, whether it be as intercessor for sinners through constant and ardent prayer, or as repairer of the insults offered to God by the absence of prayer among His devoted children, or as teachers or nurses. This work must be strengthened by the religious practices and the regular order of the Community-life laid out for fulfilment, because this religious obser-vance and this daily routine are a system established to fit us for the work we offer to God. Otherwise, religious would feel no wave of com-passion to disturb their soilitary reflections about themselves. The saints were great who could live in caves to the advantage of their fellow-beings; nor were they allowed to be perfect in absolute solitude. Their followers sprang up. Let us not copy badly the religious who escaped from the multitude with credit, but be taught by those who sought souls for their good. If we live in a Community, let us do so in order to benefit our companions by our example of loving-kindness, and the poor by that kindness. The charitable work of the Community, whatever its character, must be dearer to it than its rule or its garb, or else the "talents" will remain five. Low standards have unexpected ramifications. "The better part" comes first, but we should be ex-tremely careful to include everything pertaining to the better part of it. A great deal is involved in listening to our Lord, and certainly an active obedience to His teachings may be regarded as of the first necessity. If our Lord's commands are not carried out, there is "no truth in us;" and if we do not work with adequate effects for the multitude, we keep our "talents" in a napkin of Community stinginess. Almost the most diffi-cult problem a human being has to solve is this: how to be selfish and yet obey God. It has made sophists and self-deceivers by the million. It is better to throw the problem away altogether. The charitable work of a Community should be sacred in its eyes, and never delegated any more than its prayers, but retained in "the better part" to which it belongs, if we regard the poor and the suffering as Christ represented in each separate creature appealing justly to us. The word "justly" calls forth a series of bewildering questions, put by our meanness and impulse, unless we proceed in a simple-hearted, childlike sweetness of impartiality, often arrived at most easily by mediocrity. Here is another proof that God prefers any sincerity, even stupid sincerity, to magnificent diplomacy, just as He pardons most astonishingly even the wickedest, but the uncompromising, penitents. How He loves the multitude, He Who forgave every one composing it, and wept over a city of Pharisees and change-coats smouldering in corruption; and Who breathed an atmosphere of misinterpretation while He preached! Having given our treasure,—the work for which the Community is called together, —into the keeping of mediocrity, the directors must not expect too much. The material that failed Christ cannot but fail now, and they must reckon with its blunders and cowardice and hope only in its numerical strength and capacity for being led. To have poor external success in the eyes of men would be no spiritual discredit. But the work should continue in the midst of defeat with vital persistence. This is martyrdom, life-blood poured out, the fructifying grace of works to the death. To succeed in the eyes of the world and to let the charitable work undertaken dwindle to tepidity or policy, is to nauseate the beloved multitude, as has been proved, even while it tries to applaud. The masses are easily swayed, but only for the moment. When they settle down to an opinion it is always right, if it is the unmixed response of mediocrity, free from the bias of acumen, from the high priests whose ends are the fat of the land and erudite impressiveness. What is so dangerous as the wisdom and the observance that leave the poor in the distance for prayer at hand? What is so safe as humble work refreshed by prayer? The only dignity that is safe is that of highest holiness, such as may be seen in the face of a praying peasant or a compassionate queen, God present in them both because they serve humbly. Give a scheme for benefiting the multitude to the multitude, knowing that God loves the masses more than solitary individuals, because the masses are made up of many individuals, and He remembers "all lands;" and believe that if sincere works are to be effected in humble quarters of the race, it is by such ordinary material, infused by the light of God, which leads people to do surpassingly excellent things of which they seemed incapable.

Our resignation does not mean, however, that we cease to pray for the advent of a host of noble characters, rich in virtues and mental grasp, to guide us to better labor and purer piety.

THE GIFTS OF PETER AND PAUL
CHRIST'S POOR 1 (FEBRUARY, 1902): 24–27)

Editor's Note: The following essay represents Mother Alphonsa's effort to induce men to join her efforts. Her hopes in this matter were not to be realized, but her words suggest that male resistance to nursing, even as a gospel responsibility, proceeds from a misunderstanding of what constitutes "masculine character."

*

If we were to ask good men what had been their greatest sorrow in the round of life's experience, it may be that they would answer, "the preponderance of cowardliness and dishonor among fellow-men." Soldiers look grave in reference to war in proportion as they have been actively brave, and good men look grave when a reference is made to the generality of men. Ask men of exalted thought why the masculine character cannot be depended upon to do duty in any field but those of brute courage and intellectual grasp, and they will answer that masculine souls are not good enough for delicate and sublime sacrifices, so-called. Such sacrifices are usually of the simplest and most humble sort, perhaps considered to be beneath manly dignity.

But this is impossible of acceptance. In this men of thought are undoubtedly mistaken. It is absurd to suppose that the masculine character, wicked as it is when not good, will not display spiritual heroism at the voice of command. Men have done it; they have led the way in doing it: they are now doing it, in, perhaps, isolated cases. The Psalms of David, and the miracles of Peter and Paul, show what sinners can do who have submitted to service such as God commanded. What our Lord thought of His holy Mother, and of St. John the Baptist and of John the Disciple, our minds cannot conceive, but what He thought of repentant sinners, or in other words, men who served Him earnestly, we know. He loved them, and filled them with the Holy Ghost. They slept while He suffered, they thrust forward the evil motives of corrupt wills as He preached, they quailed in His resurrected presence like dogs, they clung to His high principles only by tortured effort, they knew and preached Him yet wallowed in temptations, but He desired to be with them with a brother's love, and to become part of their flesh in order to raise them up forever. Shall we doubt their capacities, after this? Is it to be supposed that Christ loved in this way an ineradicable and impotent wickedness, never to be separated from souls; or shall we believe that He loved souls because they can so quickly become His brothers?

Are we to speak of men as if we counted for nothing the record of twenty centuries wherein it is likely that each day has held at least one act of heroic kindness, courageous gentleness, womanly compassion in men joined to their persevering strength, deeds that poetry fails to express except at the greatest height of inspiration? In reading of a noble deed, infused with heavenly beauty, not mere hardihood, not mere integrity, but exquisitely in accord with God, do we not feel a sudden consciousness that we hear the true note of the race, that race God meant to have on earth for the purpose of glorifying Him; the vision He sees as we delay to serve?

To ask little of a country, of an army, or of a citizen, results in not getting up communication with sublime energy. The soldier will eat instead of marching, the citizen will say his nerves are too delicate for disagreeable scenes, the religious, even, will smile when it is suggested that saints kissed the sores of afflicted brethren to prove to themselves that they had made some resistance against cowardice and self-esteem. To expect people to be incapable of hardship and holy austerity is like letting rich land become poor. A discouraging view of any subject can never be a godly view. It is false to say that men are not good enough to-day for certain sacrifices that their sex formerly made. They are more capable than ever, and on a vaster scale; but these sacrifices are not properly asked of them. The man who leads is followed. Undoubtedly it is disagreeable to lead in sacrifice; probably it is the most disagreeable thing a person could do.

A look of courteous disgust overspreads a man's face at the suggestion that his sex should be represented on any noticeable scale in the holy profession of tending the sick men of destitute condition who are untended, rather than to study, or train souls at a fastidious distance from tragic complications. The vocation to nurse the sick male poor is so much beneath the notice of men to-day, that they are willing to let women nurse the poor men as well as the poor women,—and far worse than this contemptible neglect of their duties, they are willing to abandon poor men to any fate of entire neglect rather than to nurse them.

What is the reason of this deterioration on the part of men, when they are now capable of broader conscientiousness than the race ever knew before? The reason is that they are not aware of the true state of things among destitute male sufferers. They do not as a multitude know what some brave doctors and priests know, and are quite well equipped to preach about, through having themselves nursed sick men with glorious fidelity, as accidental observers can testify.

When we read that the greatest Christians in religious history are the ones who descended to the simplest and most loathsome acts of kindness (to the wonder of their fellows) it seems illogical to regard such acts as unsuited to manliness. The position often taken that the personal care of the poor sick is altogether too low for high religious quality, resembles very much a shrewd self-seeking, and is the basest insult that we can offer to Christ, Who lived among diseases in order to heal them, Who endured our loathsomeness out of loving interest in our possibilities, Who associated gently with Judas, and raised a putrifying friend with all His Heart. Is it not an insult to God, Who caused an angel to minister to the leprous bodies at Bethseda's Pool? Is it not an insult to Peter and Paul, who, loaded with sin and shame just as we are, strove so manfully that they became as angels; and proved this most convincingly by precisely that compassionate service to the poor sick which is too low for men to-day, men moreover who like to be well taken care of themselves. An age that is as remarkable for the absence of masculine care of masculine sick poor as this is must be called shockingly deficient in Christian records.

SACRIFICES FOR THE POOR—A DIFFICULTY CHALLENGED
CHRIST'S POOR 1 (MAY 1902): 34–51

Editor's Note: An appeal to the pride of Americans was part of Mother Alphonsa's approach to begging, but the appeal was genuine. She wanted, as earlier letters suggest, to love America, and believe in its best values. At the same time, she wanted to help shape those values and resisted any social hypocrisy that justified wealth at the expense of the poor. She dismisses the usual excuses for inaction on behalf of the poor with insistent, remorseless irony. ("We ask a poor person to be a saint, as though poverty gave time for an examination of conscience. . . ." "The immensity of meanness to the poor is by far the largest commodity given to them.") The conclusion of her essay is a call to social and community action, because the commitment of "individuals" is not enough.

*

I.

I have sometimes burst out, in speaking with persons interested in helping the poor who suffer most, and who asked me what I supposed would tend to hasten a really better and wide-spreading state of comfort for them, that I thought it needed the life-blood of persons working for this end. I have been pleased to discover that those who had both experience and true tenderness have eagerly responded: "This is perfectly true." By "life-blood" we mean the life we live in days and energy given, actually, with heartfelt willingness, to this object of our existence,—the being compassionate. It is "life-blood" because it is the most terrible and complete sacrifice, if thoroughly made, that we can choose, and the instinct to staunch our life-blood often strives to assert itself. Nothing less than this sacrifice will save the poor from continued degradation.

As it is the quality of good metal to cut, not to roll away from contacts like the dishonorable bayonets of contractors who cheat even in war, so it is the quality of a true man to face a disagreeable state of things with clear-eyed inspection and some sort of relief, especially if it be a case of the suffering of others. Under the latter circumstances, we cannot imagine anything meaner than a man who hastens away without doing anything,—who rolls off the enemy like a leaden blade. Yet this has been the action of the majority of people in regard to cancerous poor, not only among the very poor themselves, but among persons of intelligent and decent opportunities. I have known of a number of instances in which doctors advised those who were physically able to take care of near relatives attacked with cancer not to do so, for fear of their becoming themselves infected. The results of such advice, tempting the cowardice inherent in some souls, are more deplorable and widespread than cancer could become by association, more particularly as it is not easily communicated through mere nursing. It is not unheard of to find mistaken views, abandoned later, in the medical profession; and although no profession is nobler, or enrolls nobler men on a large scale, this very fact gives unfortunate prevalence to any mistake emanating from their non-illustrious brethren. We have had experience of three friends of the poor in this profession who have exemplified perfect charity and know that there are others equal to them; but we also know of doctors who have refused to attend cases of cancer, because they were destitute and detestable, and thereby spread the idea that the disease was too horrible to nurse. We have found this state of things when called as a last resort. Of course the sick person has no such sweeping contempt of herself (or himself), and would like attention and certain medicines and directions that soften the scourge. We have found a few heroic sons and daughters, but not enough of them to encourage a belief that help will now be given very often at home. We are many of us becoming familiar, in the second place, with the refusals of hospitals to receive inoperable and destitute cancer-cases, and even such incurables as could afford some pay, but cannot give the high price demanded for the care of cancer. There seems to be a general stampede from cases of cancer.

We have had a case from Connecticut that could not find care in all that state, and would not have found harborage in New York any-where but with us; but it was the worst case of external cancer that we have met with in a wide survey. I must not forget to add, that for large pay this poor soul was told at a distinguished hospital that she could be received. Being herself destitute, and her sister, an invalid of small means, not being able to raise the full sum, the case was set aside. Money has proved often enough that cowardice and aversion are sus-ceptible to certain treatments. What I would like to know is, why a person who cannot pay anything is regarded as not to be thought of.

If hospitals pick up their skirts and run from destitute cancer cases, what may be expected from lodging-house keepers and tenement landlords? When deception is no longer of avail, the case must go away. No one can be hired to nurse a case that might remain in tenement-rooms, because not very obnoxious, unless we are so fortunate as to secure a woman with a wise head, kind heart and starving family. She can be induced to assist in the care of room and clothing. If a photo-graph were taken of a building on fire, from which residents are scurry-ing, leaving members of the home-circle to save themselves as they may, it would illustrate the attitude of the city towards cancerous vic-tims, poor or even well-to-do. Let us make a stand, and see what can be done for the injured in this disaster of a disgusting disease. One fact ought to make us a little braver. There is no danger in handling cancer-cases, the verdict of a few unmanly doctors to the contrary. The rumor is abroad that cancer is greatly on the increase. I believe, from observa-tion, that it seems to increase because it is at last discovered. This rumor adds to the fear that is almost considered a merit in case of cancer, as it seems to be in case of smallpox or plague, if people harbor principles that are mundane and dwarfed. This belief in contagion from cancer springs and clings solely because it sanctions neglect of a responsibility that strains nature too much. Cancer is not contagious. Six years of work among its victims, under a management free from red tape and rubber gloves, has not brought on disease of any kind to a group of women crowded among the most virulent examples. We expected typhoid, but all have never been so free from sickness in our lives, (though often mortally tired). We hoped to prove cancer thus harmless by simple measures which no one else had taken, and the evidence of proof is in our opinion sufficient. Any intelligent person can guard against infection, which is a much less dangerous possibility.

Not a mere handful of women, but a large body of them, are needed to work for such sick poor in every city. In East Cambridge, Mass., there is a hospital for incurables carried on by the Gray Nuns, and they have a large ward for poor cancer-patients. I doubt if there is any other inoperable cancer-ward in the whole country. The whole country, therefore, needs groups of brave, kind women to nurse destitute cancer; or cases we will say, destitute of the help and love of kindred. These unfortunates seem to us the bitterest sufferers of the whole great crowd. Perhaps they have worked all their lives for their people, but cancer sets them apart as if they were grievously to blame, and the almshouse is pointed out to them. A man or woman of integrity, and some delicacy of thought and feeling, would rather not associate with the class to be principally met with in the almshouse hospital. We hope to grow, ourselves, into a large band of women, devoted to this and other incurable sickness among moneyless people; and if talking can convince women in many quarters that they also are needed in a similar activity, they will have to believe what we tell them so frequently. We must be so humble in our spirit and in our labor that no women could be humbler. Unless we can really forget our own, material, unspiritual interests, we are as miserable in our folly of sham assistance as the poor are in their disease, as useless in our false delicacy as the poor are in their ignorance; and so the world has but one class of fools the more, and still another class of morally sick people—those who attempt to be kind without being devoted. To be as humble as the relatives of the poorest poor, and as attentively useful as the servants of the rich,—such must be the attitude of mind of women who will do some honor to their country by curing a very terrible disease from which America suffers; its neglect of destitute persons most grievously sick. It is not worth while to include as beneficiaries of America those destitute sick who serve for the experiments of science, much to their own regret and quite without wages for this unparalleled role. Such sufferers are sometimes led on by honeyed words and assumed authority, aided by the imposing toggery of hospitals, to valleys of shadow undreamed of by the imagination, and all in the name of science. A doctor of noble qualities is superlatively a benefactor, and regards a sick person as honorably as he would a friend; and, I believe, more heartily, if I may judge by what I have seen in a number of eminent physicians, and unpromoted ones, as well. But the medical profession cannot make fine material by conferring a degree, any more than the mercantile can by bestowing a fortune; whereas great power rests still in the capacity filled by any doctor. It stands to reason that greed and deception, and the actor's faculty, will be discoverable in any large body of men, and although confidence in one's doctor is a faith hardly to be tampered with, it is time to say a good deal about the experiences of the poor under this head; and we are particularly interested in the department of operated cases, and examined and demonstrated cases, not susceptible of cure, and not treated honorably half the time. They owe no thanks to their country, but are its unwitting benefactors, even if the country pays only the medical salaries involved.

The humility which is so necessary for us in accepting repulsive conditions, and affectionate relations with rough persons, becomes pure cowardice in accepting without an effort repulsive principles, and in allowing one's self a silent tolerance of those abuses which are certain to be found where power and defencelessness meet. The women who enter into the work of properly attending to the destitute sick, will be expected to make a gradual and ameliorating change in the public estimate of the way to treat non-paying sufferers. Intelligent thought has long been brought to bear upon several phases of this source of mistake and brutality; and the testimony of great men who are doctors has always been honorably given to admit that, where surgery is abused by being allowed the rein, it lowers the nature more rapidly than any other activity.

Nathaniel Hawthorne says, in his "Outside Glimpses of English Poverty," that the "loathsome child" which he found in the Orphan Asylum which he visited with a party of friends in England, was to remind us that we are responsible, in our own degree, "for all the sufferings and misdemeanors of the world in which we live, and are not entitled to look upon a particle of its dark calamity as if it were none of our concern." He "took up the loathsome child and caressed it as tenderly as if he had been its father." We are accustomed to the gross and knavish unkindness of those low types of character which proclaim by their appearance, itself, that they will neglect all high duties. But Hawthorne was accompanied by some of the kindest and most cultivated men in England. It is a hard truth to accept, that such good people, fond of the best poetry and enthusiastic over a brave soldier or a valorous sentiment in an after-dinner speech, have duties which they refuse to admit on the ground of their being inconvenient and repulsive. Hawthorne's companions smiled patronizingly and unsympathetically at his fulfillment of this high duty, very much as boys simper when one among them confronts the group with a refined guidance of thought that had not been looked for. The pauper child, covered with sores, but carried in his arms for a considerable time, he reports to have "seemed satisfied." Peace no doubt filled the hearts of man and child, as an instantaneous evidence that God was also pleased by a tribute to human brotherhood made so unqualifiedly to little outstretched arms, held up from a destitute body and scorned soul.

It is a fallacy to think that we can deal with another person, however poor, and leave mind or soul out of the relationship. Such a superficial scheme, however, makes the dealing simple in mechanism and remunerative in apparent success; but some one has yet to give utterance to the idea that America as a nation seeks a merely worldly success in any of her principles, however much prosperity they bring with them. There is of course not one idea propounded by the nation, which she would not give up if it were proved to be wrong. American charity must be as direct, as deeply sprung and as salutary as that independence which arose at the call of masterly and devout men.

Is this a nation to slur over or deform any great department? If it is true that the charities of the race are but small matters, let Hughes, Maurico, and many others in the history of charitable thought be hushed; let the charities of the individual cease, and Florence Nightingale, St. Vincent de Paul and Clara Barton no longer be crowned with universal love. We all know perfectly well that the charitable spirit of a nation gives it rank; that if it has any genuine charities, they are its credentials with the loftiest thought discussing its advance. They are the proof of its self-control, and that magnanimity which we recognize as the hardest and the greatest victory human nature consummates. Charities are not of slight importance. Lazarus at the gate only asked for a little food,—a hideous, leprous object interested in a meal. But because Dives scorned him in his loathsome pettiness,—a momentary, trivial unkindness we would say,—the die was cast, and Dives is still pondering the result. In a great battle-scene, a little act of humility mercifully performed by a dying officer for a common soldier, gleams on England's bosom forever. Magnanimity may be no larger than a pearl, but its price is always immense; nothing less than unlimited humility and courage.

Authoritative teachers are considering social problems more and more thoroughly, or are taking up again for examination puzzles left by a past generation, that has failed like many other generations to accept the simple but physically exhausting key to the situation which a great soul held forth. There is nothing new in personal charity, but it is newly dropped by every comer as a tax upon heart and brain. Charity has been well proclaimed and exemplified from the days of the Apostles, and even from the days of Joseph, victim and magnate. While England seems to set examples in the present which her great civic apostles nobly taught seventy years ago, let America prove that her celerity can grapple with kindness as quickly and effectively as with mines and music, yachts, and war. The indications are that she will not dally in inadequate measures, as an exposition contentedly encases a detached sample of home products. We are not likely to be contented, as a nation has often been hitherto, with pretty samples of justice in fraternal love, a copy of one of its grandest forests, as it were, in photography, hung over a single tree-trunk, leaving the spectators to hear the rustle of myriad branches if they can, in fancy; a house for a handful of destitute, with a pamphlet telling how millions of them suffer. America has turned full upon actual charity, and will succeed in learning about it and excelling in it. She has passed the child's play of exposition-samples. But where personal consecration comes in, there is still a certain amount of calm expectancy, apparent inaction, germinating delay, indicating a lack of numerical strength in volunteers. As a first step towards doing something for the poor that will help them, let us have an end of the trotters on sleek, safe horses, who harangue about what they think the poor are, what they believe they do not need, and what they know they should not have. What they should not have is a fine field for eloquence, it is popular, and will last for a theme as long as people bow to inaction; it costs nothing, and even reduces expenditures as sweepingly as a mower reduces grass to unresisting hay. Let us cease to turn to the rich with commiseration for their frail hold upon their property. We do not express our mournful regrets when they expend money for colossal amusements, and it is indeed a morbid desire for justice which leads us to desire to save our millionaires added expense. The proportion of money given to charity by the rich, though generous, does not demand sympathy. So far as I have seen, the only millionaires who have suffered mental distress from giving to the charities at present existing, are those who worried themselves over trying not to give. The very arbiters between poor and rich, offering evidence against a tramp or a drunkard with microscopic care, are sure to be drawing a plump salary for foxy inspection of the masses. Christ asked the rich for their money, but we should be kinder, and will bid them to save their money, after our salaries are paid,—so the trotters harangue. We must live, we simply must, but the poor had better not. If we have cancer, we simply must be taken proper care of; but the poor can die somewhere, somehow. Charities tend to the negative, as a boy does to hesitation on his way to school. Any poor person who thinks to find a friendly greeting in neighborly style, hears that system does not include cordial trust of the poor or warm manners. Professional beggars are not numerous, and can easily be detected, and kindly dismissed; or where there is a doubt, respectful geniality will do more good than can be calculated. Our Lord did not say that the Samaritan asked who the wounded man's grandfather had been before pouring oil into his gaping sores, nor did He tell us that money was withheld for fear of tarnishing the independence of a soul. What our Lord wished us to feel was charity, simple and direct, and so He taught it.

In reading some charity pamphlets one is reminded of old-fashioned books of travel, which fail to describe important traits of nationality, for the fear that they had of banditti. Editors and clerical informants having become waylaid by a few masked roadsters in the shape of tramps and street beggars, the hand-satchel of compassion is cut open by the sword of matchless vagrant wit, and the missionary into new quarters in the city hastens home completely robbed of all interest in the interesting natives. I am sure that every pebble cast at the poor under cover of tramp stories will come back in deadly earnest, and be a particularly sharp and heavy stone when it hits any member of charitable bodies. The immensity of meanness towards the poor is by far the largest commodity given to them. Here and there over the moor of negative recoil a harebell trembles, but as a rule all is rock and stubble to a traveller who earnestly seeks for the mother earth that blossoms in positive response. Where hawk and crow patrol, there is a chill in the air. Salaries are to blame. Large organizations are demoralized by them. So long as they are the system, plated charity will be produced on a flourishing scale.

It is very difficult to persuade people to drop an attractive fashion, such as that of receiving salaries. When a nature is mean it can resist any strain of argument. But there are great indications that the salary system is becoming seriously suspected in high quarters.

It is always difficult to persuade stingy natures of existing facts. They confront one's facts with false reports from persons who cater to their stinginess of judgment, until you give up talking in amazement at the ignorance of people who declare they are informed. One learns that it is only the people who are born merciful who will open their ears to hear. The others may be made to see, if you can once lead them to a destitute bedside; and on that ground they can sometimes be converted easily enough. But it is a matter of catching your hare before you can expect to make him serve for ragout. To investigate the meagre conditions we are able to supply in our beginning of home-accommodations, for a case of cancer in man or woman, is to stir the heart in a way evidently unaccustomed to some callers; and it is as evidently a gracious emotion, which they are glad to feel. Nothing need be said. It is then seen, unanswerably, that there is need for more relief; and need also for more, or at least some, love. We then see how silly it is to haggle as to whether the poor are as hungry as we would be if we were wretchedly fed, or whether the poor feel as sick as we would feel, with our refined habits. We see a human being that has been hungry and has suffered, bearing still the marks of such piteous pain as need not have been endured if we had found them sooner. It is too bad—something must be done for those still lying untended on the field of battle—even the meanest nature feel this, as the melancholy sight stares back its appeal. This is the use of the poor.

II.

Most of us have always regarded children as subject to the laws of nature. In our eyes their parents may be scoundrels, unfeeling bundles of rubbish, as it were; they are but hungry and sick in imagination, their deceptions extending even to the astonishing pretence that they can suffer pain; or if they really suffer, it is but a mild form of punishment for sins that deserve death, outright. It would be impertinent for us to interfere in order to lessen the justice of God. It is different with children. The younger they are, the more we believe that they can feel as we do. Yet so far as our experience goes in personal pain, to grow older is to suffer more; and the callousness of a slum-dweller, it is highly probable does not affect his body, but his faith and his will, although it is a form of bravery.

A charitable review might have smiled at our concern over a poor woman who came, the other day, to our relief room, and sank, exhausted with hunger, upon the floor. Foxy wisdom would have roused itself brightly to declare that this was a case of drunkenness; but it was not. We are not incapable of detecting the difference between the effects of drinking liquor and abstaining from solids. A pale, thin child was with the woman, carrying a basket for the food which they expected us to give. We knew something of the family, that they did not like to beg, and that it was a fact that the woman had pawned her wedding-ring. But sometimes drunkards come for food. Strange to say, they can be hungry, too. I am not overwhelmed with astonishment because of the strength of my compassion in giving them food, but at the feebleness of my desire to have them call again. Charity as we enact it is usually a cold affair at heart. It is not the person we care about, but the interest they are able to excite in us. Let us strive hourly to be more generous than this; to begin once more to soften our harsh heart.

Poverty cannot make a highly honorable citizen of mean, grasping, passionate stuff. What are our own qualities? Mean, grasping and passionate, they certainly are. And yet we ask a poor person to be a saint, as though poverty gave time for an examination of conscience. A better occupation for us than to quibble about drunkenness and the dignity of independence, which we do not wait to discuss if there is a famine or a flood, is to bring our own faulty qualities to the task of relieving the good poor and the deceptive poor, when we see that either are in dire distress. Let us be careful not to refuse to look where we will find these poor people. The struggle with our faults of courage and gentleness will have a remarkable effect upon us and the poor; upon our instincts for kindness, at last nourished by veritable acts, and the hope of a soul very nearly hopeless, darkened by ignorance, and yet every inch a relative. Some destitute invalids require no strain on our part before respect and deep pity can be brought forward. They are persons of the utmost excellence, and sometimes of former ease. But any situation in life can be made heroic, according to the character placed there, and in a miserable tenement full of thieves we could use ardor. The sickrooms of the poor and the ugly proclivities of some among them change as if by magic under the influence of a holy spirit; —so we have fortunately seen. The intelligent energy of people of culture, also, can effect great good, without lowering the tone of the refined friend in contact with debasement. The good is great because it is a medium for God, Whose cooperation has the most immediate and astonishing effect in the world. To obey Him literally lets in a burst of sunlight, bringing health and joy to every soul present. Those who have observed this never wish to retreat from charity of service such as poverty invites. Some manifestations of refinement are more selfish than helpful in slum work, and cause a cessation of that mingling and companionship which is the only cure for ignorance, as everyone begins to admit. It is not easy perhaps to decide how far to go in sharing poverty, in order to know it and the lower classes; how far to go in dispensing with our accustomed style of manner and prejudices. I think the only harm is in clinging eagerly to all this. Simplicity is neither vulgar nor impressive; it is dignified and gentle. The refining of the poor cannot be done by suddenly presenting them with high art. Genius is required everywhere, and here also, that we may know how to make all the concessions ourselves, as we would to children, and how to insinuate effort towards wise living and real generosity into these lax minds by flashes of better methods and softer actions. The success of a noble heart will be so wonderful in arousing fine possibilities in the young, the renewal of determination for right behavior in the mature, and the love of God in the old, that it is not extreme to call the situation heroic, when at the command of a talent that has been given wholly to, but not wasted in, the detestable wilderness of suffering poverty. By such talent I have seen a patient who resembled a fiend in appearance and behavior, and who aroused all my own harshness constantly, cheerily soothed and amused and led into becoming one of our most consoling results.

The unwelcome lesson of the vast share which the poor absorb in all we are and have, even though we neglect them, is being diligently acquired by unbuyable and unweariable men and women. Poets and soldiers have brought their splendid perceptions to bear upon habitations that are so vile that they can wreck souls. If times were ever favorable for stirring forward in aid of light and cheer, they are upon us to-day. Women must penetrate to the dark rooms where the sick lie. If a governor is interested in a house for the poor, we need not be ashamed of pressing our plea for the house of the soul itself, the sick body. It is not a strictly intellectual department, but it is there. Of course, great thinkers endeavor to mould the future. To frustrate causes of horror is their common-sensible aim, leading to glorious fruition. In the race's battle against the dark kingdom, the commanders stand apart from the field, while smaller folk attend to marches and transfers of ammunition for emergencies. Idle people may bestir themselves to give a man and his family a meal, while it is being decided whether poor men by the million shall have a squatter's privilege to a handful of earth and sunshine. A few ideal tenements will make the twentieth century reasonably practical and fair to see, towards the middle of its course; but in awaiting a square mile of such tenements in every great city, let us nurse the sick who will die this year; and aid with various suggestions as we go and come those persons alongside of the sick who will be most undoubtedly earth, again, when false contractors shall be innocuous dust. If it were not necessary to do something while great questions are being settled, charity would be able to have a silken pillow upon which to recline a decade at a time. Were we honestly kind and honestly keen, these questions would seem to settle themselves, righteousness being contagious; and rogues would find thoroughfares too uncongenial and observant to make their peculiar life worth living. Let us take a hand's turn at some fraternal labor which is beneficial to somebody else;—we shall at once discover ourselves to be involved in life-work, we shall become more genuine, we shall exchange vanity for self-respect, and above all we shall wonder that we did not begin before. Generous simplicity should prevail in the work I refer to; a generous measure of sacrifice and great unpretentiousness of plan.

Children have been amused, washed, dressed, admonished, supplied with books, taught to sing, play the violin and to dance, and how to use doilies and forks. The mothers have been taught how to speak grammatically, and how to listen to lectures and to sew; and settlements have in other ways, also, laid down fine roads for gracious influences. Workers and the worked-for have all been gladdened. Everyone casts anchor upon the children, because it takes longer to be disappointed in them, and to see where we have made mistakes in training their virtues. I think it would be safer to take their sick mothers more seriously. We cannot influence the children profoundly for good middle-age, if we ignore these most intimate relatives because they are very sick. We cannot even point a moral by consoling the sick mothers with sweet expressions of sympathy, during calls in which we seem to fear (very likely a well founded fear) contaminating our clothes. The expression of sympathy has a pallor about it, if it is not accompanied by the necessaries which money brings. Ah, there is the boulder in the path of charity! It is provoking that money and charity must go together; but so they have ever done, immitigably, or else a miracle filled the baskets. Money is the truthful measure to show the proportions of compassion, no matter how kind we are, and though it is so necessary to speak and to look and to labor kindly, as well as to furnish the body with food and warmth, medicines and a roof. Children are at the kernel of success in clearing away ignorance and depravity; but we must include the parents in the scheme, uninteresting though they may be, and incorrigible in their ways, most probably. A juvenile group, a clever boy,—these are, more like frolic and fiction than the old folks, hard as people must work to guide the young. The older folks can certainly be the most deadly disappointment and aggravation known to existence, and it is revolting to place one's self directly in the way of their cunning and their cruelty. Their diseases are not so heart-crushing as their characters, when they are not naturally good. The only defense the heart has is to try to discover their moments of gentleness, their impulses for gratitude and generosity. They are sure to have them; and it is finally possible to believe that God likes them better than we do, these adults; and that, if we are so fortunate as to receive "a penny" at nightfall, from Him, they will also. God is more generous than any one to every one.

We are looking to the future, we say, in devoting ourselves to the children. The future is dearer to us than it should be, as almost everything is that we love. We are like worms decked with many-colored coats of theory, reaching out for a twig and overlooking it,—blind caterpillars. Children will not long be children, but will soon be grown-up monuments of selfishness, if we teach them to be brilliant and yet to neglect their invalid relatives, or to slur over their ignorant and vociferous parents. They might go so far out of our proposed course as to become as self-righteous as we have tried to make them good. They are justly recognized as very bright, in one way if not in another, and they will notice the peculiar omissions in our own charity, which skips the active agony in their homes, though handing them books that teach consideration for sufferers, no matter what labor it entails; they will notice that we ask as few questions as we dare about a bedridden member of the family; and that if we should see her, we recommend "the hospital," not minding which or where, and not reflecting whether her heart—in a bedridden person hardly to be supposed a heart— breaks at the suggestion. The children may overhear us say, that it would be better if such difficult cases of penury and pain were to make haste and die. Good people say this sometimes. The sick woman (or man) never consents to be regarded as on a level with broken furniture, no matter how disjointed their skeleton is. The children can only so catalogue their parents by losing those qualities that give us our hope in them. In fact, children love their parents; and because the young poor are so susceptible to good precepts and manners, and so soon lose traces of low origin, may we not infer that the adult poor are more revolting than deeply depraved? I firmly believe it, from close contact, at all hours and in all events. Of the better class of poor I am not speaking; but of those who seem drunk with chaotic moral aberrations, their children often being pretty and clever as the best. These adults darken the slums, and the decent poor close to them barely console us, good as they are. But the children see frequently the kindly traits we notice at intervals; their voices therefore rise in sincere and affectionate plaint to heaven when the parents dangerously engage in combat, or when the half-cruel mother refuses to leave the rum-shop. The Bible, Tennyson, Thackeray, almost any good book, will not distract the attention of a good child from its relatives, but will teach him that to refrain from giving what money will bring to the afflicted poor, and to give maxims instead, is economical nonsense. The plea of "pauperizing" belongs to the lips of dabblers,—by this plea you shall know them.

The "visitors" of rich organizations come to us with requests for money. We have all the evidence that we need as to their finding—because they look to see the truth—that to work without money is rank hypocrisy, and not to be thought of unless one draws a salary for doing it. One young woman, sparkling with intelligence and kindness, admitted that she had but five dollars a month to expend upon fifty families, in each of which was a sick person. I was some weeks in recovering from the shock this statement gave. She used her car-fares to eke out the insolently small pittance for supplying some necessaries; we can but guess what for and how many. She was loth to tell me what her salary was—it was fifty dollars a month; not so small. The male cancer-case which I helped through this young woman needed everything but the rent; and his mother, half crippled, needed coffee and tea. While drawing children to the settlement and opening their minds to receive our light, let us not leave them to grope their way through such darkness as this charity that has forgotten its ammunition against the wolf, this theorizing that has to beg from the first person who comes along untrammeled by a theory. There is nothing so absurd as charity without money beyond salaries, except sacrifice without pain. Let the children see that we, who set out to help the poor in brain or bodily well-being, are willing to give our life-blood in honor of the "heavenly country," as soldiers give theirs for their native land, which is but a symbol of the land that is more real. The youngsters will then know that God is the Father of good, and very good hearts, not of half-hearted people, whose pretty manners, without nobility of action, lead away from Christ.

The first firm step in social reform must be to attend to the worst, most evident disorder. This is the physical sickness of poverty. Then, and not till then, comes the second step of the care of the moral sickness of poverty. I do not mean that we are to stand on one foot for a long time after taking the first step. Care of the mind and soul may easily accompany care of the wretched sufferer; but when we postpone the latter duty, we are re-arranging the order of our Lord. Not that the body is of value in comparison to the soul, but that other people's bodies have a peculiar value for our soul. The body was put outside of the soul for some reason, and when we ignore it, we assume that we have a more reliable judgment than the Creator's. He says that we are to take care of people physically, when they are afflicted physically, and this is because we cannot help aiding the soul at the same time. The body which we are at liberty to ignore is the one we do not—our own. Many activities, then, can proceed from, and flourish alongside of, this nursing of the poor; but it is a blunder to suppose that it is not itself the preliminary of fraternal comradeship, since Christ said it was. It is the vantage ground from which to elaborate our tactics.

To have only one hospital for the incurable sick is not to take a firm step in the advancement of charity; moreover, it is not charity if it is self-preservation. The state induces support of incurable destitute consumptives, because it is sure people are afraid of consumptives, and would rather not have it spread. Charity is the opposite of policy, and I am not speaking of the care of the poor from low motives, but high ones. We may argue that the populace is not made up of angels, and that it is better to accomplish projects by recognizing limitations, than, by forcing exalted notions not likely to be assimilated, thus to fail. The only things that we care about in history, however, are the exalted standards which were expected to fail, but came off victorious. One hospital attached to an almshouse where a city needs half a dozen generously managed, is but an advertisement of the dwarfed stature of the state's charity; it is a pigmy monstrosity. If there is no state hospital for an certain incurable disease in all the Empire state or all the country —words fail to describe the stupid neglect.

It is a mistake to erect a hospital which is a model of inventions, a triumph of arrangement, if the building is to be serviceable to the destitute. Every penny accumulated should go to the benefit of the poor; not the greater share to the benefit of superintendent, doctors, nurses and visitors, and the external dignity of the state. A fine building, marble floors, and all that fiddle-faddle, making a good appearance, are impediments to the comfort of the destitute. As a rule, large debts ensue, and pay-beds magically appear in the very place of the endowed beds given for non-paying need. Put on shabby clothes, and find out the truth of this statement. It is safe to assert that a hospital which would please God, would be one that was adequate to relieve the abject poor,—if one were not sufficient, then as many as are needed.

Not merely fifty persons are needed in a city to attend to the sick poor by living near them, or, one might better say, slowly dying near them. Such fraternal laborers must lead "a dying life," do violence to their memories and their tastes, testifying to the truth in defense of the poor, in aid of the needs of the poor, and from the point of view of the poor. The entire devotion of great individuals in the past must be imitated by groups of individuals,—not in the easy "future"—but to-day. These groups must be multiplied, until the unpicturesque work of attending to the sick poor and all accompanying miseries begins to show great results, by doing away with the worst conditions.

Having faced the disaster and looked upon the injured, let us act, remembering God's words, not men's. Diplomacy and moral courage are strangers to each other; excessive business prudence and charity will not shake hands; but God and the poor await us, side by side.

RELIGION AND WORK, PART I
CHRIST'S POOR 1 (JULY 1902): 38–44

Editor's Note: Before "holiness is wholeness" became an axiom in spiritual writing, this 1902 essay urges that more critical attention be paid to bodily needs, especially the bodily needs of religious women engaged in active ministry. Part II of this discussion is an urgent insistence upon the necessity of active service, willingly undertaken and faithful to gospel values, which Mother Alphonsa distinguishes from "mechanical usefulness" and contrasts with a flight from service disguised as a longing for recollection.

*

Work is so necessary to religion that even those religious who do not set out to work as the form of prayer which is most distinctive in their service of God, make the flesh work in actual miseries of austerity and inflicted pain. The religion that does not work to the suffering point, with hands and if possible with brains too, is the sort of worship that splits into a hundred sects, because although endeavoring to satisfy most fully and delightfully it never does so at all, but nauseates. A name and a definition carry people along to a certain stage, but when the suction of truth draws them back to the starting point once more, they wish that they had struck deeper for the answers to their prayers.

Possibly we enter religion with the perfectly secure conviction that we are going to pray vocally all the time, or at least remain in peaceful contemplation of God, when we reject all labor whatsoever; and we are appalled to discover that we must scrub, cook and obey as forms of prayer, and an evidence of religious sincerity, whereas the prostrations and ecstasies which we had regarded as signs of grace are received as dubious testimony. We learn, in short, that what we find to be nice our superiors have judged to be fraud; that what benefits our own fancy may weaken the community and its object of the public weal. The apparent contradictions of the religious life are as opposite as the mud which our Saviour took from the ground to heal blindness, and the miraculous power which He mingled therewith. Though we must regard our soul's salvation as our chief concern, the religious who thinks of nothing else will be damned; but he who regards himself as worthy of hell, and denies himself every attempt to secure spiritual consolation that he may labor for the good of his community and its charitable object, will be saved. In the midst of desolation and fatigue, opprobrium and honest labor, the flashes of divine mercy or direct communication with God give rest to the weary and heavily laden, though the sanctimonious humbug will be growling over the fatigue of the beads themselves, and wondering if his Paters and Aves amount to a row of pins. The spirit of labor in the most humiliating directions, and the spirit of piety, which finds in the Rosary a cradle of peace, are kindred. Great suspicion attaches to those who regard it as far more agreeable and holy to read spiritual books, and repeat prayers, than to prepare a meal or hoe cabbage, or nurse the sick; far wiser to immerse ourselves in paints or embroidery than to regard kettles or brooms; to pray to God in calm seclusion than to beg for alms in humility and generous intent for others. Religion is work, and it is a proverb that those who will not work cannot genuinely pray; and that when they meditate they refreshingly sleep.

The problem, therefore, comes up again,—how to believe the impossible can be done because everything is possible with God; how to believe that when so far as we can understand we are too busy to think of God, our sacrificed desire to think of Him brings Him closer than a Gregorian chant would do, supposing that it were sung at the expense of needed labor. "God comes first;" but God is in His commands, and He has bade us to work for others; and though we must retire to pray, let us not desert to pray. Christ's admonition that we should do all things spiritual, yet not leave the material necessities unfulfilled, renders the religious life a closely mosaiced labor of exalted observance and diligent work. A good religious very nearly accomplishes the impossible by the help of a miraculous Master.

Men effect wonderful results for money and for fame. We all know how they are rewarded for their pains. Not one of them is glad for a very long time. All are like creatures who are penned up in a small yard surrounded by a bare brick wall,—self. They throw a million dollars or a great novel over the wall, and they hear shouts of praise in response, and the shouts are flat as an old piano. They become enormously sad as time goes on, and the wall is all they see, however keen their imaginations are to fancy that they see a world. Now, a good religious has no personal liberty, but his impersonal soul is never confined; his nature obeys, but his supernatural life is in God. God contains every art, every glory of the physical world, every joy that man would desire to remember at the approach of death. Not seeing all these, but seeing God, we have the elevation of the superior senses which such contacts could in actual life bring. Our hand is clasped in that of a power which raised the dead, gave sight to the blind, and redeemed a world, and by a submission of our will we become the slave of men, but the master of heavenly expansion. Working at the beck of our own will, we become (possibly) famous and forlorn—working at the command of religion we become (perhaps) abject and rapturous, being God's friends forever, and rewarded by One Who never fails to satisfy.

It is an absolute physical and mental necessity that persons who pray much should work actively with the body. The ideal sort of relaxation for the forces which are drawn upon in religion is found in the outdoor air, where nature contributes a thousand harmless interests and delights. Those who have tried outdoor life in the secular state know the effect produced upon minds that think. It is a reckless thinker who never resorts to work of the muscles, and the ease of the brain that comes from active labor, especially in the open. In short, it is necessary to have some sort of outdoor exercise in order to preserve life fit to be called such, and possibly sanity. The Trappists are especially devoted to this clause because they are particularly taxed as to concessions of normal manners. Women are only relegated to indoor limits, even the little yard of old being often absent in their present reckoning, because no one will remember their physical and mental interests when they themselves ignore these requirements. It is a serious question as to how valuable they will be as instruments in the hands of God, if they prefer the piety of invalid pallor to the piety of energy and length of useful days. That the melancholy diseases and deaths of religious of both sexes are not welcomed by their Superiors seems abundantly to prove that religion is for developing, not extinguishing the workers who make up the body of the house.

If good sense in regimen for the rank and file does not prevail, we must expect consumption, cancer and aberration. All communities which set out to ignore (we do not criticise those who voluntarily forego for a noble purpose) these needs of the fibres which, so long as we live, require reasonable support (unless, again, we are of that class of spiritual guides who most help and teach the world by their death in life and final martyrdom), all communities so poorly reckoning their economic management, become pale, weak and ineffective, diseased and short lived. Postulants who enter in a condition which is sturdy, rosy and cheerful, in a few weeks take on the pallid stolidity of contemned physiques. Their prayers may become purer and their patient resignation in deadly conditions is often beautiful to see, holy and edifying; but it is assuredly obstructive to the object of the community's existence to let them fade and die, always supposing that some labor for the public good has been assumed, such as teaching or nursing. The good religious will be, in her approaching death, pure spirit very shortly at best, though we give her twenty years of labor; and so let her try to do the good others leave undone before this little season of the world's need ceases to pain, annoy and interrupt her. A teaching Sister who is fed on sham food (most probably many a religious knows what that term means) and is expected to teach in a confined room in a nauseatingly vitiated atmosphere, which no sensible person could defend as coming within the laws of the Board of Health; who walks through rain and snow storms to her classroom, as is done in mission-schools (branches not yet fully equipped, even if near the richest centres in cities) and using every spare moment for her own study, or the hand-sewing a Sister is expected to do for fetes;—this little angel, or perhaps nervous and acid being, develops a cough because she must, and then the Superiors tearfully wonder why some of their most efficient subjects last so short a time. The same need of health-preservation applies to a cancer-nurse,—no doubt to any nurse,—and success in the attempt for far-reaching usefulness cannot be expected if the root of the plant is above-ground. Nurses of cancer were thought, by the most liberal religious estimate, to need much less air and relaxation and contrasting activity than has proved to be the case. A brief, early walk to Mass was thought, by those not engaged in the service, to be ample breathing-space, though the city air was dead in summer and forbidding in winter, and the church was filled with a quality of air close and soiled beyond recognition as oxygen. An abundant addition was supposed to be given in allowing an occasional visit to a noisome tenement, to find out the needs of revolting sick and dirty poor, usually consumptive or cancerous. These nurses were kept alive only by the genuine quality of their simple food, and the regularity and interest of their routine. After a year of inherently healthy but paling physiques, more air and exercise were adopted, and are so far only limited by necessity and certainly never forestalled by theory.

That asceticism produces conditions favorable to holiness and spirituality is too evident to need argument with the least informed; but having offered a work to God it must not be deterred but brought to its goal, which is, of course, vigorous usefulness. Nursing, and teaching also, will not flourish upon asceticism, although mortifications can be hourly, and include abstinences and other hardships. Religion deserves at least as much study of the fitness of different manifestations of religious feeling as the science of chemistry needs for its effects of color and influence. Apply the right manifestation of religious sincerity to the work to be benefited by this spiritual treatment, and success is probable. Perceptive work will be aided by the slow death of the body;

supernatural growth is wholly independent of the mental nourishment
we may or may not fall in with, and is wholly opposed to physical
nourishment. But a badly nourished student, in all his manly strength,
will die of pneumonia or typhoid fever or become insane, or feel for the
next fifty years the ravages of constant prayer and study, if without an
intelligent and conscientious cherishing, in adequate food and recreation, on the part of the shepherd set over the novitiate. Witness the
difference between the advice of a Provincial and a petty official.
Rough nurture must be given, but with a scientific knowledge of what
and how to give suffering in that direction, care being taken to avoid
killing your spiritual athlete, or your laboring machine, thus hastening
the denouement of emptying your religious life of its living quantity.
Supernatural strength and supernatural capacity for length of days is
not to be expected in the rank and file, although God builds the house
that is holy, and the saints led a dying life with prowess of extraordinary
usefulness and ceaseless toil. It must be remembered that, in very essential matters, at any rate, almost all the greatest workers or founders
among the saints had their own way, which is meat and drink in itself.
Most probably St. Simeon Stylites for the first time felt really faint
when he proceeded to obey his Superiors, and to rise from his station at
the top of his column, agonizing as his position had been upon that
form of torture. We must remember that the hidden and ordinary
religious is always under some one's feet, as a mat which it is thought
meritorious to flatten still more. God may easily supply a happiness to
this poor soul that is sweeter than power or completed projects; but
alas, not every ordinary soul deserves this peaceful and untold bliss.
Supposing that it is admitted that religious are needed to work in very
practical ways, because seculars are in arrears with these works, it then
seems a logical conclusion that a scientific care should be taken to keep
the convent peopled by its community. No doubt when conventual life
was young this was understood so well that the Superior was the least
fed and hardest worked member of the band; and although fasts were
more frequent, a vigorous regime was not forbidden when it could be
adopted in its season, speaking always of life not deliberately ascetic as
a form of service for souls. But communication with the saints who
planned regimes is becoming less and less intimate and vivid among
the majority; and the majority, apt as they are to misinterpret because
their inspiration may be wholly lacking, since their gift of the Holy
Ghost is still to be bestowed, find it most facile to make mistakes about
the unspoken meaning, or even the directions, of founders. One little
word is enough, from the inspired saint, to set their plodding brains on
fire with the unholy flame of spurious interpretation, as was the case

with the disciples of Christ when He most trusted them, in uttering a sublime guidance. Custom soon makes that meaning seem true which has crept slyly to its authority.

Work that is neglected but commanded by God, must be done. Religion, the holding back of the body, religion, the source of divine union for the soul, must prepare the being for its work. If one force retards the other, if one virtuous effort debars the other, will God be served? No sane thought can aver that work deserving the title can go on unswervingly and faithfully without religious aids, because God accomplishes all that is its honest success. And no sane thought can aver that religion is union with God which is not united to mercy in diligence for the general good. A glance at the Bible sometimes helps one to see what mercy is, and it is almost safer to refer to it than to read a passage in the life of a saint; for even religious are heard to say that the saints were "made so." There is no class of persons who have so little credit done them as the saints. They and their true followers alone are sufficiently jealous of the requirements of an exact harmony between devotion which fits for action and action which imitates Christ.

RELIGION AND WORK, PART II
CHRIST'S POOR 2 (AUGUST 1902): 33–41

We human beings will do nothing without looking for a reward. God is so munificent that we can do nothing harmless without being rewarded. The religious understand that the most generous of acts, hidden, apparently seconded only by greater sufferings or persecution, is rewarded in such a manner, were it only at the end of a century, we will say, that the sane mind realizes how selfish it has been in being unselfish; how its loss of self has resulted in the finding of self in God, where all is joy and vigor, though the body be but a skeleton of severities. The work attempted for God, with all its renunciations, weariness, incurred scorn, floutings of one's personal tastes and sensibilities, is never anything but a self-interested proceeding—its goal is heaven. The simperings of conscious rectitude are absurd; rectitude alone is prudence, and heroism is the best calculation for returns in the world. The great God is so good a Master as this; and if He has made it impossible for us to lose by suffering for Him, our contemptibleness, in sublimity itself, is so only because His glory casts light into the shade. Let us understand clearly, in the beginning of religious service, that there can be no question of pride or complacency, but only humble thanksgiving, abashed shamefulness, that we can do so little for the gift that will be given to us by God, Who rushes His rewards upon us for the least loving act on our part, or causes us to wait patiently for still greater treasure. It is not that we are not sublime when true to Him in entire obedience; but that He is so unforgetting, so faithful, that the more we think we are doing for Him, the less we should imagine that we are to be pitied. Pagans alone could deserve to be commended or wept for in a generous deed.

We will work marvellously as seculars for the rewards of money and fame; we have a passion (in the world) for being paid. This is the perverted sense of God's readiness to pay, for Redemption by His Blood, and for good works by His eternal peace; and as a degenerate creature apes the external manifestations of its class by some antics distantly resembling their qualities and abilities; so the degenerate soul imperfectly goes through the actions of the soul that is united to God. It strives to win or steal returns for its efforts, from the child's bribed toy to the millions of a laboring financier. Oh, corrupt, theatric imitation of the energy that unfailingly wins the treasures of spiritual riches by its spiritual nobility in work and word! As the flower turns to the light, and enjoys a flood of sunbeams, so does the ugly weed fatten upon the same ray, not discouraged by the Creator, though thus blazoning forth, in characters that no one finds it difficult to understand, how immitigably true it is that there are creatures who defy God's holy influence and become hideous, although they might have grown to be creatures who listen to His word, becoming fair and sweet. Shall we labor to become hideous, or labor to grow fair? For this beauty of God can make even a physically ugly form radiant to contemplate, whereas the beauty of Satan will make a faultless contour repulsive. Labor there must be, of some sort, in any one not physically or morally impotent. Yes; and to the morally impotent an eternity of penitential life—no sinecure.

As said previously, nursing and teaching will not flourish upon asceticism. But there never was a full-fledged religious who did not inflict unceasing denial of mental requirements, and the suffering of physical violence in abstinence and fastings, watchings and silences, upon himself or herself. Consumption, cancer, general decline are usual among the saints; who, inspiring their disciples to do that work which is more mundane, outwardly useful and far easier than their own exalted labors, yet do this secondary work themselves long enough and well enough to prove that a human being can be a drudge and closely resemble Christ at the same time. The hour of a saint's death is not really of the smallest consequence to the race; but the glorious manner of it is of unending importance. In the case, however, of a disciple, the length of life is of the greatest importance, because he will do useful, faithful work, but his death can never be so sublime as to be a legacy; no miracles could possibly attend it. Yet we know well that the ordinary worker for God could be a great saint, if he tried. He does not try, and on such a huge numerical scale is this so that we may be pardoned for assuming that he never will try, or the millions like him.

We desire to be paid for what we do; and when we are truly wise, we work for God: we choose that profession, of good works, which He patronizes, and we are certain of our wages. We desire to pray, we look for work under religious rule, because this is the apprenticeship for good works. Religion and work should never be disjoined. Good works without religious observance are a strange group of unblessed efforts, from hearts that are a confusion of good and harmful impulses; hearts abortive, passionate, ever an-hungered.

For every good work, every kindly thought, or tiny act of humble helpfulness, God gives a reward, a merited return of sustenance for our souls, or answer to our pleading for some purpose. The orderliness of heaven cannot be disturbed, and if our free will is not given wholly to the act, in a consecration clear and sweet, the corresponding mercy cannot approach us. This is our dignity—we are not paupers before God, though poor. We are not His impotent and lackadaisical children, when we are His; but manly, though crushed to the earth in adoration. For God's mercy, we give our free will, in each moment of our life. This giving of a work to merit a petitioned benefit bestows the definiteness and worth upon every hour of religious life. It may be fatiguing to think of meriting at each step, but it is also fatiguing to study Greek or Mathematics. The things of most worth are not cultivated without labor. And to imagine that it would be more generous to do something for God without reckoning at all upon merciful return from Him of any sort, is not intelligent virtue—though it may be stupid and mistaken virtue—for God will give mercy for return to every act worthy of reward, and when He does not so give reward, we have failed to recollect ourselves; that is, to act religiously.

Like the soil to be prepared for different vegetables, the body and mind must be prepared in religion for the usefulness expected. This has not been sufficiently remembered, so that charity in religion has dwindled to a degree that has left very necessary works to their fate in abandonment, or so sparsely and inadequately accomplished that there is more blame than praise to accord. A big, expensive building and a staid manner, and an appearance of starched perfection, will not fit the inmates of an institution for charitable labor, and may, if too artificial, hinder the poor heart from following its simple and divine instincts. Until secular aid attends adequately to the severest needs of the poor, religious aid must, as in the early days of Christianity, grasp the dilemma, and help the needy in Christlike fervor of gentleness and completeness. To help the needy is not enough: it must be done in a Christlike manner. To edify the populace by external success and stylish forms may be a great mission in missions, but dry-rot supervenes unless the edification is based upon some pith and marrow less spurious than masonry and primness, however much these solid attributes of a charity may seem to promise integrity. The investigator sees really more than can be expressed with tact, in the charity of to-day; it is too sad to dwell upon. The only hope is in hoping, and the only remedy is a religious observance in the general body of workers more like the observance of the saints among the body of workers of hundreds of years before now. We see individuals who are profoundly charitable, but there is a plausible assumption of doing remarkably well by the crowd of those who are at work, and those who, looking on, find it kindly and convenient to assume that this is so. Undoubtedly there were few really noble workers in the past, as now; but it is probable that they were less complacent triflers—they had the saints to match by, and blushed occasionally at their own sourness towards the representatives of Christ whom they were serving.

The low standards praised by some people may be practical, but, like all concessions to what is human, will deteriorate even good quality coming into acquiescent contact with them. It makes these tepid people furious on their own account to say that human charity can be criticized with any justice, as if human beings were already heavenly bodies. They think that only a little can be done in charity and that it is heroic to do it. It is moreover pathetic to listen to the discourse of those who have no knowledge of the history and literature of the true faith. They hammer away at rocks with their watery weapons, saying that this or that cannot be accomplished, because they do not recognize the power that moves mountains, even if they believe that somewhere there is a power which can. They laboriously trail their steps over leagues of desert,—the laziness and meanness of the race,—whereas a dove of inspired thought has swept across the sands with one motion of the wings; such as a saint's consecration to God, acknowledging himself to be a vile worm capable through Him of resurrection; and this consecration grants the efficiency needed for every sacrifice and every labor which the saint will attempt. Charitable travellers on humdrum feet might begin to work aright if they would dare to look at the homilies or the recorded lives of the doctors of the Church. That Catholics often do not equal their Protestant or Agnostic brethren in ardor of charity, is but the just punishment of the negligence with which they ignore their treasures; is because they shut their Christian ears as the Jews shut their less gifted ones. Catholics in America, at any rate, are often willing to dwell in a routine that possesses no reflection upon real thought, no richness of reference to real events of a high order. A body of people so vast, so blessed, so powerful for right and example, should cease to disregard their riches for development in all that is meritorious. What religion has done for charitable workers is, in the aggregate, to make them far superior to irreligious or misguided charity-workers; but because these privileged workers are lukewarm, and are uncultivated in their own science, they are becoming second-rate professors; and those whose work can never be so true or persevering, because not receiving the daily inspiration of the true faith, the Protestants, Jews and others, can find many a laughable crudity and defect, even many a sham and fraud, in Catholic labor for the poor and the good of souls. The poor themselves laugh, decorously, and with as much secrecy as they can, at the strangely unsuccessful spurts of a flagging Catholic effort to be the messenger of God. Certainly this fruitlessness would be lifted, as a curse is brushed away by an angel's hand, if the life of St. Vincent de Paul, or the accumulated glories of the Breviary, were familiar to those who follow great Catholic standards, but are rigging up little sticks and rags, because they have lost sight of their leaders, and only know that they are plodding along in a duty assigned them, for which somehow or other they are getting the applause of the people who are doing even less. Some cultivation of opportunities is necessary, though the aim be so simple as to serve with hands and feet and purse. In working religiously elaborateness is not desirable. Religion is, we know, eminently childlike, and works of mercy certainly should be simple. Elaboration has no part in the mind of a child; but his intuitions are marvellous, if he is a child of healthy abilities. A brief sentence written by a saint will be moral provender for a good Catholic for many a day—his heart will develop the words, as the saint's calculated simplicity intended, into a long sermon. Our Lord as a child taught the doctors; but any intricacy of knowledge is far from the equipment needed in the preparation of a devout but ordinary soul which is desirous of serving the suffering brothers and sisters who are poor, oppressed, ill, as our Lord indicates to be His wish. But as children eagerly listen to tales of adventure and prowess, kindness and fairy beauty, so does the faithful religious read tales of the matchless sweetness, the majesty and loveliness of the saints and their trusty men. Children like to learn simple lessons in many avenues of fact; and so may the religious rejoice in the direct and sublime teachings of Popes and martyrs, who speak as no other men speak, and cannot be gainsaid, though persons of alien faith, who do not read what they said, will deny their speech to be true. It is not enough to know that this sweet eloquence is being read somewhere near us, but we must grow under the rain of instruction. This we should do, who would carry any light ourselves into the darkness we shall find around the poor, even though many of the poor will prove to be already gentle children of light. Intelligent simplicity in religious training all must seek; pompous emptiness of head we must fear. It is true that we cannot wholly change by any system from fools to useful servants; but there can be a principle that to know and to think the fair realities of supernatural value is decidedly meritorious, instead of contemptibly superfluous. A mechanical usefulness, that, to be sure, never disturbs routine, but also never evolves the slightest ability to act nobly when left to itself, is the bane of religious development, producing weeds, spurious growths, and encouraging a lack of real piety in those who meet it or submit to it. Bright, childlike simplicity should be the criterion of the rank and file of religious workers; but also there must be the child's penetration, courage, apprehensive quickness, and the generosity that gives with the folly that is dear to God—the child's unwearyingness. The divine estimate of the highest religious type for the masses is good enough for all, even though upon its faultlessness the greatest saints lay added perfections. Nothing can make us children or keep us such, except the practice of realizing the presence of God; this being the highest prayer, for in this practice we must think about Him. In striving to fulfill this act, we would gather together all definite references to Him that are to be read or heard, which we have at command. Neglected opportunities are too likely to be points against us, for us to depend upon the fact that without any opportunities some people have learned of God, (as St. Rose did, at three months old)—in other words, without any medium from Himself. Religion being the science of the knowledge of God, we should certainly study it in order to do good, of which it is the source, under God. The constant recurrence of vocal prayer through the day soothes the nerves, and helps a deficient capacity to realize the presence of God, lost sight of in hard or bewildering work, from a lack of self-training in mental prayer, or even the most primitive recollection. The selfish, lovingly selfish soul, desirous of basking in the light of this consciousness of the most faithful of friends, the best Friend, will seek more and more to avoid work and conjunctions of circumstance that dispel the sublime peace of recollection in God. It is a temptation, wound about with the veil of piety, cloaked well to deceive us, to cater to our greediness, our more human judgment. We are tempted to give up works of mercy, in spite of the Epistle of St. James. At last a whole community may (and have done so) drop all but a perfunctory connection with the poor, distort the decrees of a founder, unslip the connection, and float away into space free of the divine inspiration which gave the corporate workers life. Witness the inferior and perfunctory school for poor children which dwindles from the original intention before the onset of a school for more elevated children, who are supposed to be entitled to first attention, though the foundress had quite intelligence enough to weigh the pros and cons of this question, when decreeing that her foundation was principally for the poor. Ways and means are usually more urgent than their terrorized victims acknowledge to themselves, who image they are doing a charity practical service by doing homage to the element which pays. Witness also the charitable foundation for the service of the sick poor, which relinquishes its active works for those neglected creatures in order to help them by ritualistic devotions. If one is called to the lower and more obvious kind of usefulness, it is certainly best to carry it out thoroughly and unswervingly, that this side of service may be offered to God, as well as the higher side, of impetratory prayer. And unquestionably a great soul will be able to serve the sick as well by corporal deeds that are prayer, as by prayer without corporal deeds. Of a charitable institution that is carried on without prayer, we may say that it is a harborage for animals; kind animals, and needy ones. The concession of some time and strength to religion must be given, as we build a house against the storm; for the evil day will come to all earnest charity workers when the best one can effect will seem futile and the greatest need of the suffering but a shadow in the night, not worth laboring to aid or contending to ameliorate; and gratitude will show itself to be but a dove's feather in a field of thorns. Dejection and cruelty take possession of one who has not seen that God does all that we do which is beneficent, and that we can live at His feet, even though we must fly upon His errands, only to return, for ever and ever.

"What shall it profit, my brethren, if a man say he hath faith, but have not works? Shall faith be able to save him? And if a brother or sister be naked, and want daily food: And one of you say to them: Go in peace, be you warmed and filled: yet give them not those things that are necessary for the body: what shall it profit? So faith also, if it have not works, is dead in itself. . . . For even as the body without the spirit is dead: so also faith without works is dead."—St. James.

And lo, the Apostle places faith on a level with the body, and works on a level with the soul.

A LEGACY FROM HAWTHORNE

Editor's Note: The following personal essay was solicited by Maurice Francis Egan for inclusion in his own review of the *Reports* of the Servants of Relief for Incurable Cancer, January, 1908 to October, 1912 and January, 1921 to January, 1922 and published in The *New York Times Book Review and Magazine* Sunday, April 16, 1922. His editorial comment is somewhat romanticized, but he was motivated by Mother Alphonsa's cause at the time. She needed publicity and was struggling to get money for a fireproof building at Rosary Hill in Hawthorne, New York, to replace the dangerous wooden structure which the congregation had purchased in 1900. Of her reports he writes, "They are the kind of reports that St. Francis d'Assisi might have made if reports had been considered necessary in his time, and the spirit of St. Francis d'Assisi dominates their every page. They are the reports of the voluntary poor ministers of the involuntary poor." The entire essay from the *Times* was reprinted in *The Nathaniel Hawthorne Review* 12 (Spring 1986), 1, under the title "On Founding a Home for Destitute Victims of Cancer." What is important about Mother Alphonsa's account is its tribute to Nathaniel Hawthorne's own spirit of charity, a spirit that became transformed by his daughter's enduring and concrete response to human need. The autobiographical elements of the essay are significant to any understanding of Rose Hawthorne's spirituality. The following selection from the review omits only Maurice Egan's brief introduction and short history of Mother Alphonsa's work.

*

In looking back after a windy walk which has somewhat bewildered eyesight and reflection, the trees and hills are noticeable for having kept their places, and for preserving their traits steadily, so that they give the pedestrian a pleasant sense of the secondary importance of wind. In such a way, my twenty-five years of strenuous and bewildering work for a few hundred cancerous poor, and daily anxiety for these guests, gives place to a keen memory of former days when in my half thoughtless life, the strong facts and beautiful sublimities which I could observe here and there in the human scene taught me the best, humanly, in my life. But to be definite, I am asked to say what it was that first made me interested in this especial nursing to which I have given half of my trifling existence, to the great surprise of the majority of those who have noticed my joyful selection of cancer cases rather than of the blind and others. One of my acquaintances, putting her opinion baldly, asked me what (she read French fiction constantly herself) made me "choose such a dirty occupation."

The first influence came from the attitude of my father's mind toward both moral and physical deformity and corruption. Some critics call his mental inclination morbid, using the word in the wrong place. It is the sinner who is morbid, not the man who pities him and devotes his abilities to helping others to sin no more as he did, even if the sinner himself is beyond reclaim. Extraordinary sinners, as has been said elsewhere, came to my father with their woes of conscience (much to his innate horror) because they knew from his writings that he was full of compassionate insight; and at the cost of his equanimity he consoled them, in so far as this life holds consolation for enormous wrongs.

Those readers who have come upon the chapter in *Our Old Home* which deals with "English Poverty" will have seen how far his practical pity reached down, both in observing the exterior aspects of the lowest class, and the inner misery out of which they spring; and the yet more stunning truth that the lowest class is the composition of the neglect of the highest one. In his writings he shows clearly that he is "brother" to the abject element in mankind, and perhaps in no place more sharply revealed than in the chapter referred to. The subject, as he treats it there, had in my early days of reading a hold upon me which remained; and in long spaces of loneliness the firm touch could be perceived, and was indeed chilling.

This importance of his respect for all misery, so that if it was the misery of poverty he did not lessen his regard, gave me, as I read the account of the child covered with sores in the hospital of horribles, instruction that harmonized with the melodious verities of Christ, and by its connection with my life gave no excuse for a forgetting. I detested the reading of such evidence of truth, which justly damned denial of it, and that urging to self-abnegation which has the finality of the woolsack, made me wish to be yet more self-indulgent. But I knew in my heart that this evidence was sublime wherever it might assert itself, and at last I did try to accept it to the point of sacrifices for the poor. The words in "English Poverty," which seemed to me the greatest my father ever wrote, are the following:

What an intimate brotherhood is this in which we dwell, do what we may to put an artificial remoteness between the high creature and the low one! . . . Let the world be cleansed, or not a man or woman of us all can be clean. . . . And here a singular incommodity befell one member of our party. Among the children was a wretched, pale, half-torpid little thing (about six years old, perhaps, but I know not whether a girl or a boy), with a humor in its eyes and face, which the Governor said was the scurvy, and which appeared to bedim its power of vision, so that it toddled about gropingly, as if in quest of it did not precisely know what. This child, this sickly, wretched, humor-eaten infant, the offspring of unspeakable sin and sorrow, whom it must have required several generations of guilty progenitors to render so pitiable an object as he beheld it, immediately took an unaccountable fancy to the gentleman just hinted at. It prowled about him like a pet kitten, rubbing against his legs, following everywhere at his heels, pulling at his coattails, and at last, exerting all the speed that its poor limbs were capable of, got directly before him and held forth its arms, mutely insisting on being taken up. It said not a word, being, perhaps, under-witted and incapable of prattle. But it smiled up into his face—a sort of woeful gleam was that smile, through the sickly blotches that covered its features—and found means to express such a perfect confidence that it was going to be fondled and made much of that there was no possibility in a human heart of balking its expectation. It was as if God had promised the poor child this favor on behalf of that individual, and he was bound to fulfill the contract or else no longer call himself a man among men. Nevertheless, it could be no easy thing for him to do, he being a person burdened with more than an Englishman's customary reserve, shy of actual contact with human beings, afflicted with a peculiar distaste for whatever was ugly, and furthermore, accustomed to that habit of observation from an insulated standpoint which is said (but I hope erroneously) to have the tendency of putting ice into the blood.

So I watched the struggle in his mind with a good deal of interest, and am seriously of the opinion that he did a heroic act and effected more than he dreamed of toward his final salvation when he took up the loathsome child and caressed it as tenderly as if he had been its father. To be sure, we all smiled at him at the time, but doubtless would have acted pretty much the same in a similar stress of circumstances. The child, at any rate, appeared to be satisfied with his behavior.

As *Notes of Travel* later explained, though without my father's intention, this man was Nathaniel Hawthorne, at whom all the others "smiled," as if they thought he was posing for admiration and was really unaccountable. But he himself felt that he had never before approached so near to God. When speaking to my mother wonderingly of this episode, after my father's death, but before *Notes of Travel* was printed, she said that my father had told her that it was to him that the child had come. She called it the most extraordinary evidence of his correspondence with the highest principles, for she had never known anyone so peculiarly sensitive to even the slightest deformity, ugliness or disease as he; and she gave me a number of illustrations to show how she had endeavored to shield him from the inevitable disagreeables of life, or any shocks of an unexpected sort that would trouble his refinement, taking the brunt upon herself. Yet he fondled a loathsome, half-witted child who was in profound neglect, and held it in his arms for some time, knowing that its human property had been the product of evil; and he so thoroughly evinced his brotherhood that the darkened mind within the abhorrent personality fully recognized it. Half-witted that mind certainly was, but not wholly without wit, and the waif waited for him at the entrance of the hospital until he had retraced his steps—and then was gone forever from its presence.

My father gives also a second description, of a baby in arms, which brought to a climax in the chapter the extreme of his moral theme in which cowardice had no right, and that acceptance of co-responsibility which unhesitatingly gleams in all his books, and which the persons of distinction grouped near him could not prevent him from manifesting, although he had no doubt of their quick scorn. Strange! On a battlefield these aristocrats would undoubtedly have become normal, and served the lowest as well as the highest victims of ghastly wounds.

I tried to acquire a fondness for the very poor, and I finally came to like them very much if they were rather good. But I was not satisfied with liking them; I wanted to love all the poor whom I met. I did anything I could that happened to be possible, to prove to them that I did not merely greet them in passing, but knew their claim to be identical clay with the rest of mankind to be absolute truth. My mother was very charitable, and I tried to emulate her in various ways, such as carrying her gifts to an old woman in our Concord neighborhood and sitting for an hour with her in her stuffy cottage. I thought that I had shown a loving interest in the old woman when I listened admiringly to her slow but unceasing chatter upon her own philosophical convictions, and I admired my marvelous self-control when partaking of a large slice (and on other occasions, although then knowing the ground) of mince pie made, in her dire poverty, of apples from her one tree, possibly molasses, and probably pepper, closing this ordeal with a downright lie as to my feelings. These visits to Abigail Cook always ended by her reading aloud a Gospel page from her greasy Bible, to which she was devoted and of which the delicious beauty was not obscured even by a tremendously long nose charged with snuff. My efforts were grotesque and somewhat insincere, but the humble people I wished to love knew that I did not any more cling to the crass belief that I was superior porcelain, and they liked me for that. In later years my sister, Una, crowned a life of kind deeds by becoming the good support of a little orphanage in London, both by her small means and her actual labor, which was an example of the highest calibre. Of course, many congruous inducements caught upon the magnet of my fervent desire somehow to help others, which means the loss of one's own affairs. One goad was the book which made so many readers stop, though we all passed by again—*Joshua Davidson*. After closing the covers of this noble appeal, I was ready to give myself to those who needed friends, and to cut off my personal likes and gains. And whenever a serious friend came into my world of musings the crowd of aspiring thoughts started to agility, and this companion would have leave to tear up by the roots customary satisfactions and legitimate indulgences. This reflective discontent is universal, since everybody who thinks has a longing to cease the jellyfish period, and I am speaking sparingly of what so many minds discourse about at length. Fraternal charity abounds in literature. However, as best I can, I am answering the question that has so often been put to me: "Why in the world did you set out to nurse this unattractive disease?"

When it came to giving part of a life not greatly valued in itself to the care of cancerous poor, many reasons, little and large, had removed any heaped-up impediment that would have been in the way. To tell the truth, I was shocked to discover how unusual my new endeavor seemed to people—they seemed to be acknowledging that they were asleep in the midst of a great disaster, that of the misery of a class which they could so justly serve. Among my valuable friends at one time was Miss Emma Lazarus, the poetess, whose mind was lofty, brilliant and pathetically unsatisfied. I met her in the perfect artistic atmosphere— never to be equaled—of the studio-home of Richard Watson Gilder and his wife, Helena de Kay. Here the genius of the young Jewess was recognized to the brim, held up and rejoiced over in its rare vintage and purity. Miss Lazarus and I sometimes walked and talked together, and in her sweet delicacy of spirit she would not show in the least that she did not find a very secure footing for her mental explorations while accompanying a person who knew little Latin and less Greek, whereas she herself commanded both and had read voluminously. On the contrary, she assured me that I was a paragon for "stirring her up with suggestions." I doubt if two more such fundamentally disconsolate minds, trying to carry a corner of the woes of the world upon their quivering shoulders, could have been found together in a search of years. But early discontent can sometimes produce a result. This young woman of finest promise and exalted perceptions died in her prime of cancer; but, though I grieved deeply for her, I would not pity her, for she never knew unaided suffering, but every amelioration. On the other hand, I finally heard of a case of abandonment to death which no one of any sensibility could ignore. The victim, a young seamstress of refinement, had recently died without relatives or friends. She had been obliged by cancer to give up work, and was operated upon at a hospital, where she had been told to expect a cure. When found to be incurable (some six months later), she was given one day's notice before being sent to Blackwell's Island—that den of mixed souls—and her despair was, most reasonably, complete. There was no one to stand forth and forbid the immolation of this young woman upon the altar of fraternal indifference. A fire was then lighted in my heart, where it still burns, to do something toward preventing such inhuman regulations for those who are too forlorn to protest. I set my whole being to endeavor to bring consolation to the cancerous poor.

When I had settled down, over a year later, as a nurse in the lower east side slums, Miss Josephine Lazarus, the sister of Emma, wrote me that what I was trying to do "could not be done." She had tried herself to establish a little hospital for this class, in memory of Emma, and had failed in spite of wealth, paid trained nurses and every advantage. The nurses would not stay put. Out of the kindness of her generous heart she sent me a donation for my mendicant and, as she thought, doomed labors, and my cancer cases, for whom I did not depend upon paid assistance, but upon service that cannot be bought.

To voices of discouragement, derision and indignation I had a strong answer—that I knew I was incapable of doing much, but that I was going to carry out my idea precisely as I had at first received it, warm from the fire of compassion, in so far as I could. As no one felt able to say just how far I could go, the discussion was stalled. Aid of this sort was a just need of the poor, and therefore it should be met by someone. Impudent as it may seem, I declared that I was going to keep on in the somewhat unique work until that unidentified personality turned up. I have been surprised to find that persons of eminence and the highest intelligence praised our idea, developing well as it has done, having been useful to thousands of cancerous poor, until death. And these words of our friends have sanctioned the cry I uttered to New York over the deep seas. New York answered with a ringing cordiality.

"I have known about this lofty work of yours since long ago—indeed from the day you began it; I have known of its steady growth and progress, step by step, to its present generous development and assured position among those benefactions to which the reverent homage of all creeds and colors is due; I have seen it rise from seedling to tree with no endowment but the voluntary aid which your patient labor and faith have drawn from the purses of grateful compassionate men; and I am glad in the prosperous issue of your work, and glad to know that this prosperity will continue and be permanent—a thing which I do know, for the endowment is banked where it cannot fail until pity fails in the hearts of men. And that will never be."

Samuel Clemens to Mother Alphonsa, October 19, 1901

INDEX

Alcott, Bronson, 5, 162–64
Alcott, Louisa, 163
Aldrich, Thomas Bailey, 22, 24
Alphonsus, Saint, 76
Alter, Mary Theresa, 81 ("M.T. Elder"), 81–82
American Catholic Quarterly Review, The, 30

Blackwell's Island, 3, 48, 235
Bochen, Christine, 30
Bok, Edward, 42, 89n.68
Brook Farm, 4, 25
Brown, Lucy Madox, 16
Browning, Elizabeth Barrett, 9
Browning, "Penini," 9
Browning, Robert, 9–10
Brownson, Orestes, 24

Caldwell Dominicans, 126–29
Callan, Father Charles, 72
Carroll, Bishop John, 26
Catholic Columbian Congress, 31
Catholic Summer School, 36, 117
Channing, Dr. William Ellery, 4
Channing, William Ellery II (Ellery), 164–65
Chappell, Adelaide (Huntington), 31

Chappell, Alfred, 31
Chinicci, Joseph, 77
Christ's Poor, 64, 67, 182–83
Clark, James Freeman, 26
Clemens, Samuel ("Mark Twain"), 68, 237
Cohan, George M., 67
Conway, Katherine, 40, 46, 47, 78, 90n.79
Corrigan, Archbishop Michael, conservatism of, 30, 31, 87n.88; confirmation of Rose and George, 32; establishment of reading circle, 37; early resistance to Rose, 54–55, 57, 121; opposition to "Americanism," 57; permission given for religious habit, 59; authorization of property purchase, 60
Cothonay, Father I.M. (*Couthenay* in some sources), 60
Council of Baltimore, First Plenary, 27; Third Plenary, 28, 93n.105
Crimmins, John D., 55, 67, 92n.98, 157
Cronin, Cornelius F., 67

238

Other Volumes in This Series